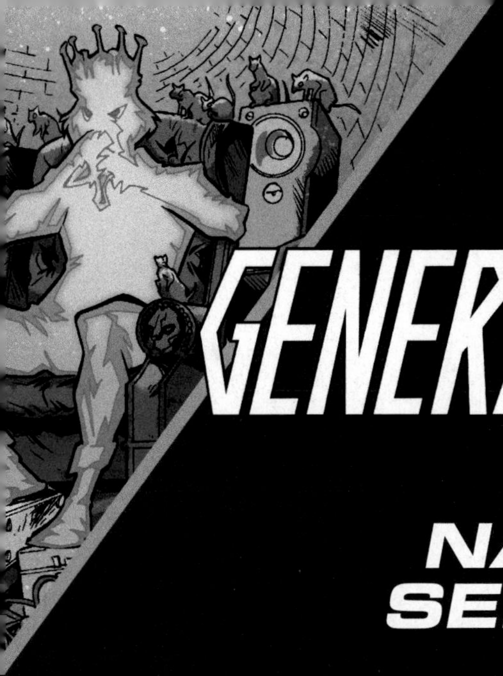

GENERATION X

NATURAL SELECTION

Writer/**CHRISTINA STRAIN**

Pencilers/**AMILCAR PINNA** (#1-4),
ALBERTO ALBURQUERQUE (#5)
& **ERIC KODA** (#6) with **MARTÍN MORAZZO** (#4)

Inkers/**AMILCAR PINNA** (#1-4),
ALBERTO ALBURQUERQUE (#5)
& **ERIC KODA** (#6)
with **ROBERTO POGGI** (#3-4) & **MARTÍN MORAZZO** (#4)

Color Artists/**FELIPE SOBREIRO**
with **JAY DAVID RAMOS** (#2),
CHRIS SOTOMAYOR (#2) & **NOLAN WOODARD** (#3)

Letterer/**VC's CLAYTON COWLES**

Cover Artists/**TERRY DODSON** & **RACHEL DODSON**

Assistant Editor/**CHRIS ROBINSON**
Editors/**DANIEL KETCHUM** & **DARREN SHAN**
X-Men Group Editor/**MARK PANICCIA**

Collection Editor/**JENNIFER GRÜNWALD** • Assistant Editor/**CAITLIN O'CONNELL**
Associate Managing Editor/**KATERI WOODY** • Editor, Special Projects/**MARK D. BEAZLEY**
VP Production & Special Projects/**JEFF YOUNGQUIST** • SVP Print, Sales & Marketing/**DAVID GABRIEL**
Book Designer/**JAY BOWEN**

Editor in Chief/**AXEL ALONSO** • Chief Creative Officer/**JOE QUESADA**
President/**DAN BUCKLEY** • Executive Producer/**ALAN FINE**

1

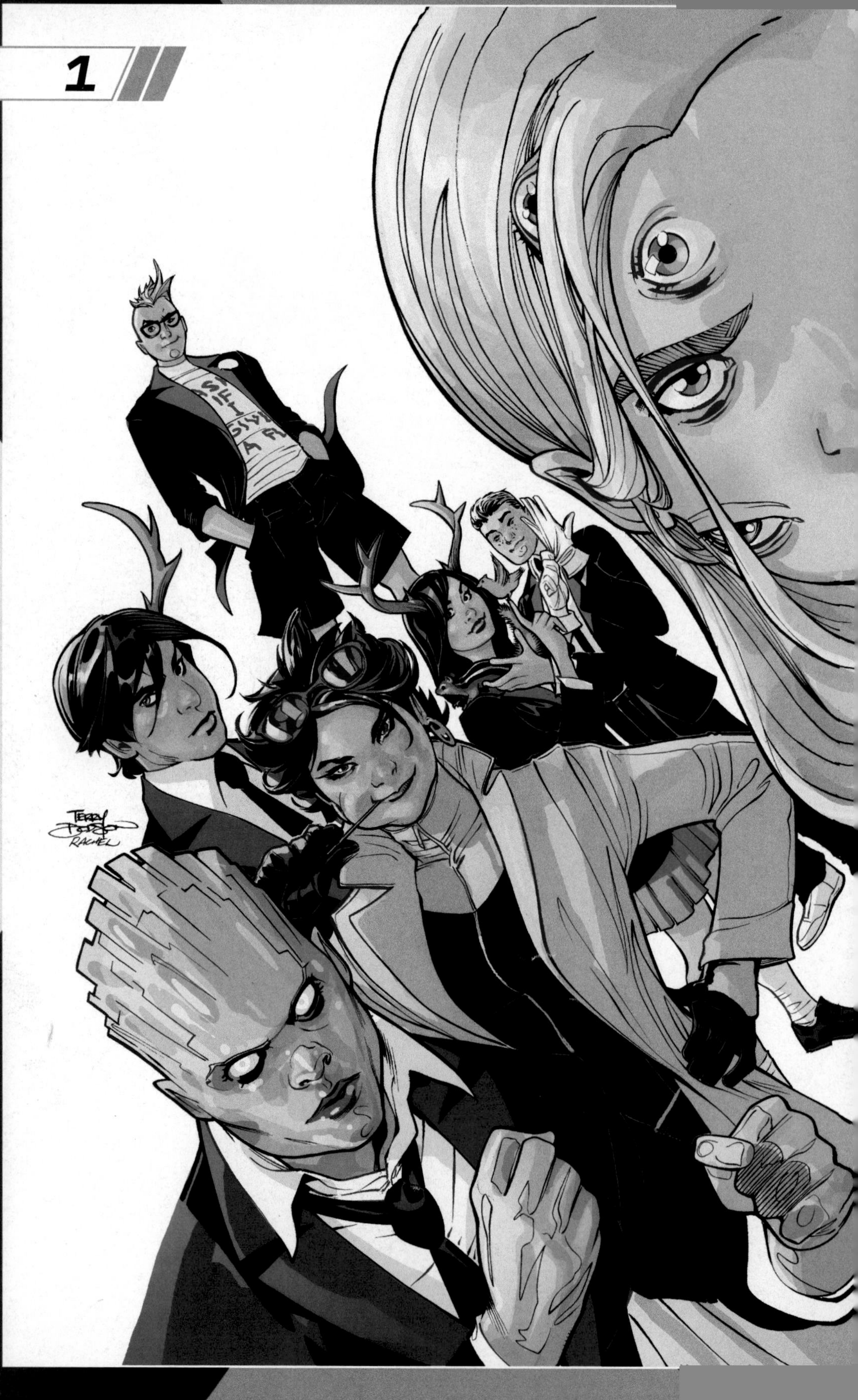
TERRY DODSON
RACHEL

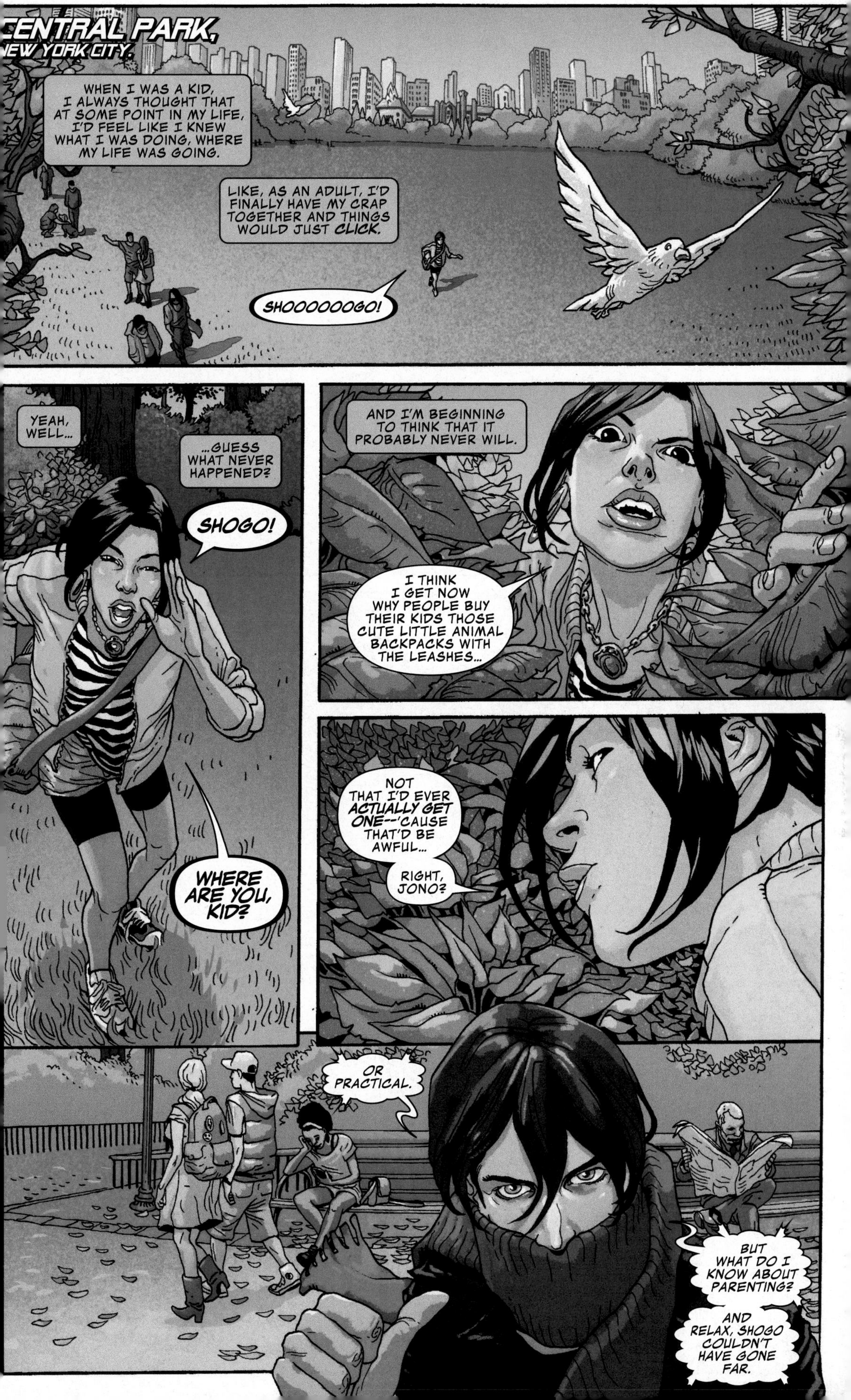
CENTRAL PARK, NEW YORK CITY.
WHEN I WAS A KID, I ALWAYS THOUGHT THAT AT SOME POINT IN MY LIFE, I'D FEEL LIKE I KNEW WHAT I WAS DOING, WHERE MY LIFE WAS GOING.
LIKE, AS AN ADULT, I'D FINALLY HAVE MY CRAP TOGETHER AND THINGS WOULD JUST CLICK.
SHOOOOOOGO!
YEAH, WELL...
...GUESS WHAT NEVER HAPPENED?
SHOGO!
WHERE ARE YOU, KID?
AND I'M BEGINNING TO THINK THAT IT PROBABLY NEVER WILL.
I THINK I GET NOW WHY PEOPLE BUY THEIR KIDS THOSE CUTE LITTLE ANIMAL BACKPACKS WITH THE LEASHES...
NOT THAT I'D EVER ACTUALLY GET ONE--'CAUSE THAT'D BE AWFUL...
RIGHT, JONO?
OR PRACTICAL.
BUT WHAT DO I KNOW ABOUT PARENTING?
AND RELAX, SHOGO COULDN'T HAVE GONE FAR.

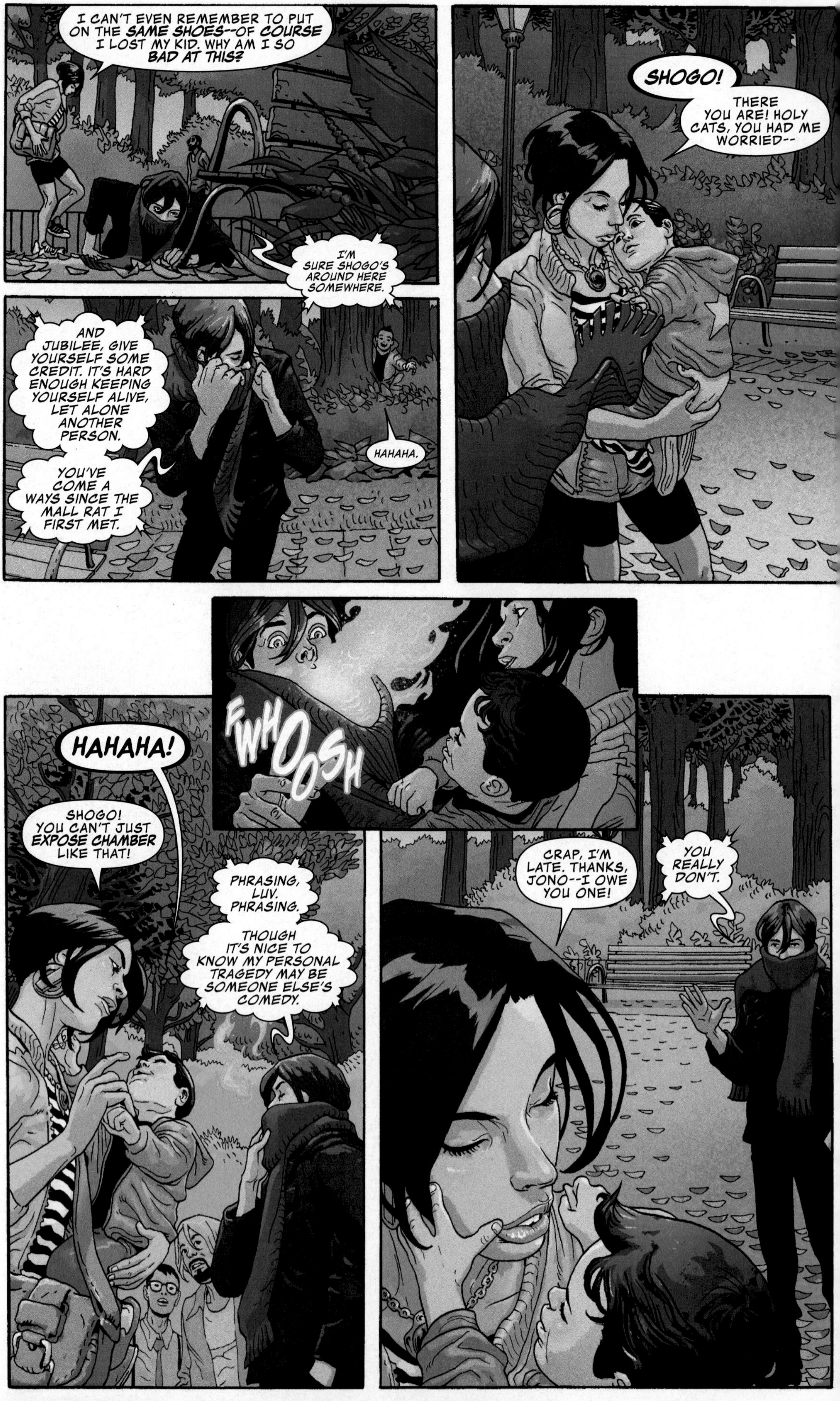

I CAN'T EVEN REMEMBER TO PUT ON THE SAME SHOES--OF COURSE I LOST MY KID. WHY AM I SO BAD AT THIS?
I'M SURE SHOGO'S AROUND HERE SOMEWHERE.
AND JUBILEE, GIVE YOURSELF SOME CREDIT. IT'S HARD ENOUGH KEEPING YOURSELF ALIVE, LET ALONE ANOTHER PERSON.
YOU'VE COME A WAYS SINCE THE MALL RAT I FIRST MET.
HAHAHA.
SHOGO!
THERE YOU ARE! HOLY CATS, YOU HAD ME WORRIED--
FWHOOOSH
HAHAHA!
SHOGO! YOU CAN'T JUST EXPOSE CHAMBER LIKE THAT!
PHRASING, LUV. PHRASING.
THOUGH IT'S NICE TO KNOW MY PERSONAL TRAGEDY MAY BE SOMEONE ELSE'S COMEDY.
CRAP, I'M LATE. THANKS, JONO--I OWE YOU ONE!
YOU REALLY DON'T.

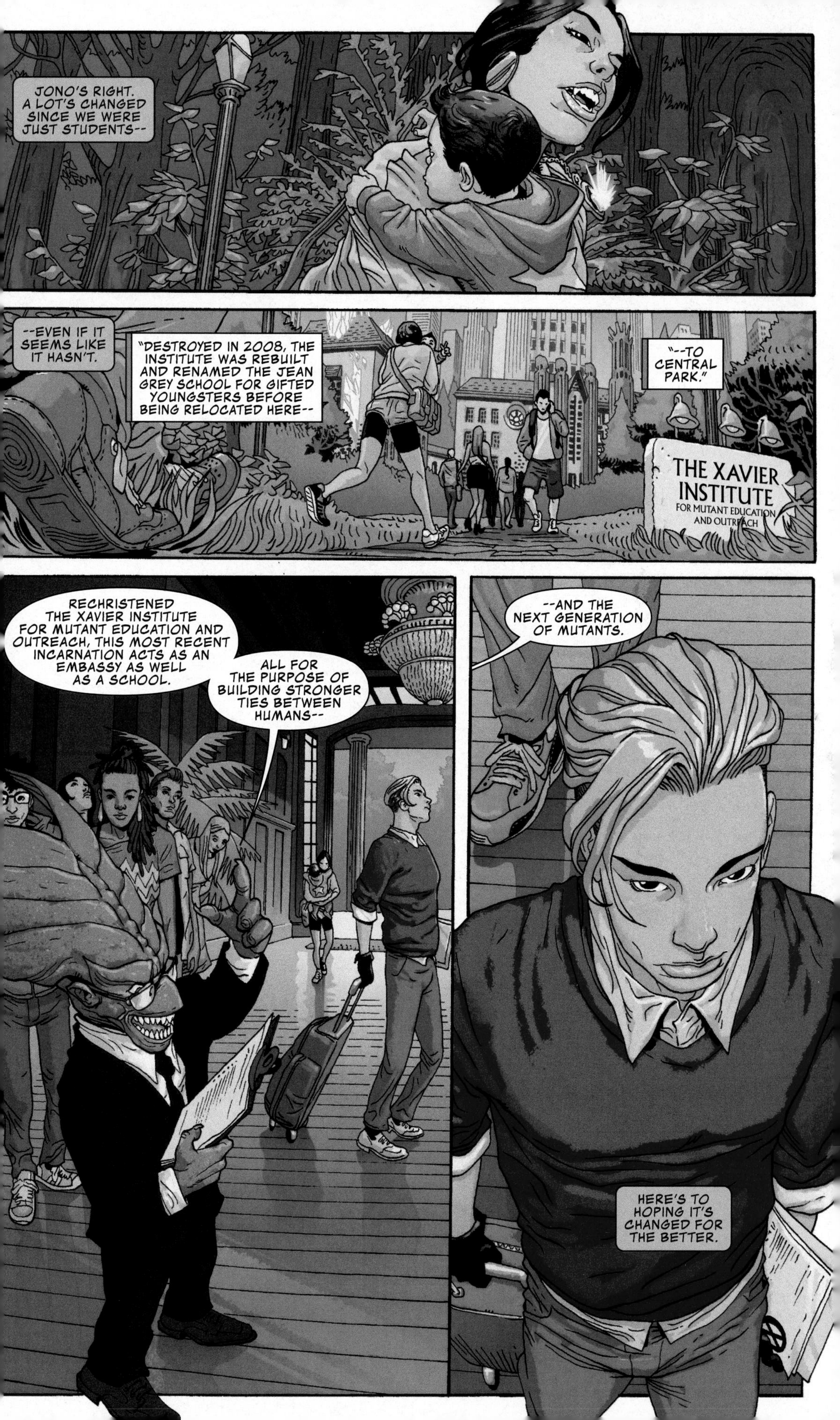
JONO'S RIGHT. A LOT'S CHANGED SINCE WE WERE JUST STUDENTS--
--EVEN IF IT SEEMS LIKE IT HASN'T.
"DESTROYED IN 2008, THE INSTITUTE WAS REBUILT AND RENAMED THE JEAN GREY SCHOOL FOR GIFTED YOUNGSTERS BEFORE BEING RELOCATED HERE--
"--TO CENTRAL PARK."
THE XAVIER INSTITUTE
FOR MUTANT EDUCATION AND OUTREACH
RECHRISTENED THE XAVIER INSTITUTE FOR MUTANT EDUCATION AND OUTREACH, THIS MOST RECENT INCARNATION ACTS AS AN EMBASSY AS WELL AS A SCHOOL.
ALL FOR THE PURPOSE OF BUILDING STRONGER TIES BETWEEN HUMANS--
--AND THE NEXT GENERATION OF MUTANTS.
HERE'S TO HOPING IT'S CHANGED FOR THE BETTER.

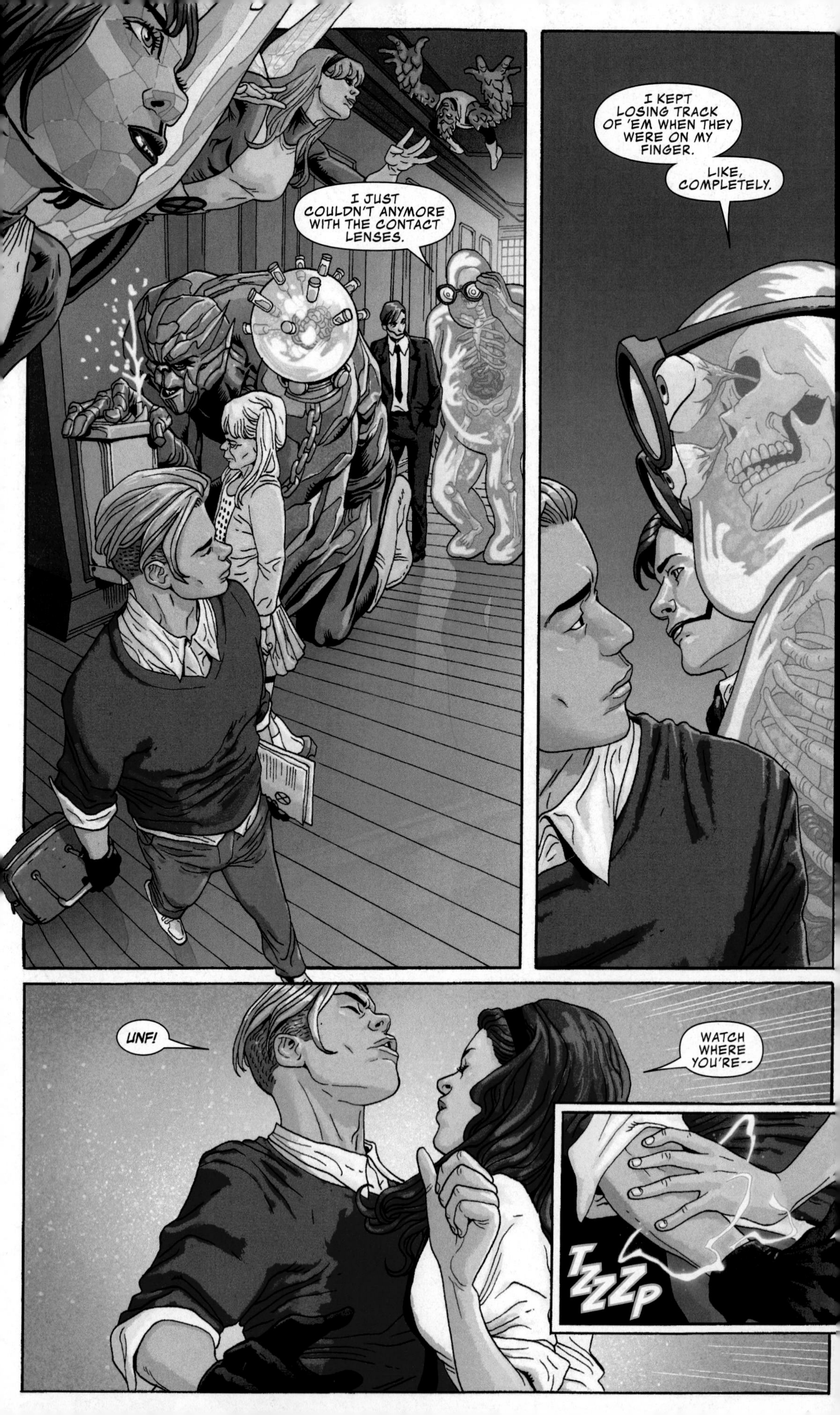

I JUST COULDN'T ANYMORE WITH THE CONTACT LENSES.
I KEPT LOSING TRACK OF 'EM WHEN THEY WERE ON MY FINGER.
LIKE, COMPLETELY.
UNF!
WATCH WHERE YOU'RE--
TZZZP

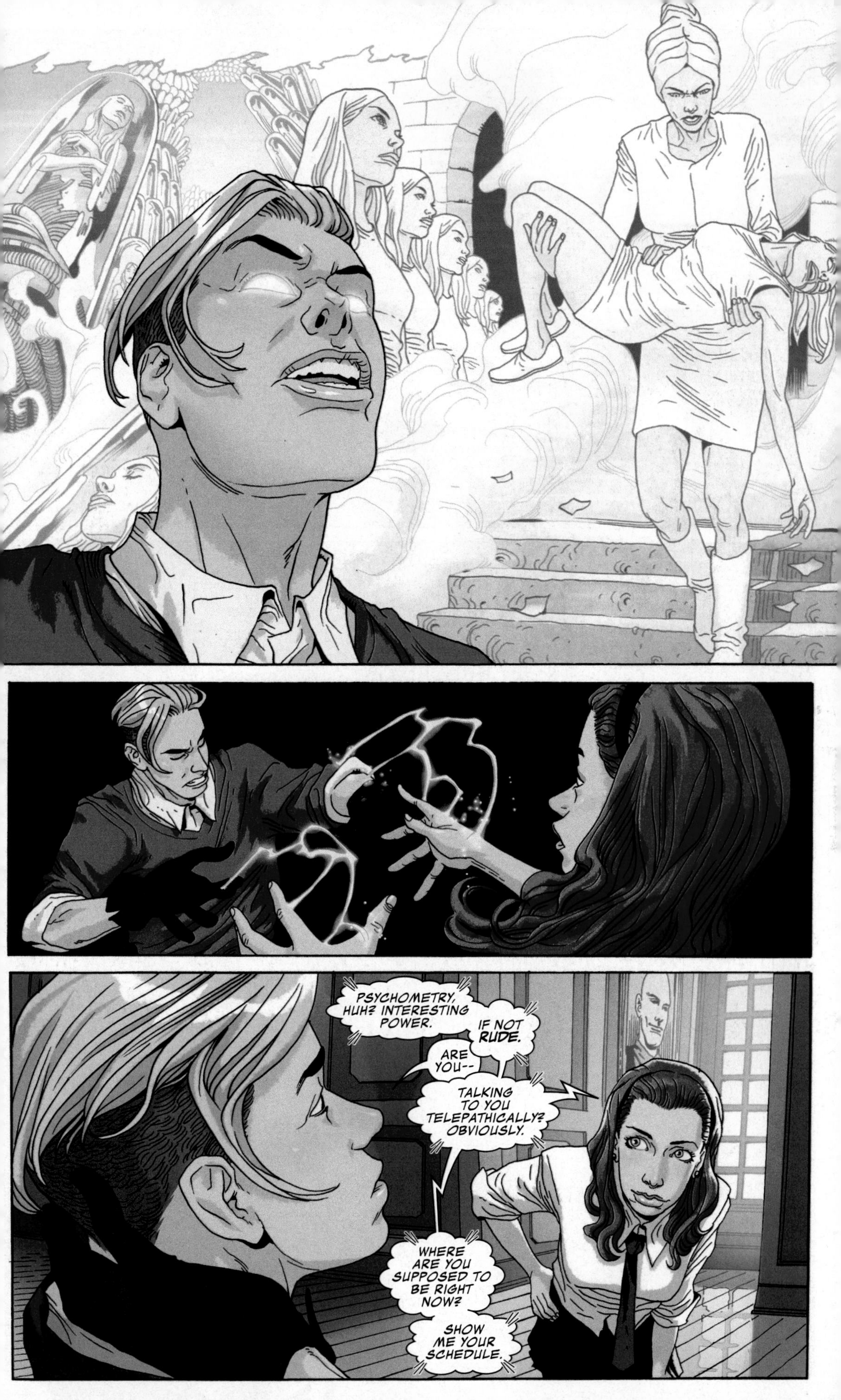
PSYCHOMETRY, HUH? INTERESTING POWER.
IF NOT RUDE.
ARE YOU--
TALKING TO YOU TELEPATHICALLY? OBVIOUSLY.
WHERE ARE YOU SUPPOSED TO BE RIGHT NOW?
SHOW ME YOUR SCHEDULE.

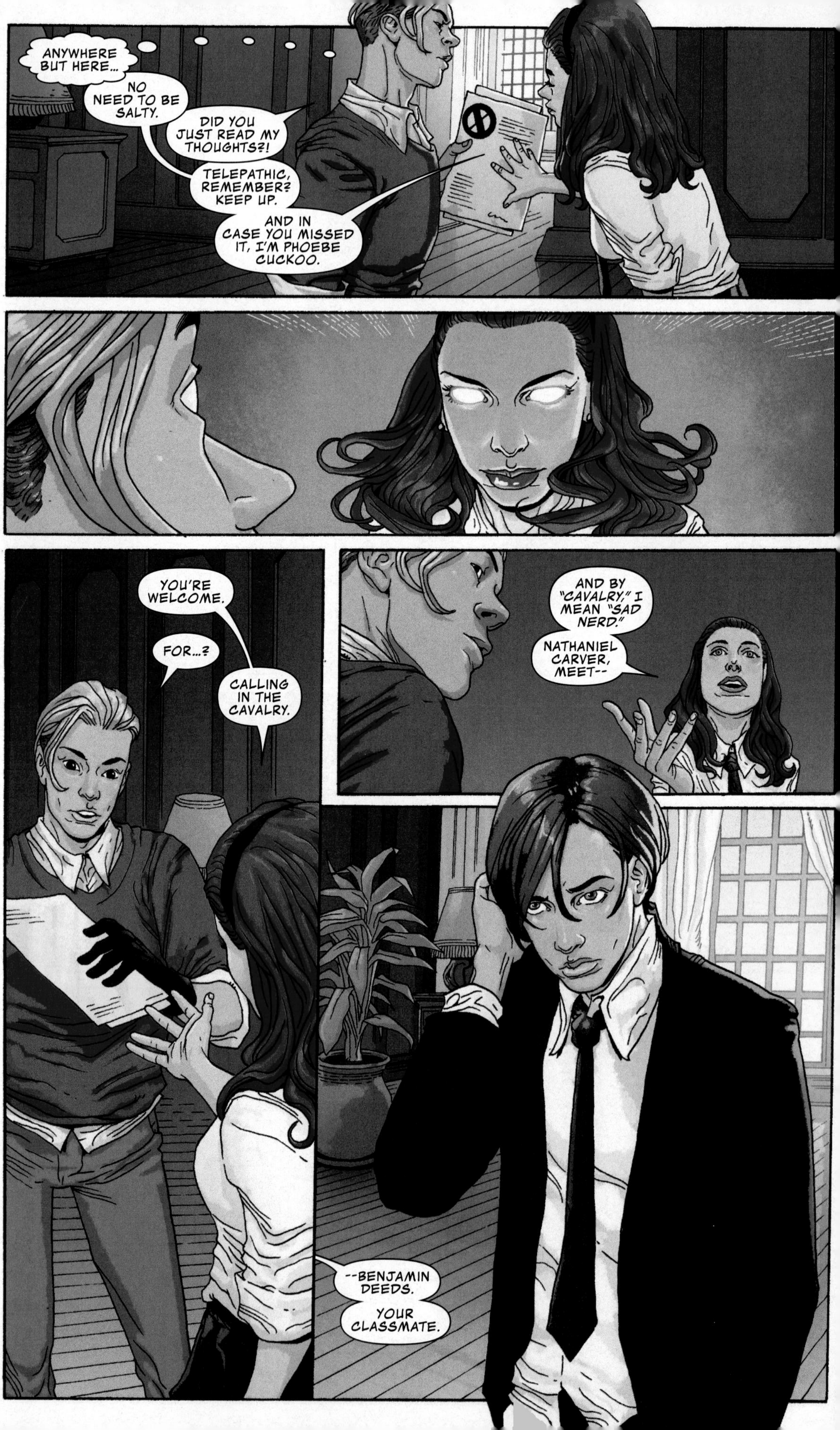
ANYWHERE BUT HERE...
NO NEED TO BE SALTY.
DID YOU JUST READ MY THOUGHTS?!
TELEPATHIC, REMEMBER? KEEP UP.
AND IN CASE YOU MISSED IT, I'M PHOEBE CUCKOO.
YOU'RE WELCOME.
FOR...?
CALLING IN THE CAVALRY.
AND BY "CAVALRY," I MEAN "SAD NERD."
NATHANIEL CARVER, MEET--
--BENJAMIN DEEDS.
YOUR CLASSMATE.

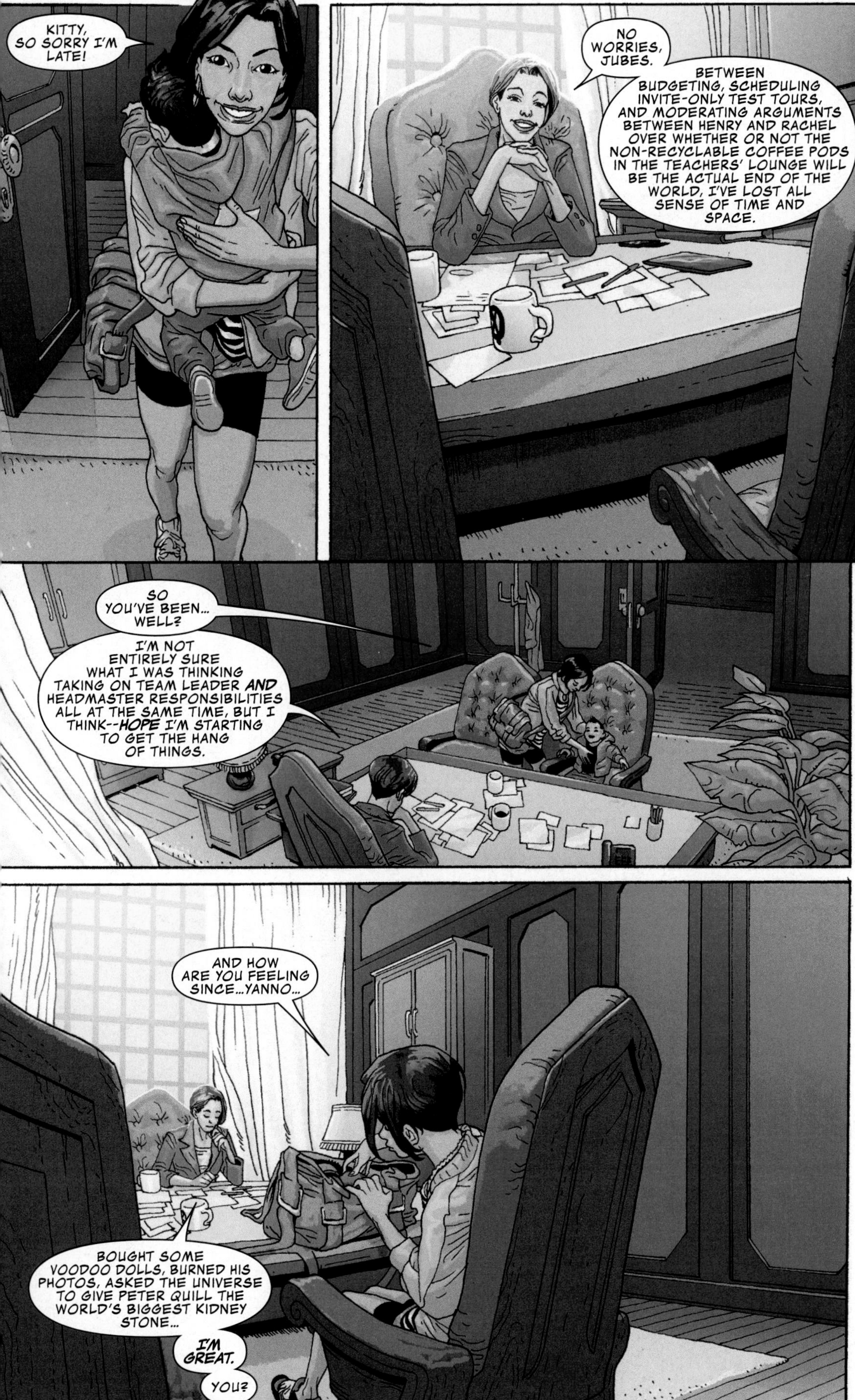

KITTY, SO SORRY I'M LATE!
NO WORRIES, JUBES.
BETWEEN BUDGETING, SCHEDULING INVITE-ONLY TEST TOURS, AND MODERATING ARGUMENTS BETWEEN HENRY AND RACHEL OVER WHETHER OR NOT THE NON-RECYCLABLE COFFEE PODS IN THE TEACHERS' LOUNGE WILL BE THE ACTUAL END OF THE WORLD, I'VE LOST ALL SENSE OF TIME AND SPACE.
SO YOU'VE BEEN... WELL?
I'M NOT ENTIRELY SURE WHAT I WAS THINKING TAKING ON TEAM LEADER AND HEADMASTER RESPONSIBILITIES ALL AT THE SAME TIME, BUT I THINK--HOPE I'M STARTING TO GET THE HANG OF THINGS.
AND HOW ARE YOU FEELING SINCE...YANNO...
BOUGHT SOME VOODOO DOLLS, BURNED HIS PHOTOS, ASKED THE UNIVERSE TO GIVE PETER QUILL THE WORLD'S BIGGEST KIDNEY STONE...
I'M GREAT.
YOU?

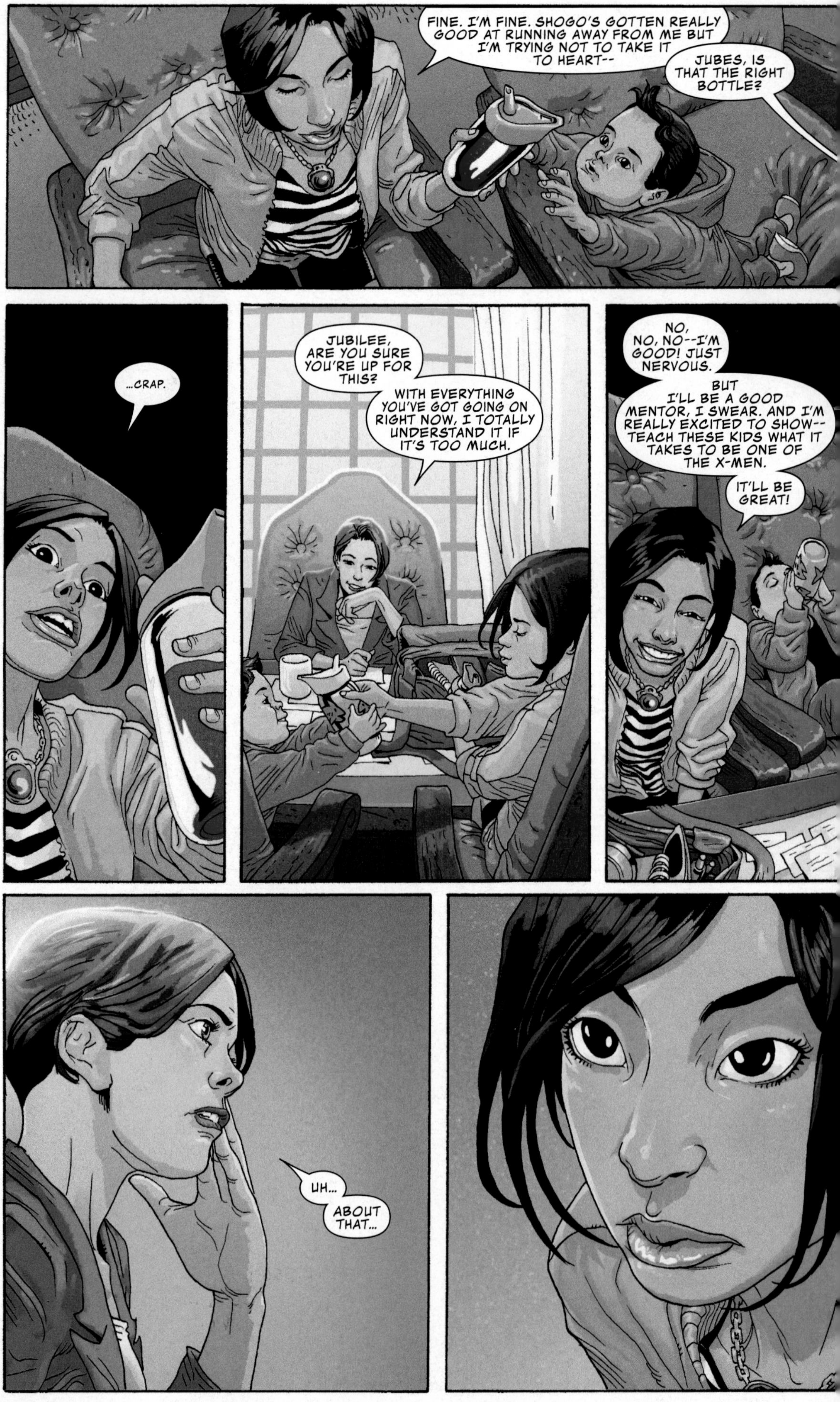
FINE. I'M FINE. SHOGO'S GOTTEN REALLY GOOD AT RUNNING AWAY FROM ME BUT I'M TRYING NOT TO TAKE IT TO HEART--
JUBES, IS THAT THE RIGHT BOTTLE?
...CRAP.
JUBILEE, ARE YOU SURE YOU'RE UP FOR THIS?
WITH EVERYTHING YOU'VE GOT GOING ON RIGHT NOW, I TOTALLY UNDERSTAND IT IF IT'S TOO MUCH.
NO, NO, NO--I'M GOOD! JUST NERVOUS.
BUT I'LL BE A GOOD MENTOR, I SWEAR. AND I'M REALLY EXCITED TO SHOW-- TEACH THESE KIDS WHAT IT TAKES TO BE ONE OF THE X-MEN.
IT'LL BE GREAT!
UH...
ABOUT THAT...

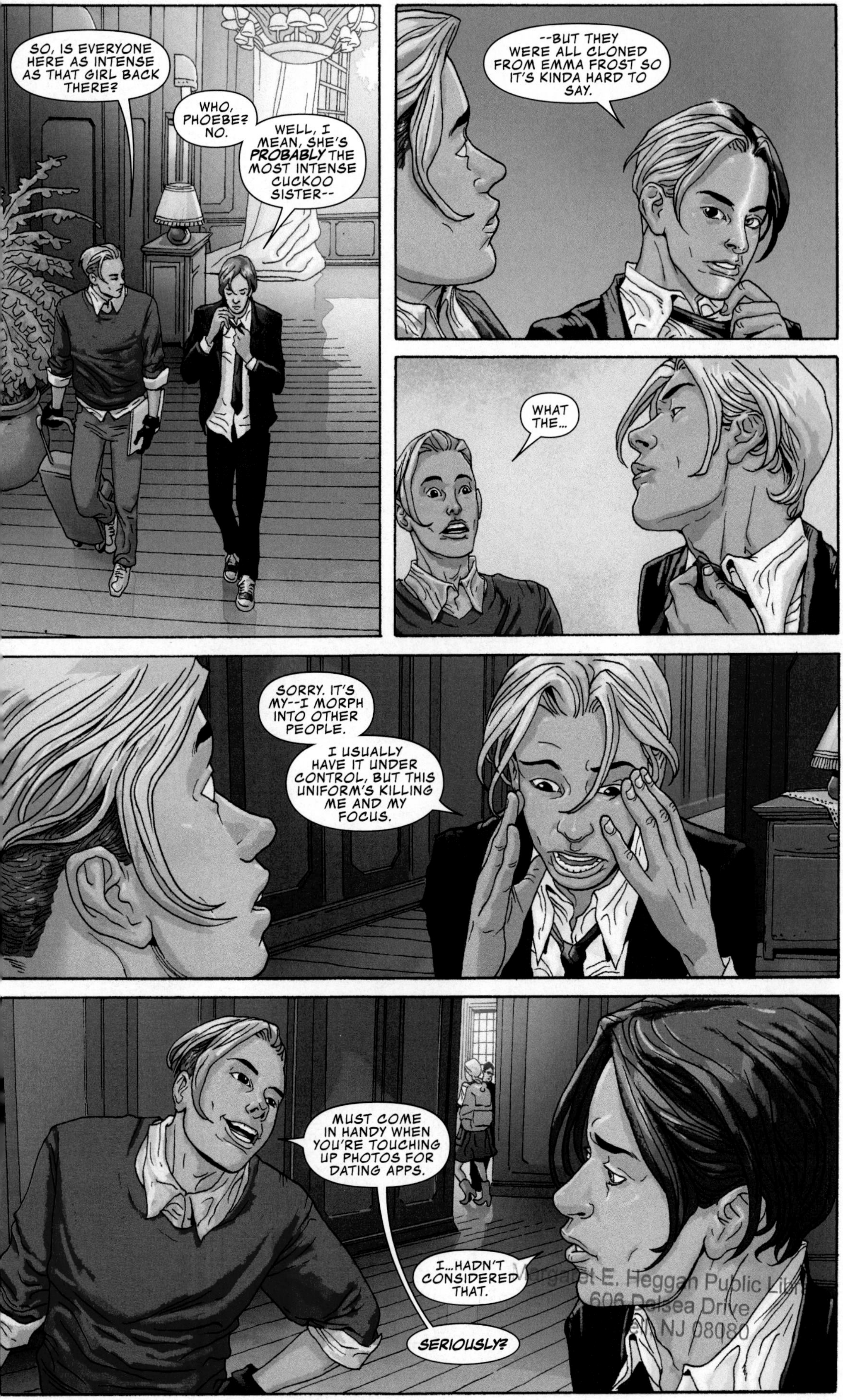
SO, IS EVERYONE HERE AS INTENSE AS THAT GIRL BACK THERE?
WHO, PHOEBE? NO.
WELL, I MEAN, SHE'S **PROBABLY** THE MOST INTENSE CUCKOO SISTER--
--BUT THEY WERE ALL CLONED FROM EMMA FROST SO IT'S KINDA HARD TO SAY.
WHAT THE...
SORRY. IT'S MY--I MORPH INTO OTHER PEOPLE.
I USUALLY HAVE IT UNDER CONTROL, BUT THIS UNIFORM'S KILLING ME AND MY FOCUS.
MUST COME IN HANDY WHEN YOU'RE TOUCHING UP PHOTOS FOR DATING APPS.
I...HADN'T CONSIDERED THAT.
SERIOUSLY?

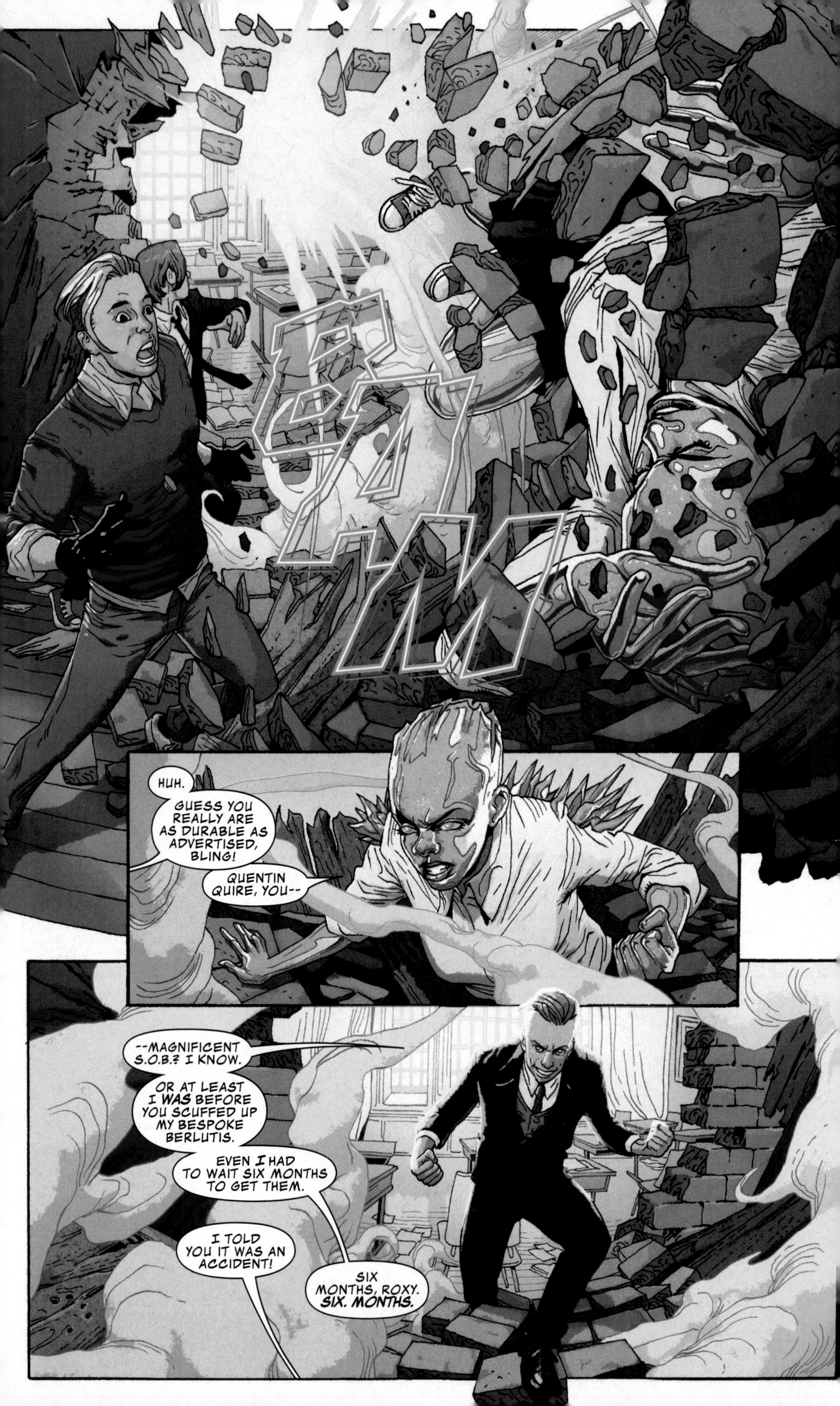
BRAM
HUH.
GUESS YOU REALLY ARE AS DURABLE AS ADVERTISED, BLING!
QUENTIN QUIRE, YOU--
--MAGNIFICENT S.O.B.? I KNOW.
OR AT LEAST I WAS BEFORE YOU SCUFFED UP MY BESPOKE BERLUTIS.
EVEN I HAD TO WAIT SIX MONTHS TO GET THEM.
I TOLD YOU IT WAS AN ACCIDENT!
SIX MONTHS, ROXY. SIX. MONTHS.

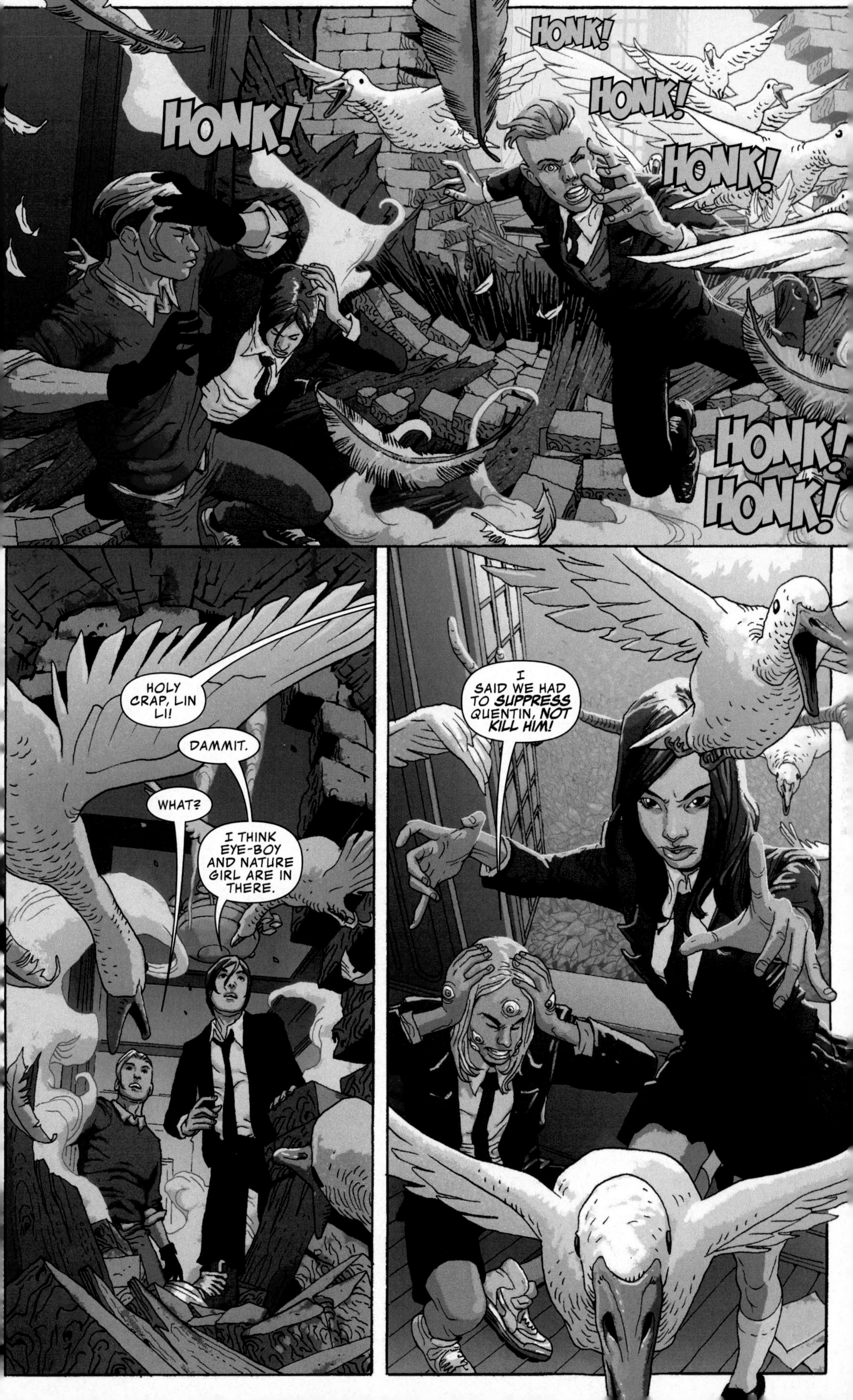
HONK!
HONK!
HONK!
HONK!
HONK!
HONK!
HOLY CRAP, LIN LI!
DAMMIT.
WHAT?
I THINK EYE-BOY AND NATURE GIRL ARE IN THERE.
I SAID WE HAD TO SUPPRESS QUENTIN, NOT KILL HIM!

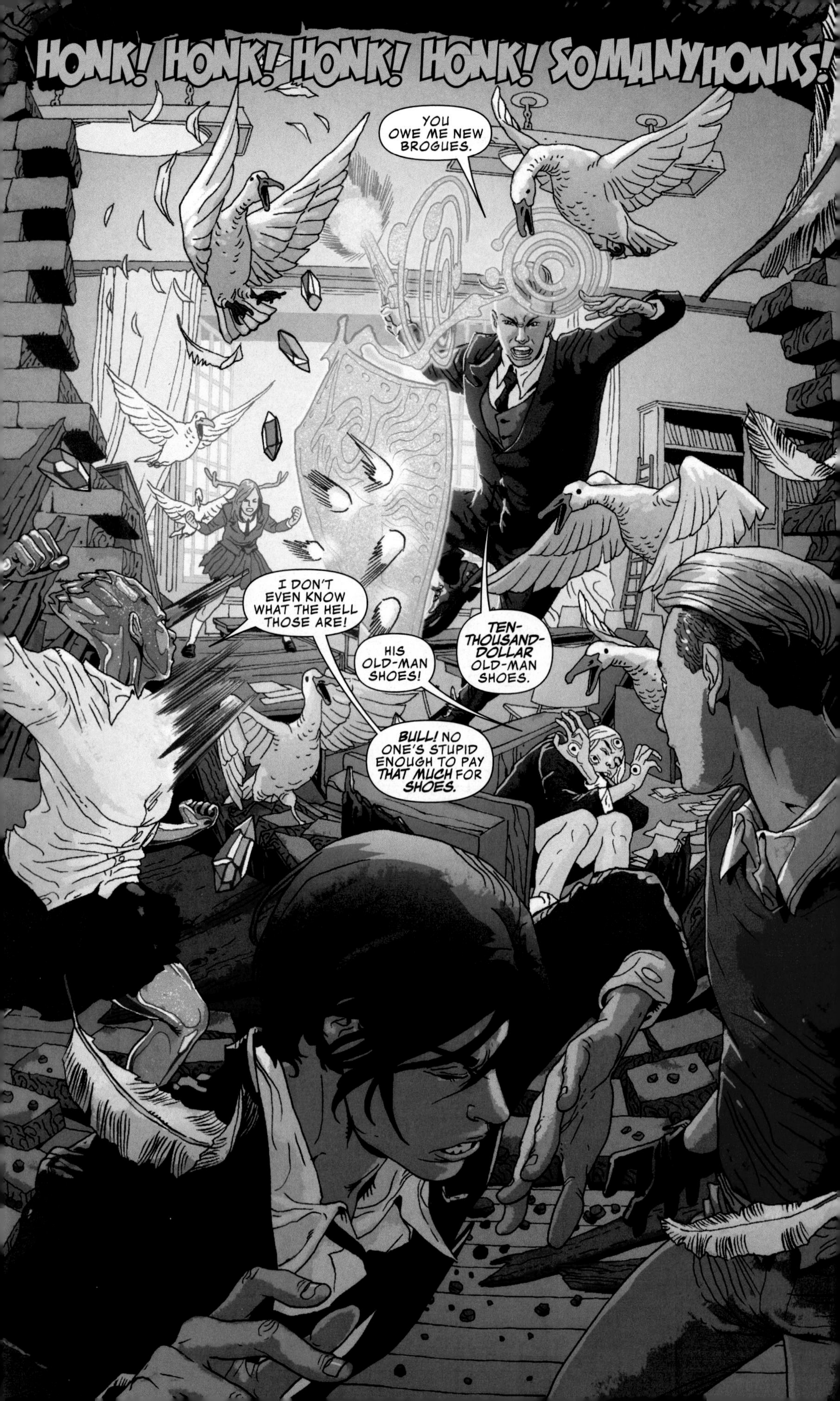
HONK! HONK! HONK! HONK! SOMANYHONKS!
YOU OWE ME NEW BROGUES.
I DON'T EVEN KNOW WHAT THE HELL THOSE ARE!
HIS OLD-MAN SHOES!
TEN-THOUSAND-DOLLAR OLD-MAN SHOES.
BULL! NO ONE'S STUPID ENOUGH TO PAY THAT MUCH FOR SHOES.

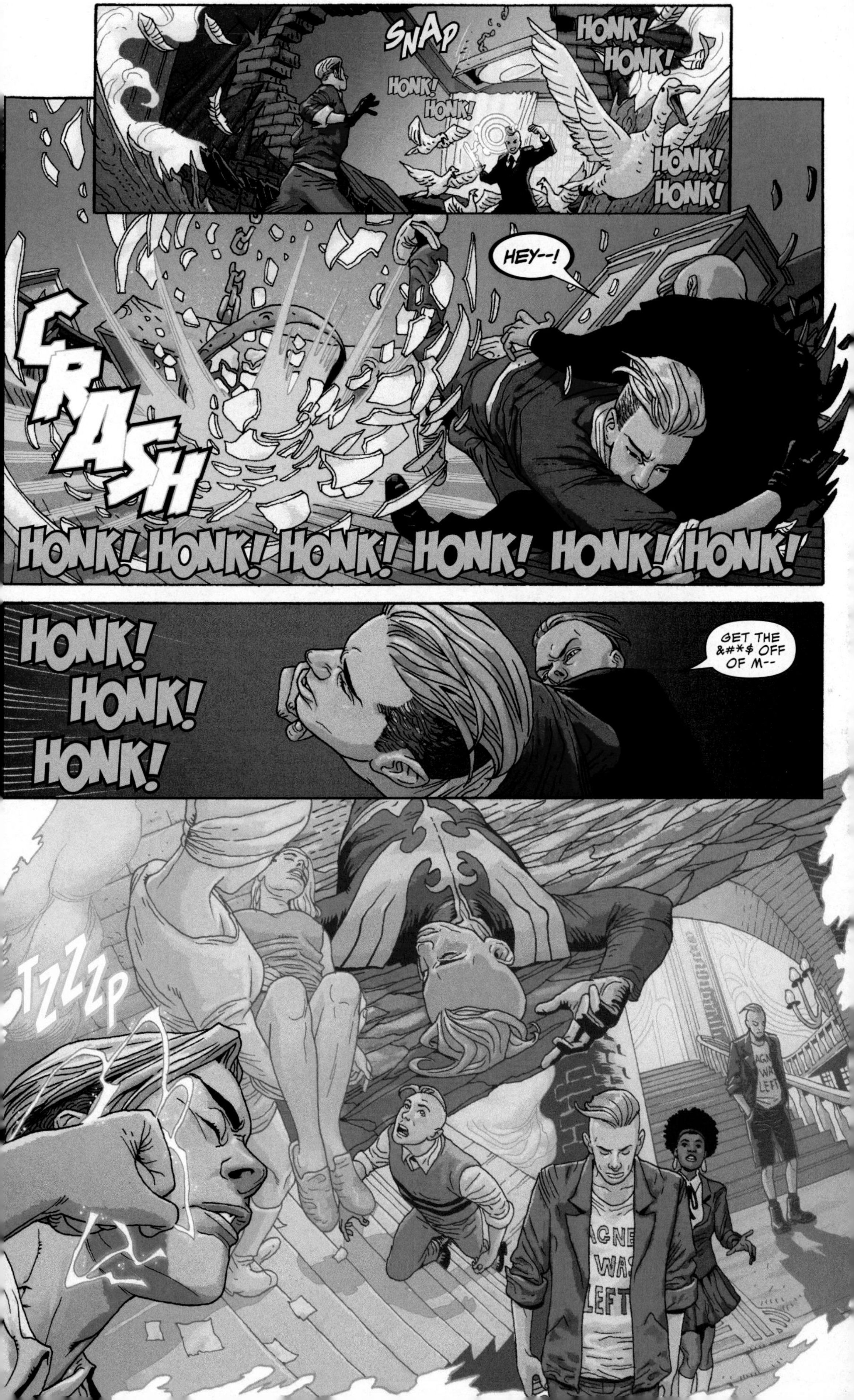
SNAP
HONK! HONK!
HONK! HONK!
HONK! HONK!
HONK! HONK!
HEY--!
CRASH
HONK! HONK! HONK! HONK! HONK! HONK!
HONK! HONK! HONK!
GET THE &#*$ OFF OF M--
TZZZP
AGNES WAS LEFT

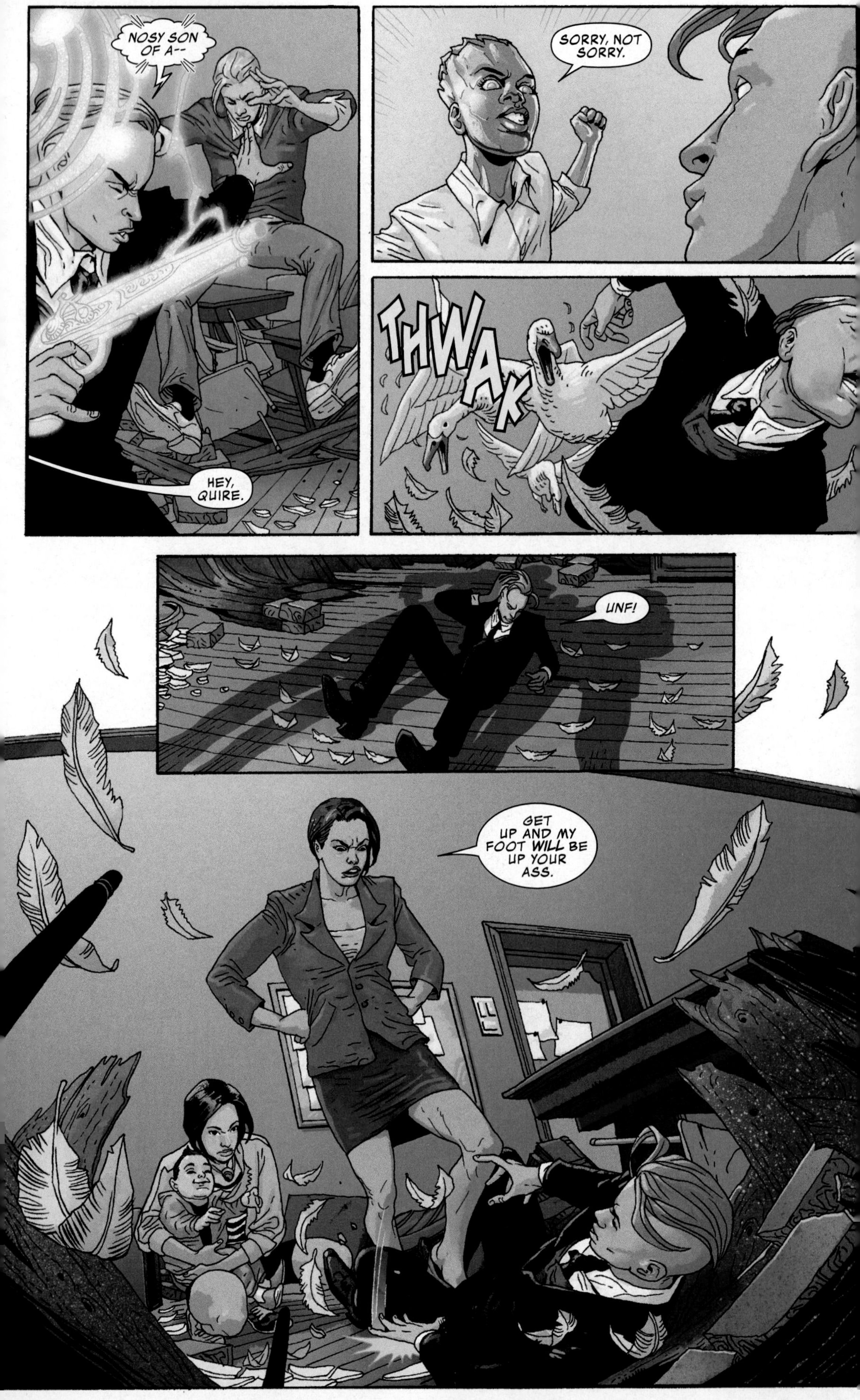

NOSY SON OF A--
HEY, QUIRE.
SORRY, NOT SORRY.
THWAK
UNF!
GET UP AND MY FOOT WILL BE UP YOUR ASS.

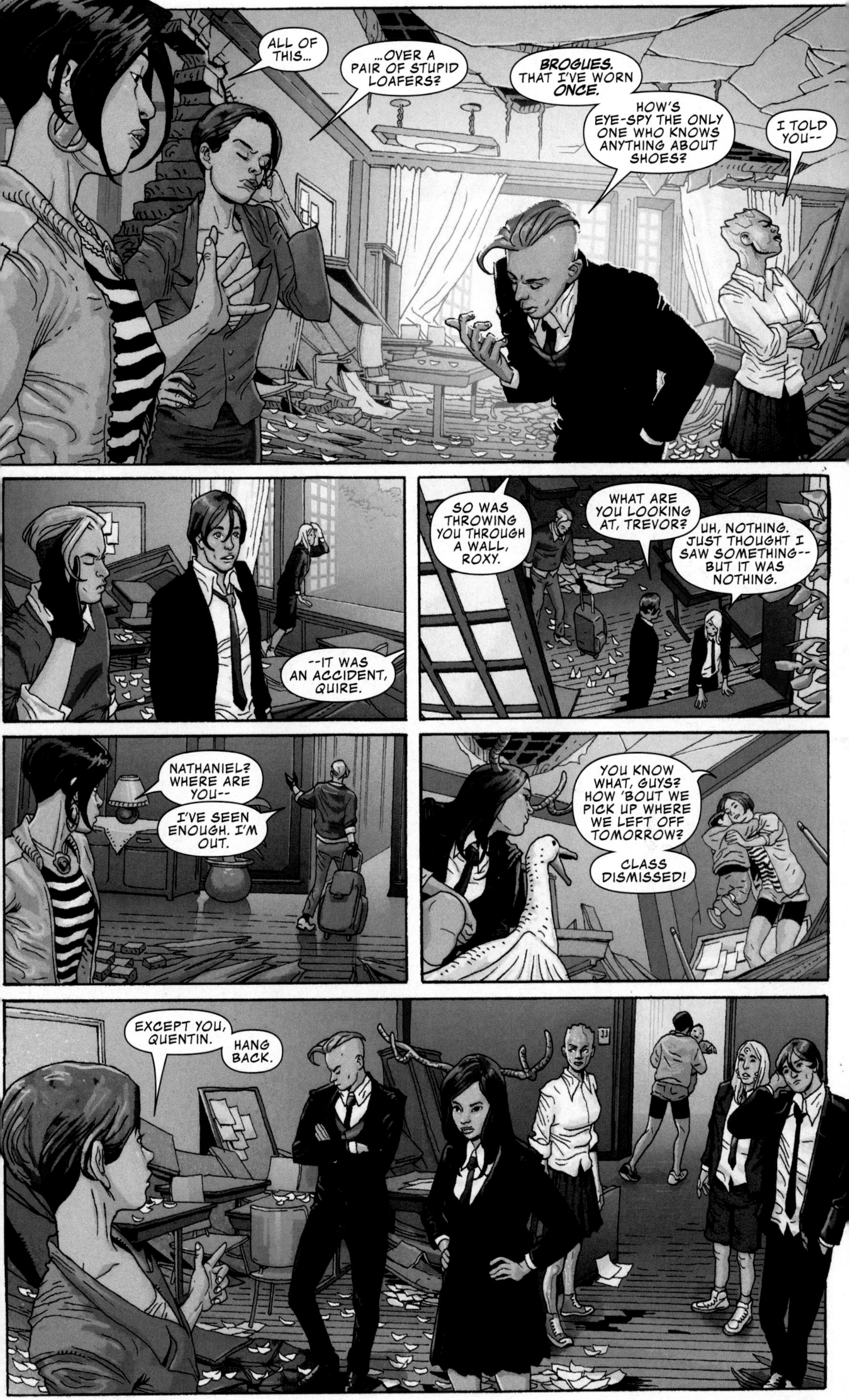
ALL OF THIS...
...OVER A PAIR OF STUPID LOAFERS?
BROGUES. THAT I'VE WORN ONCE.
HOW'S EYE-SPY THE ONLY ONE WHO KNOWS ANYTHING ABOUT SHOES?
I TOLD YOU--
--IT WAS AN ACCIDENT, QUIRE.
SO WAS THROWING YOU THROUGH A WALL, ROXY.
WHAT ARE YOU LOOKING AT, TREVOR?
UH, NOTHING. JUST THOUGHT I SAW SOMETHING-- BUT IT WAS NOTHING.
NATHANIEL? WHERE ARE YOU--
I'VE SEEN ENOUGH. I'M OUT.
YOU KNOW WHAT, GUYS? HOW 'BOUT WE PICK UP WHERE WE LEFT OFF TOMORROW?
CLASS DISMISSED!
EXCEPT YOU, QUENTIN.
HANG BACK.

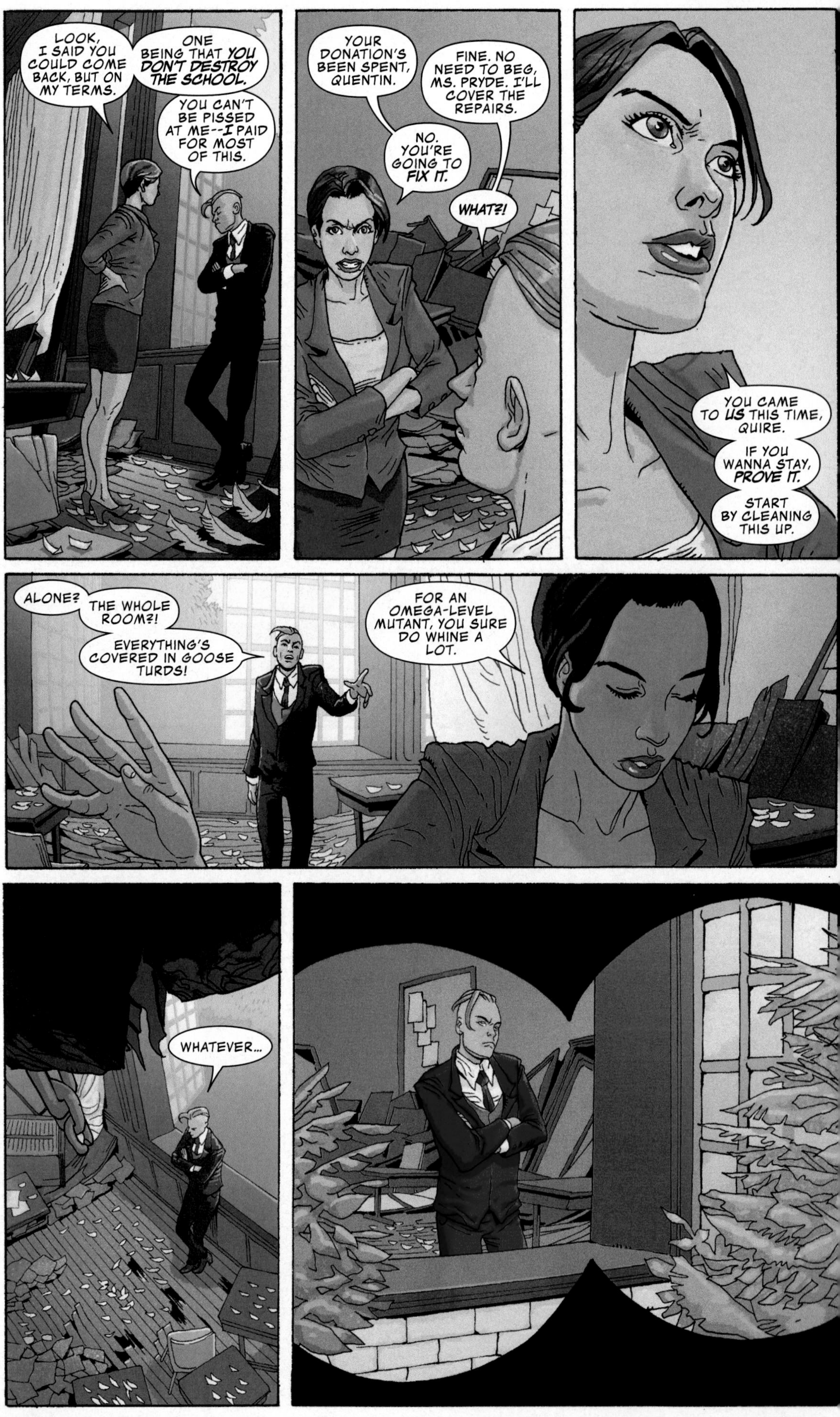
LOOK, I SAID YOU COULD COME BACK, BUT ON MY TERMS.
ONE BEING THAT YOU DON'T DESTROY THE SCHOOL.
YOU CAN'T BE PISSED AT ME--I PAID FOR MOST OF THIS.
YOUR DONATION'S BEEN SPENT, QUENTIN.
FINE. NO NEED TO BEG, MS. PRYDE. I'LL COVER THE REPAIRS.
NO. YOU'RE GOING TO FIX IT.
WHAT?!
YOU CAME TO US THIS TIME, QUIRE.
IF YOU WANNA STAY, PROVE IT.
START BY CLEANING THIS UP.
ALONE?
THE WHOLE ROOM?!
EVERYTHING'S COVERED IN GOOSE TURDS!
FOR AN OMEGA-LEVEL MUTANT, YOU SURE DO WHINE A LOT.
WHATEVER...

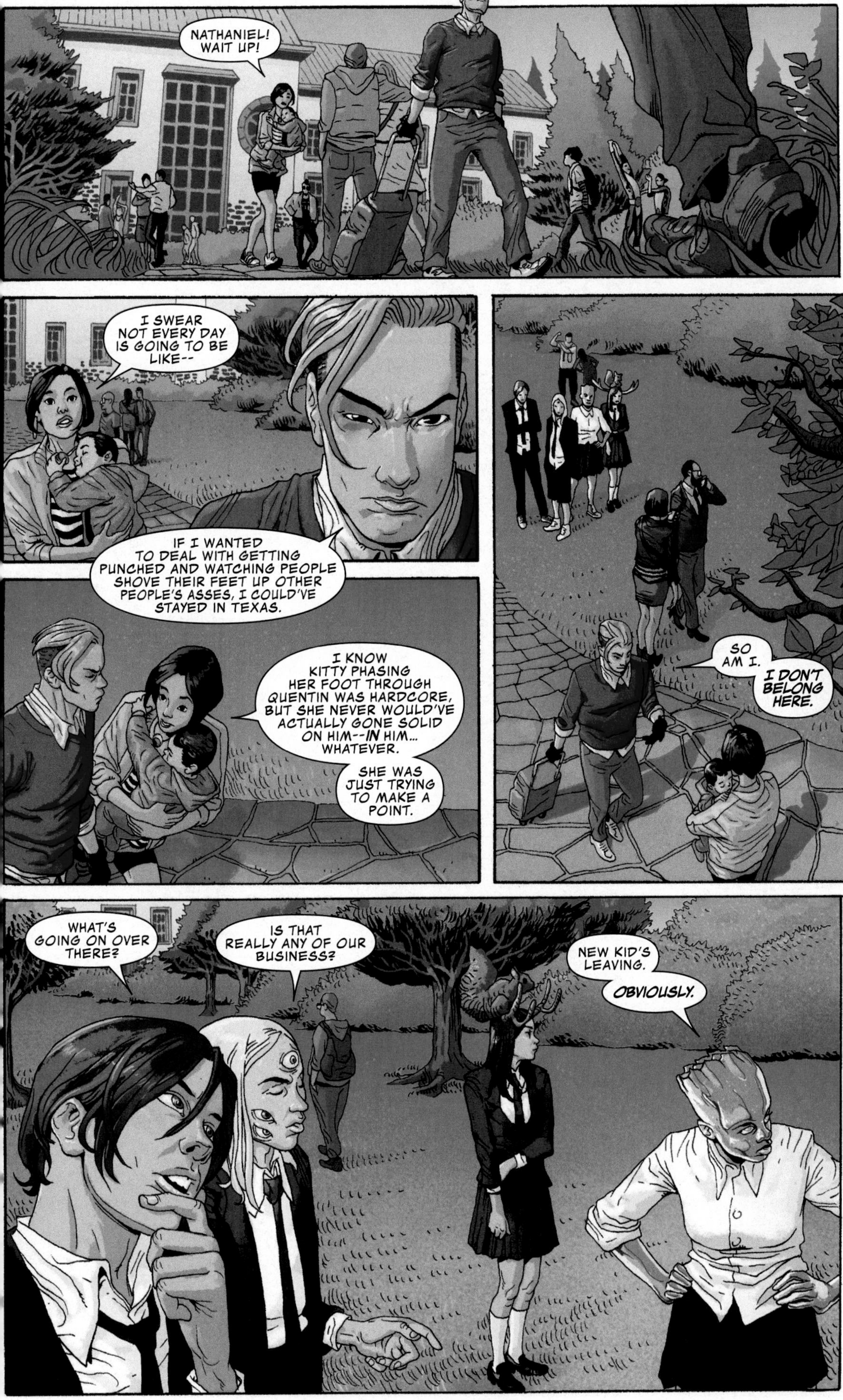

NATHANIEL! WAIT UP!
I SWEAR NOT EVERY DAY IS GOING TO BE LIKE--
IF I WANTED TO DEAL WITH GETTING PUNCHED AND WATCHING PEOPLE SHOVE THEIR FEET UP OTHER PEOPLE'S ASSES, I COULD'VE STAYED IN TEXAS.
I KNOW KITTY PHASING HER FOOT THROUGH QUENTIN WAS HARDCORE, BUT SHE NEVER WOULD'VE ACTUALLY GONE SOLID ON HIM--*IN* HIM... WHATEVER.
SHE WAS JUST TRYING TO MAKE A POINT.
SO AM I. *I DON'T BELONG HERE.*
WHAT'S GOING ON OVER THERE?
IS THAT REALLY ANY OF OUR BUSINESS?
NEW KID'S LEAVING.
OBVIOUSLY.

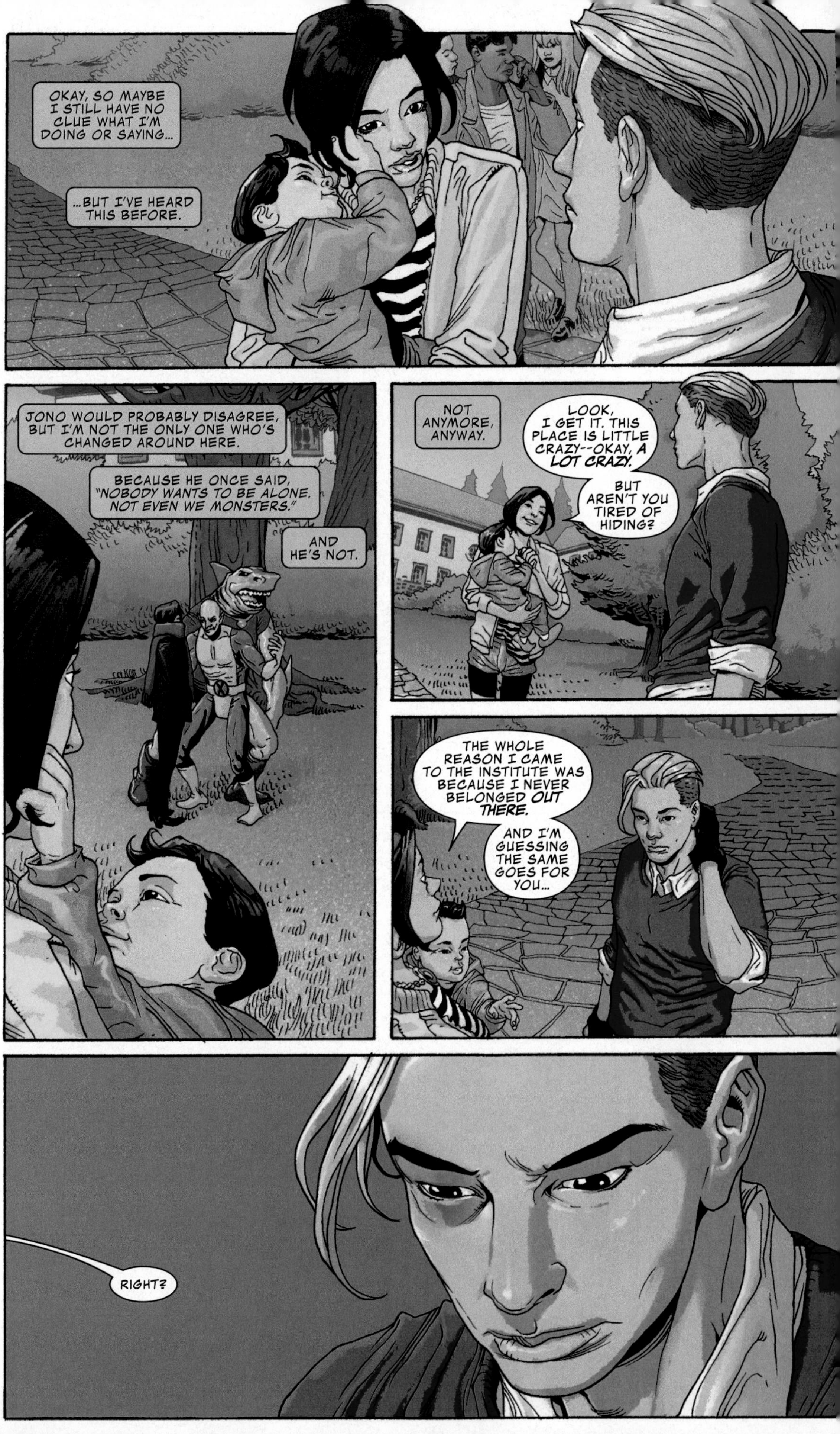
OKAY, SO MAYBE I STILL HAVE NO CLUE WHAT I'M DOING OR SAYING...
...BUT I'VE HEARD THIS BEFORE.
JONO WOULD PROBABLY DISAGREE, BUT I'M NOT THE ONLY ONE WHO'S CHANGED AROUND HERE.
BECAUSE HE ONCE SAID, "NOBODY WANTS TO BE ALONE. NOT EVEN WE MONSTERS."
AND HE'S NOT.
NOT ANYMORE, ANYWAY.
LOOK, I GET IT. THIS PLACE IS LITTLE CRAZY--OKAY, A LOT CRAZY.
BUT AREN'T YOU TIRED OF HIDING?
THE WHOLE REASON I CAME TO THE INSTITUTE WAS BECAUSE I NEVER BELONGED OUT THERE.
AND I'M GUESSING THE SAME GOES FOR YOU...
RIGHT?

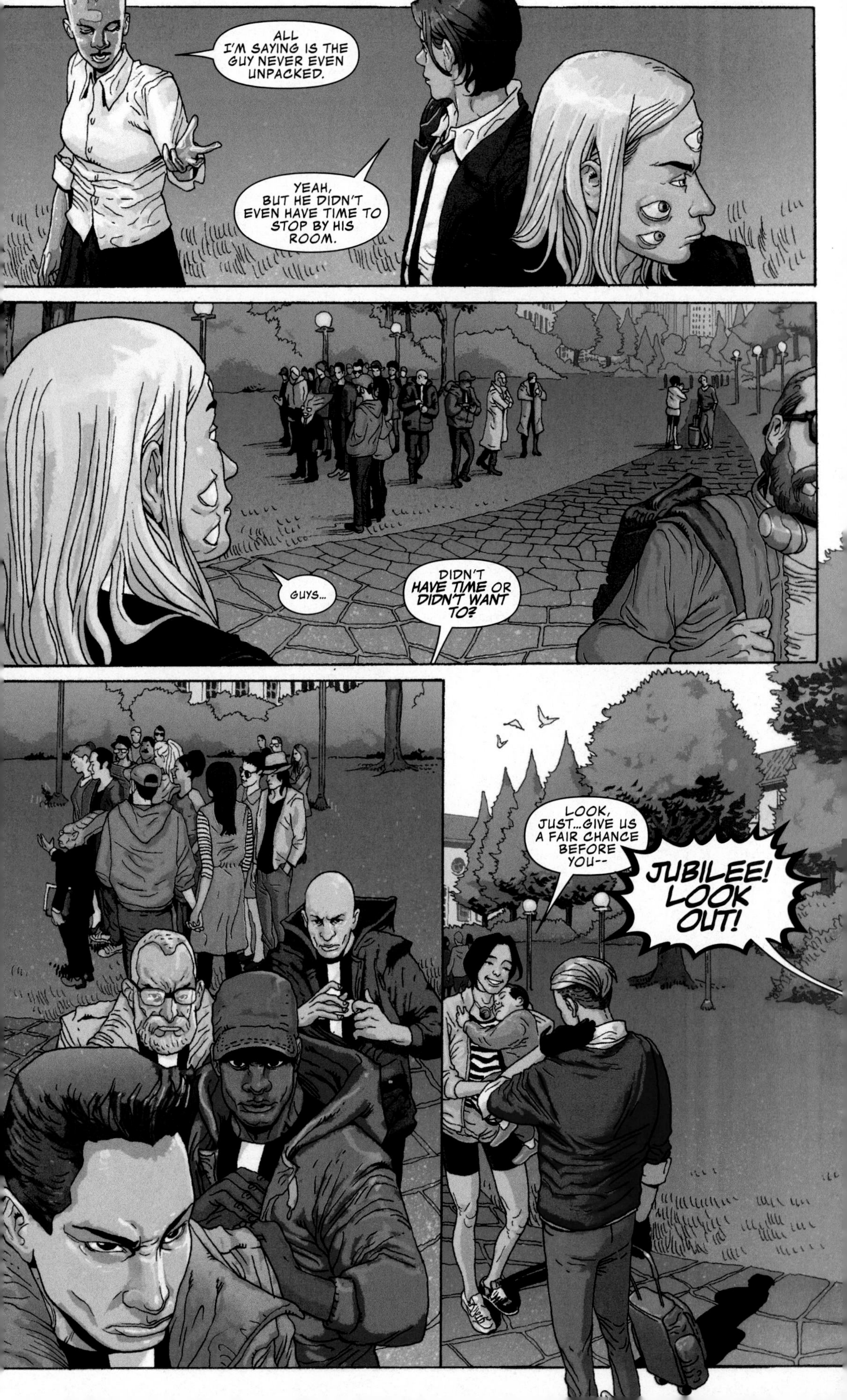
ALL I'M SAYING IS THE GUY NEVER EVEN UNPACKED.
YEAH, BUT HE DIDN'T EVEN HAVE TIME TO STOP BY HIS ROOM.
GUYS...
DIDN'T HAVE TIME OR DIDN'T WANT TO?
LOOK, JUST...GIVE US A FAIR CHANCE BEFORE YOU--
JUBILEE! LOOK OUT!

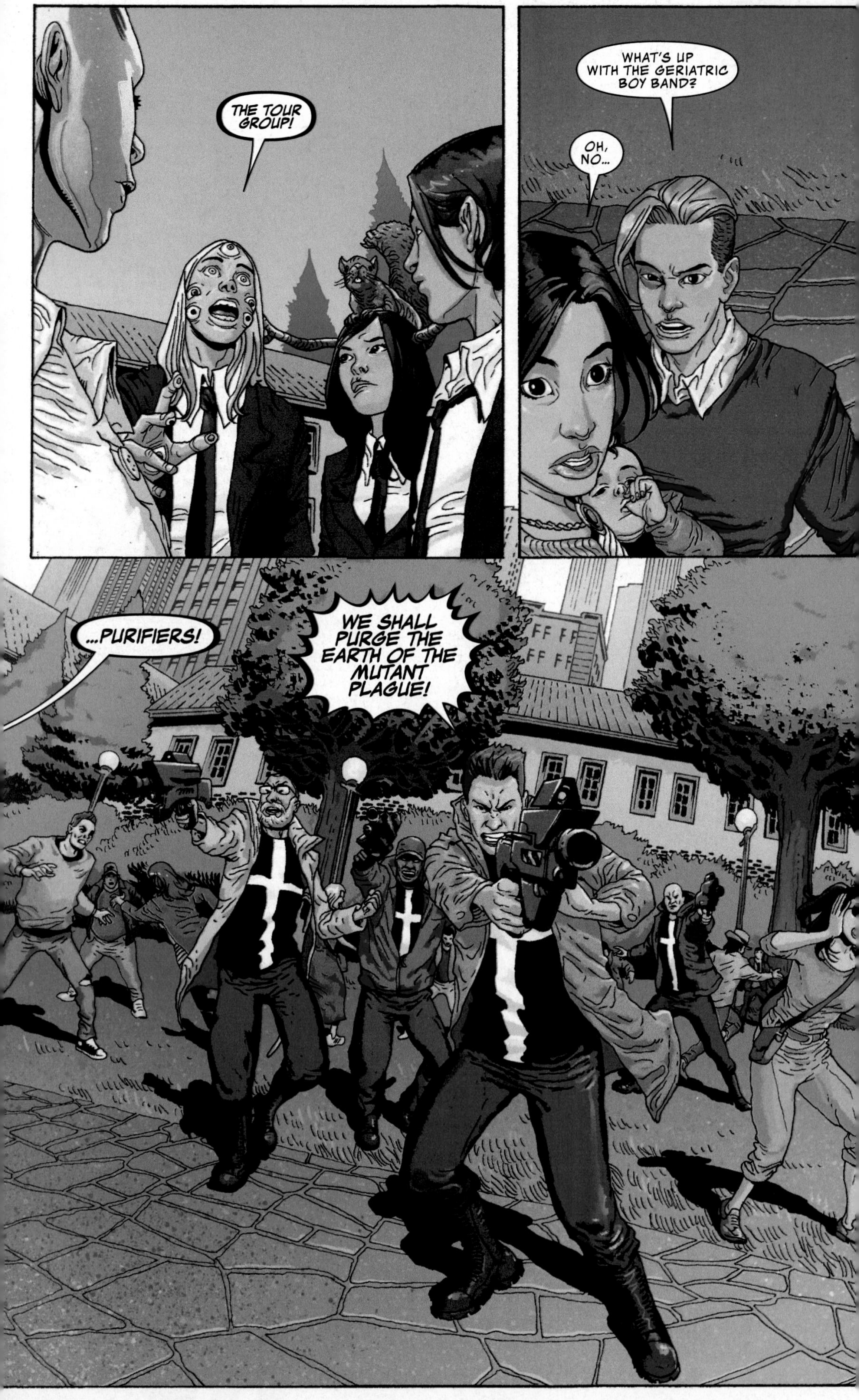
THE TOUR GROUP!
WHAT'S UP WITH THE GERIATRIC BOY BAND?
OH, NO...
...PURIFIERS!
WE SHALL PURGE THE EARTH OF THE MUTANT PLAGUE!

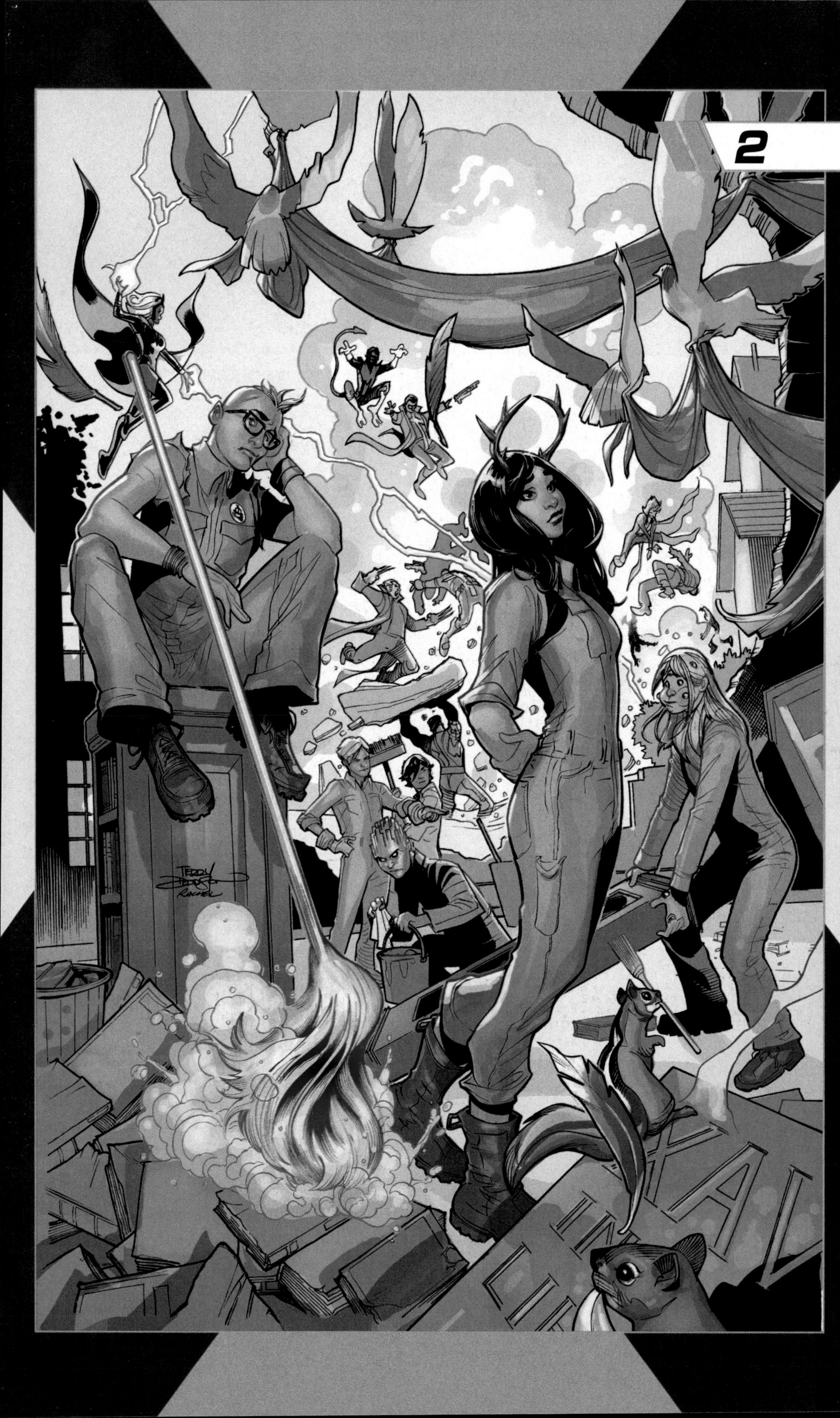
2

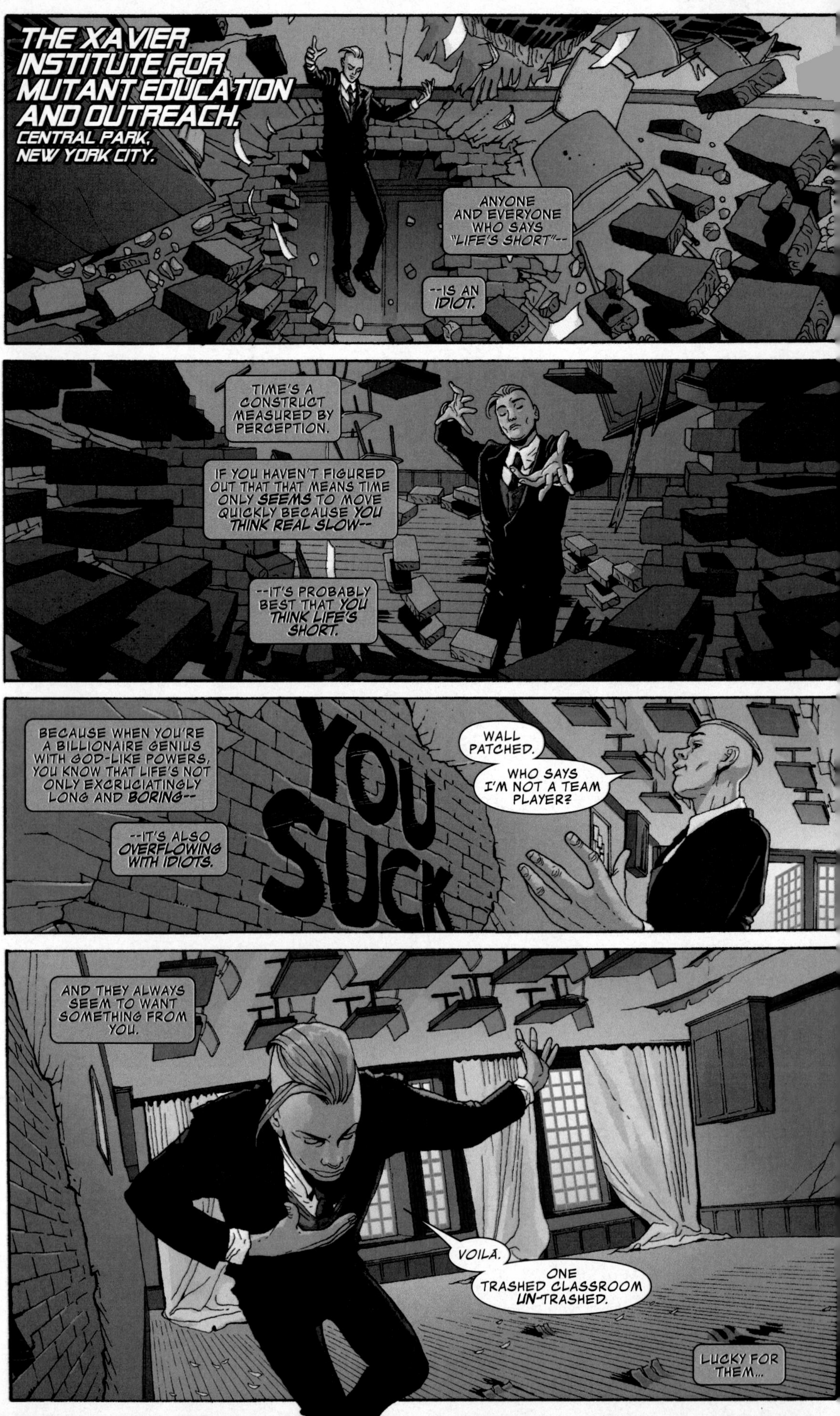
THE XAVIER INSTITUTE FOR MUTANT EDUCATION AND OUTREACH.
CENTRAL PARK, NEW YORK CITY.
ANYONE AND EVERYONE WHO SAYS "LIFE'S SHORT"--
--IS AN IDIOT.
TIME'S A CONSTRUCT MEASURED BY PERCEPTION.
IF YOU HAVEN'T FIGURED OUT THAT THAT MEANS TIME ONLY SEEMS TO MOVE QUICKLY BECAUSE YOU THINK REAL SLOW--
--IT'S PROBABLY BEST THAT YOU THINK LIFE'S SHORT.
BECAUSE WHEN YOU'RE A BILLIONAIRE GENIUS WITH GOD-LIKE POWERS, YOU KNOW THAT LIFE'S NOT ONLY EXCRUCIATINGLY LONG AND BORING--
--IT'S ALSO OVERFLOWING WITH IDIOTS.
YOU SUCK
WALL PATCHED.
WHO SAYS I'M NOT A TEAM PLAYER?
AND THEY ALWAYS SEEM TO WANT SOMETHING FROM YOU.
VOILÀ.
ONE TRASHED CLASSROOM UN-TRASHED.
LUCKY FOR THEM...

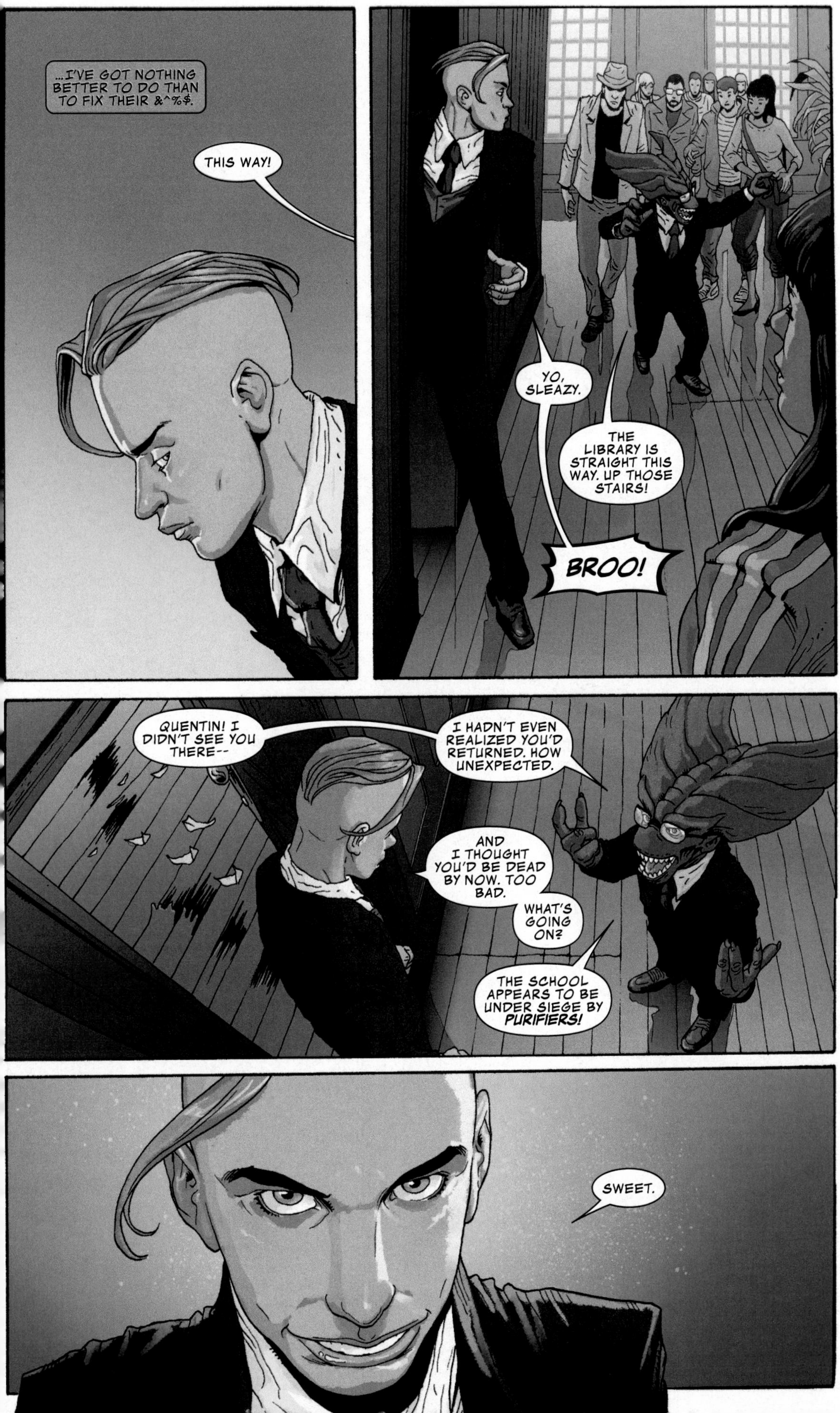

...I'VE GOT NOTHING BETTER TO DO THAN TO FIX THEIR &^%$.
THIS WAY!
YO, SLEAZY.
THE LIBRARY IS STRAIGHT THIS WAY. UP THOSE STAIRS!
BROO!
QUENTIN! I DIDN'T SEE YOU THERE--
I HADN'T EVEN REALIZED YOU'D RETURNED. HOW UNEXPECTED.
AND I THOUGHT YOU'D BE DEAD BY NOW. TOO BAD.
WHAT'S GOING ON?
THE SCHOOL APPEARS TO BE UNDER SIEGE BY PURIFIERS!
SWEET.

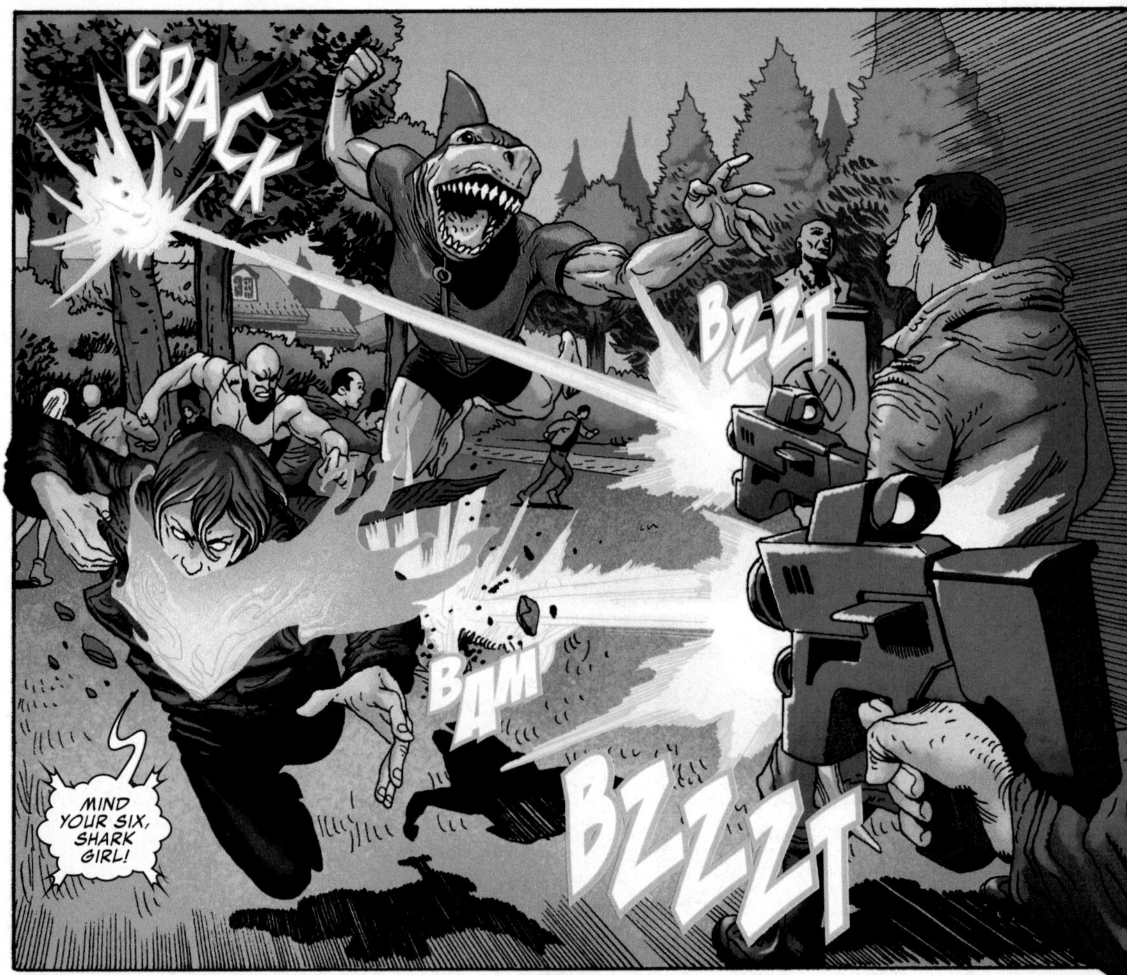
CRACK
BZZT
BAM
MIND YOUR SIX, SHARK GIRL!
BZZZZT

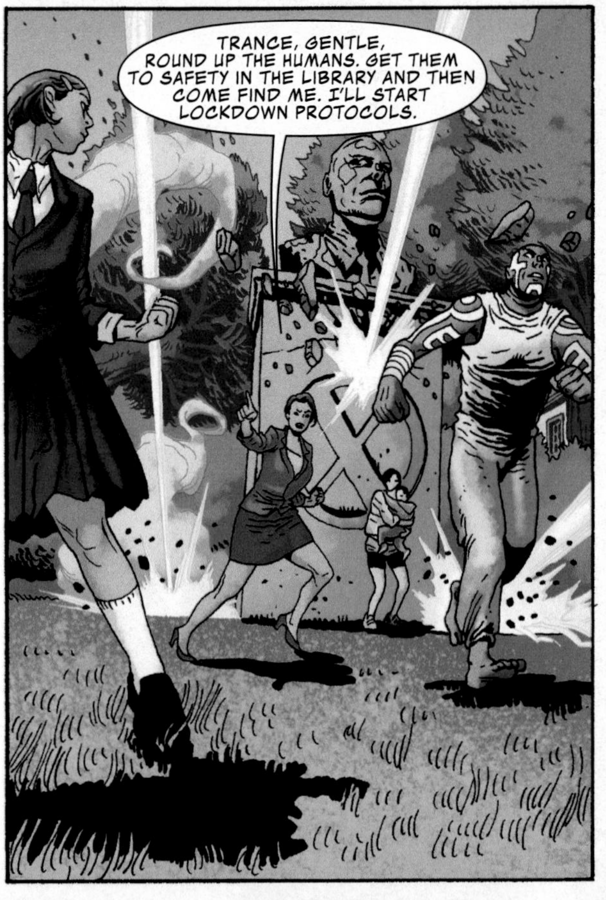
TRANCE, GENTLE, ROUND UP THE HUMANS. GET THEM TO SAFETY IN THE LIBRARY AND THEN COME FIND ME. I'LL START LOCKDOWN PROTOCOLS.

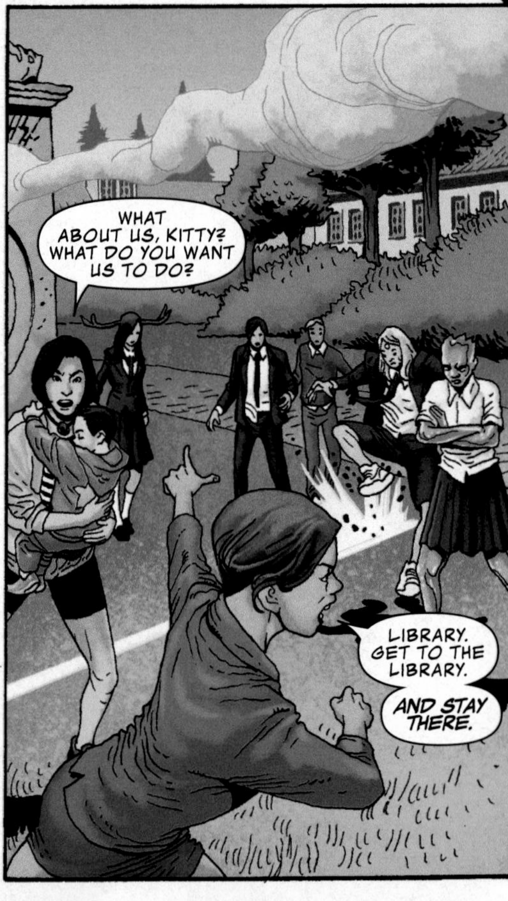
WHAT ABOUT US, KITTY? WHAT DO YOU WANT US TO DO?
LIBRARY. GET TO THE LIBRARY.
AND STAY THERE.

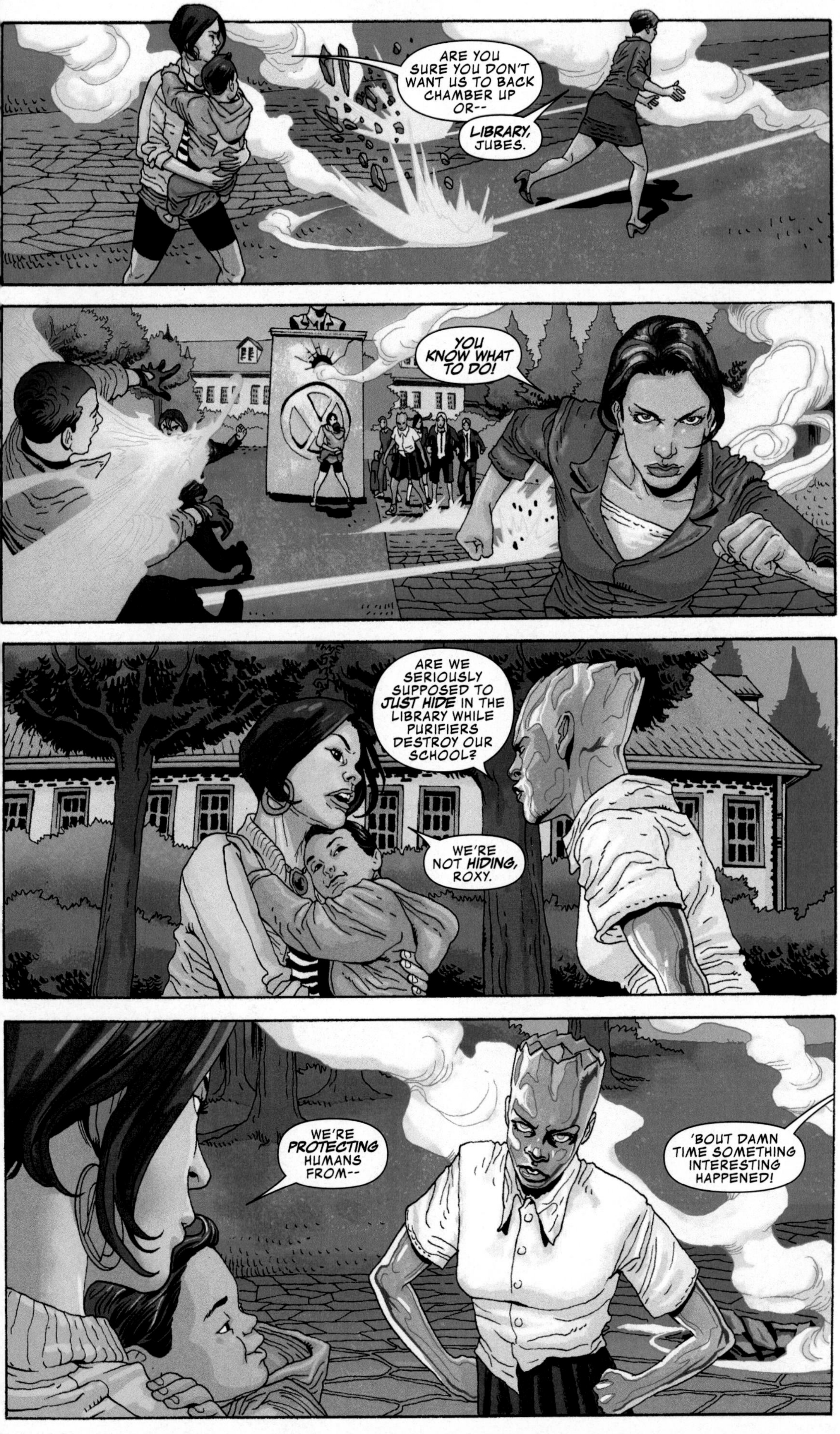
ARE YOU SURE YOU DON'T WANT US TO BACK CHAMBER UP OR--
LIBRARY, JUBES.
YOU KNOW WHAT TO DO!
ARE WE SERIOUSLY SUPPOSED TO JUST HIDE IN THE LIBRARY WHILE PURIFIERS DESTROY OUR SCHOOL?
WE'RE NOT HIDING, ROXY.
WE'RE PROTECTING HUMANS FROM--
'BOUT DAMN TIME SOMETHING INTERESTING HAPPENED!

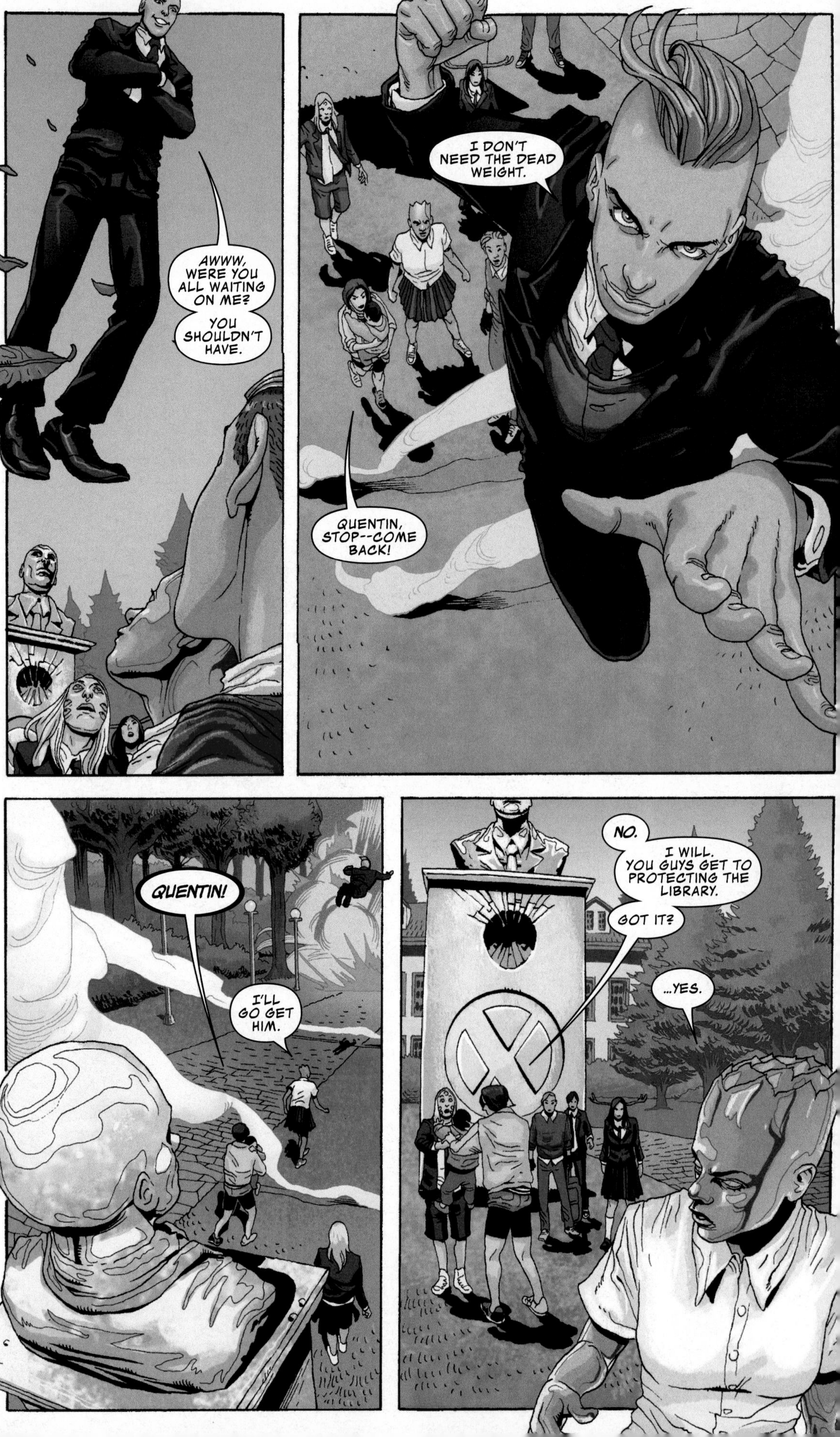
AWWW, WERE YOU ALL WAITING ON ME?
YOU SHOULDN'T HAVE.
I DON'T NEED THE DEAD WEIGHT.
QUENTIN, STOP--COME BACK!
QUENTIN!
I'LL GO GET HIM.
NO.
I WILL. YOU GUYS GET TO PROTECTING THE LIBRARY.
GOT IT?
...YES.

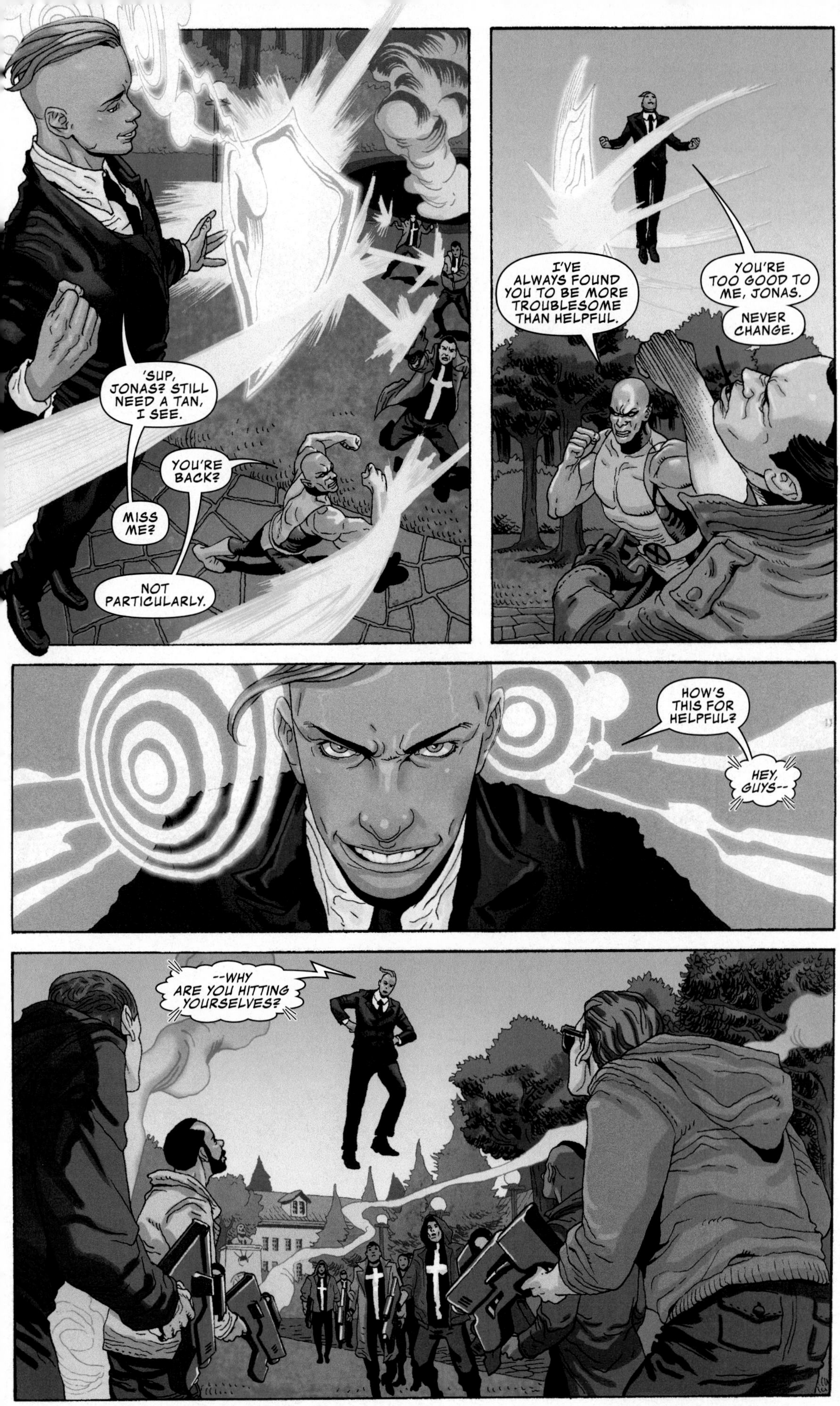
'SUP, JONAS? STILL NEED A TAN, I SEE.
YOU'RE BACK?
MISS ME?
NOT PARTICULARLY.
I'VE ALWAYS FOUND YOU TO BE MORE TROUBLESOME THAN HELPFUL.
YOU'RE TOO GOOD TO ME, JONAS.
NEVER CHANGE.
HOW'S THIS FOR HELPFUL?
HEY, GUYS--
--WHY ARE YOU HITTING YOURSELVES?

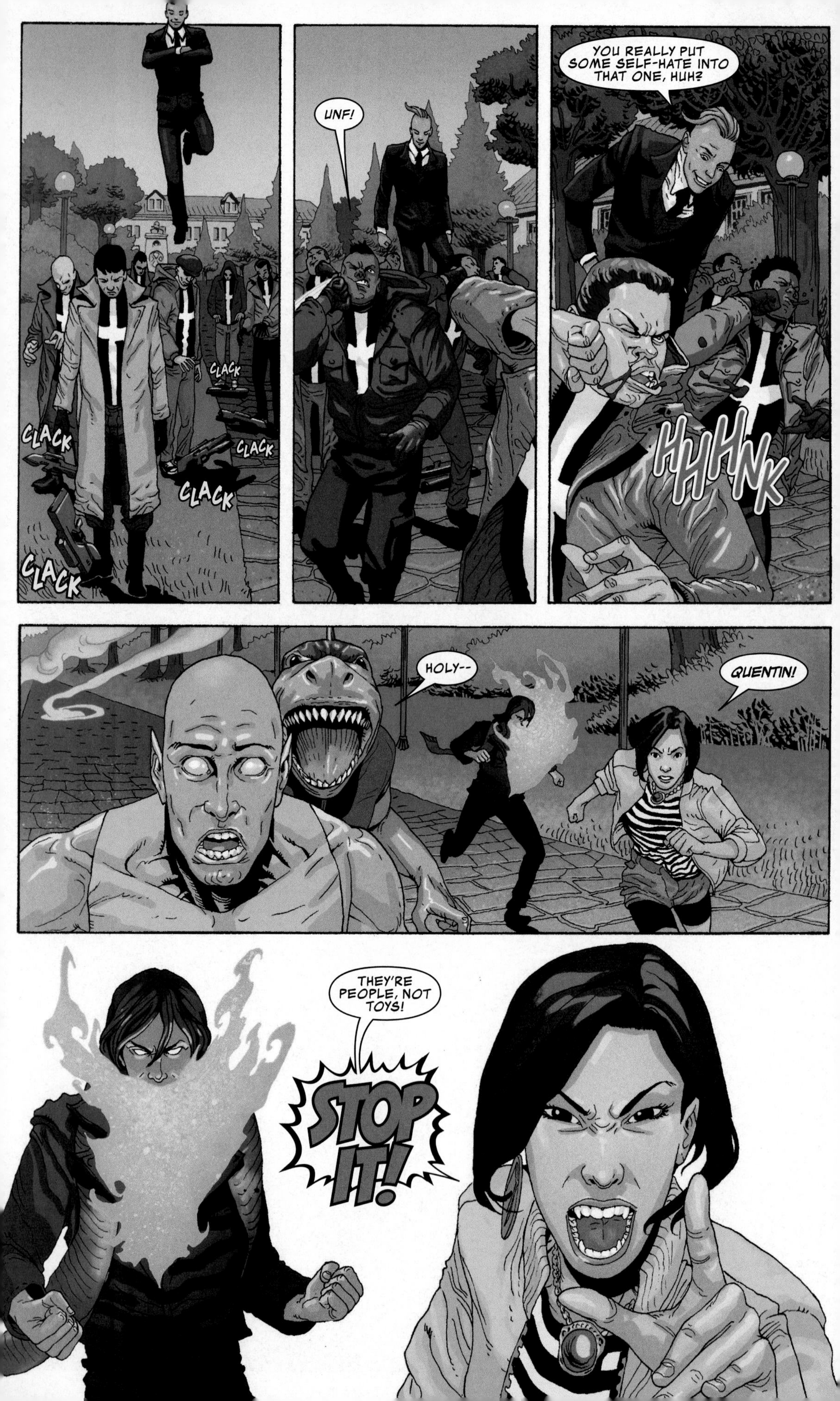
CLACK
CLACK
CLACK
CLACK
CLACK
UNF!
YOU REALLY PUT SOME SELF-HATE INTO THAT ONE, HUH?
HHHHNK
HOLY--
QUENTIN!
THEY'RE PEOPLE, NOT TOYS!
STOP IT!

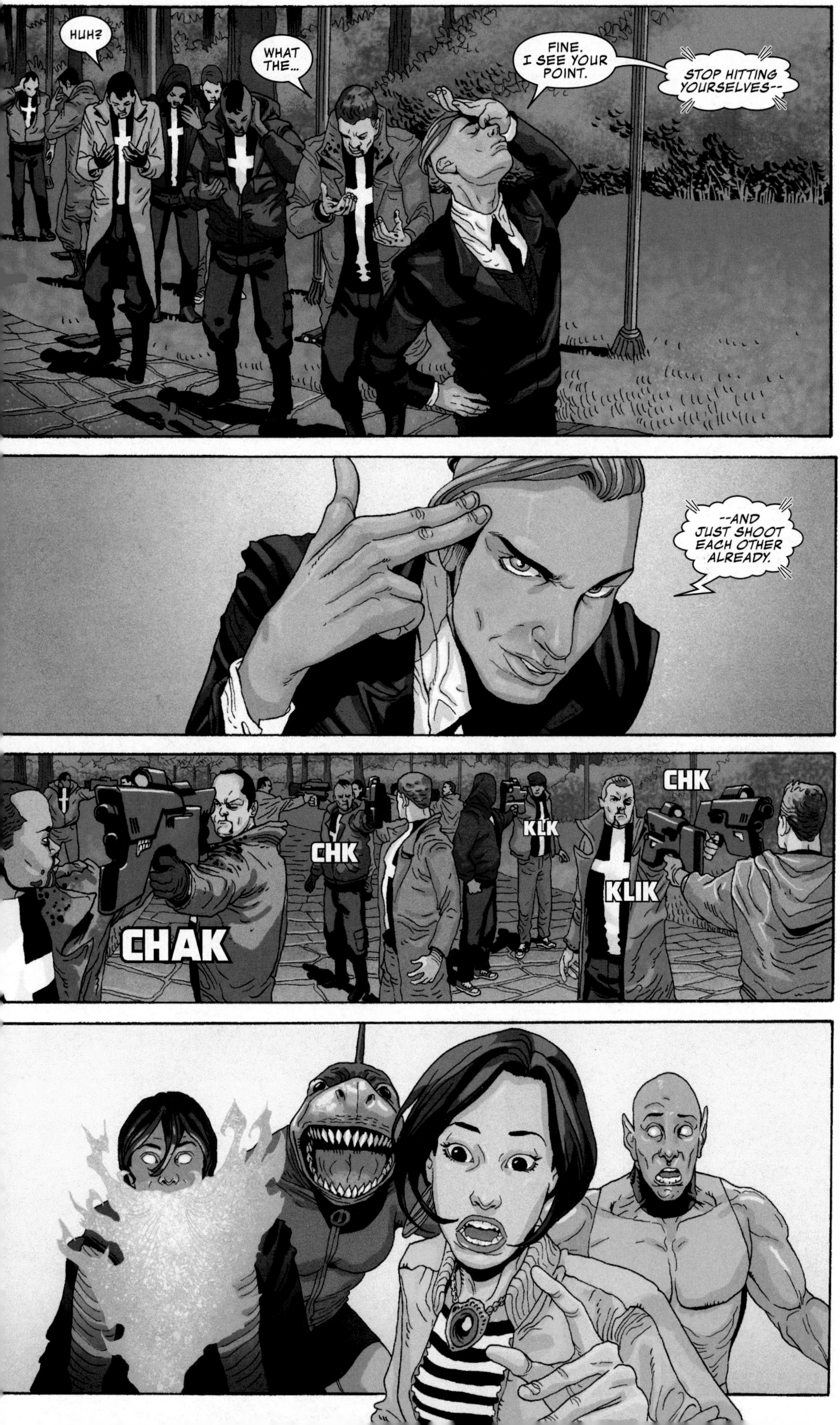
HUH?
WHAT THE...
FINE. I SEE YOUR POINT.
STOP HITTING YOURSELVES--
--AND JUST SHOOT EACH OTHER ALREADY.
CHAK
CHK
KLK
KLIK
CHK

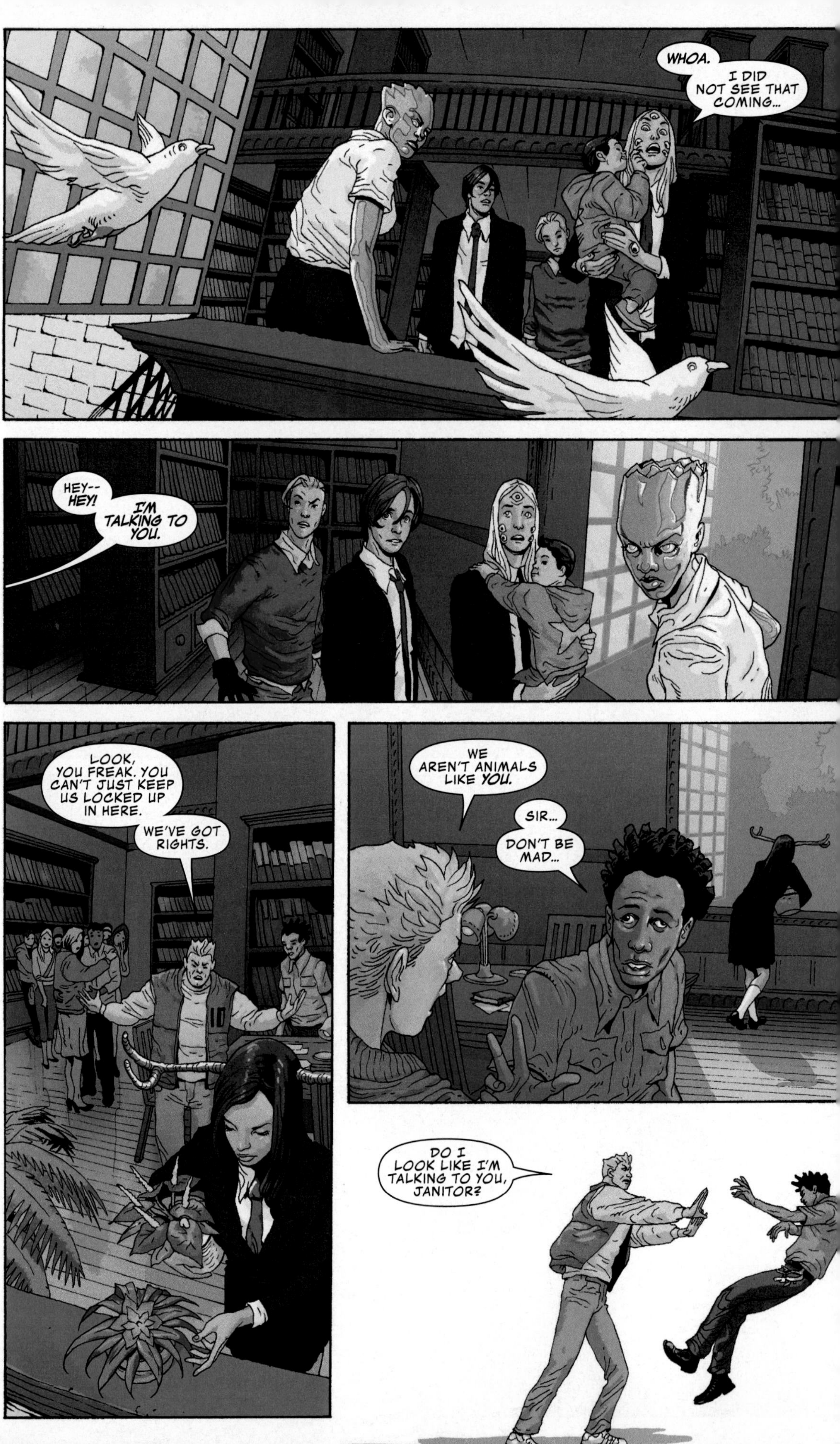
WHOA.
I DID NOT SEE THAT COMING...
HEY-- HEY!
I'M TALKING TO YOU.
LOOK, YOU FREAK. YOU CAN'T JUST KEEP US LOCKED UP IN HERE.
WE'VE GOT RIGHTS.
WE AREN'T ANIMALS LIKE YOU.
SIR...
DON'T BE MAD...
DO I LOOK LIKE I'M TALKING TO YOU, JANITOR?

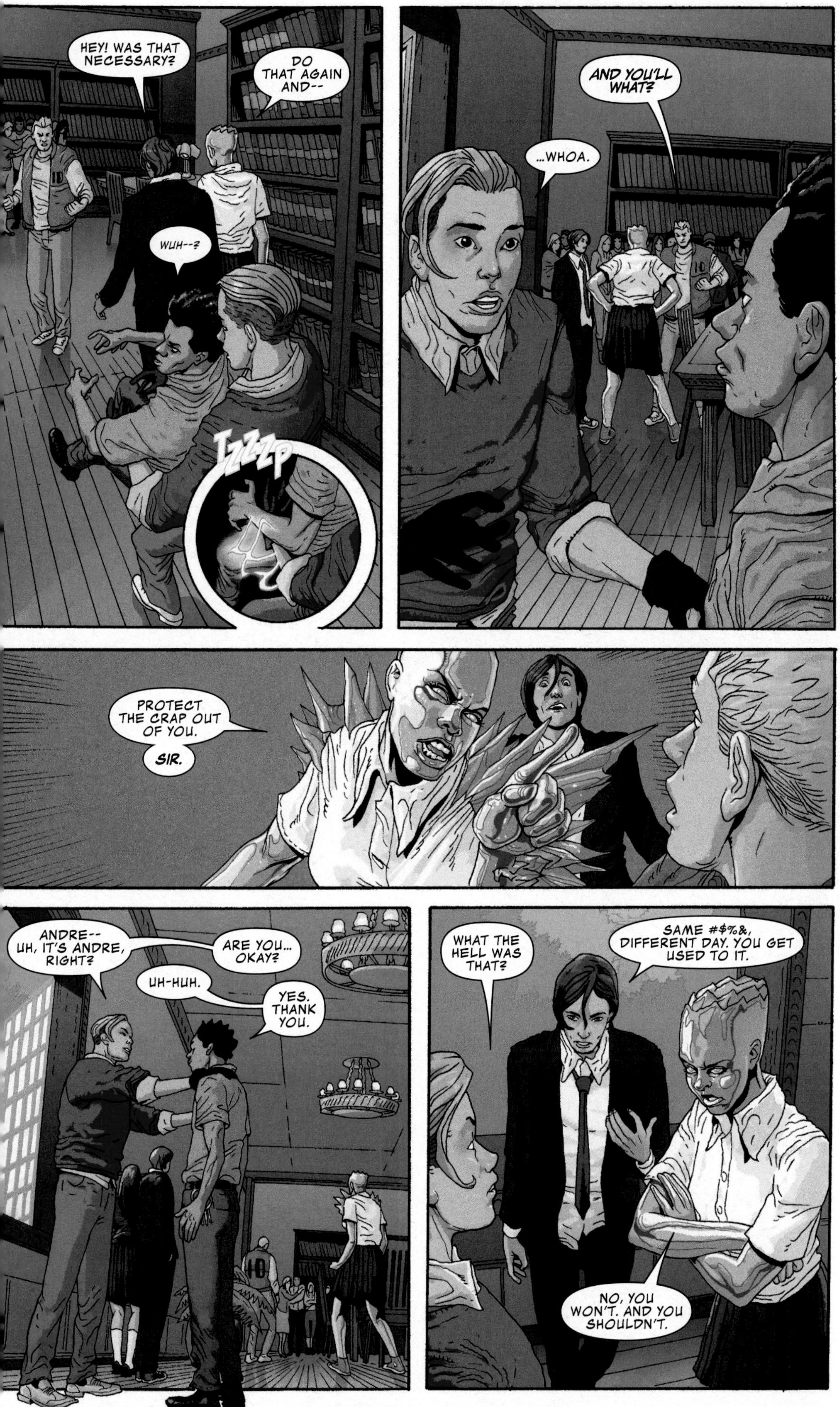

HEY! WAS THAT NECESSARY?
DO THAT AGAIN AND--
WUH--?
IZZZZP
AND YOU'LL WHAT?
...WHOA.
PROTECT THE CRAP OUT OF YOU.
SIR.
ANDRE-- UH, IT'S ANDRE, RIGHT?
ARE YOU... OKAY?
UH-HUH.
YES. THANK YOU.
WHAT THE HELL WAS THAT?
SAME #$%&, DIFFERENT DAY. YOU GET USED TO IT.
NO, YOU WON'T. AND YOU SHOULDN'T.

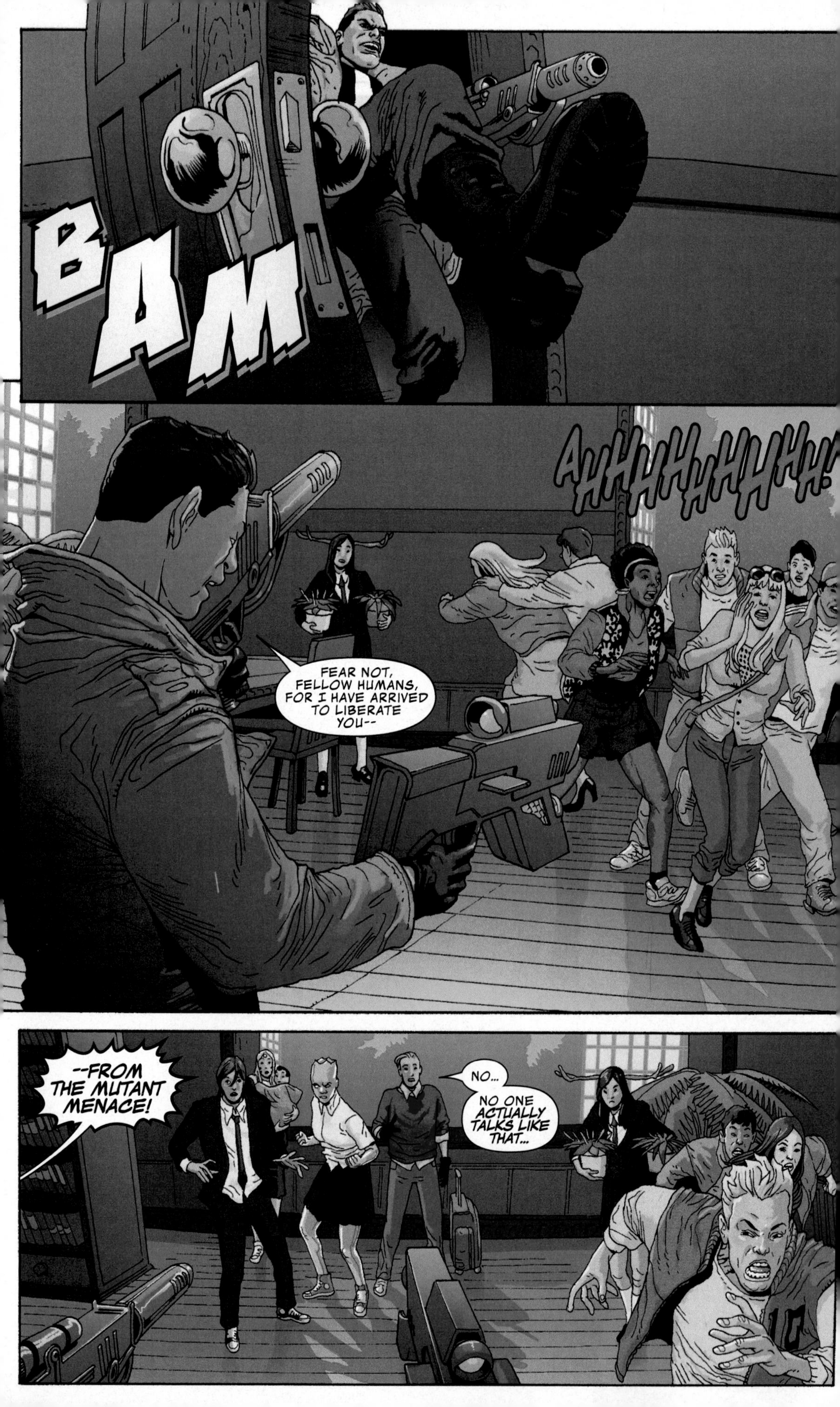
BAM
AHHHHHHHHH!
FEAR NOT, FELLOW HUMANS, FOR I HAVE ARRIVED TO LIBERATE YOU--
--FROM THE MUTANT MENACE!
NO...
NO ONE ACTUALLY TALKS LIKE THAT...

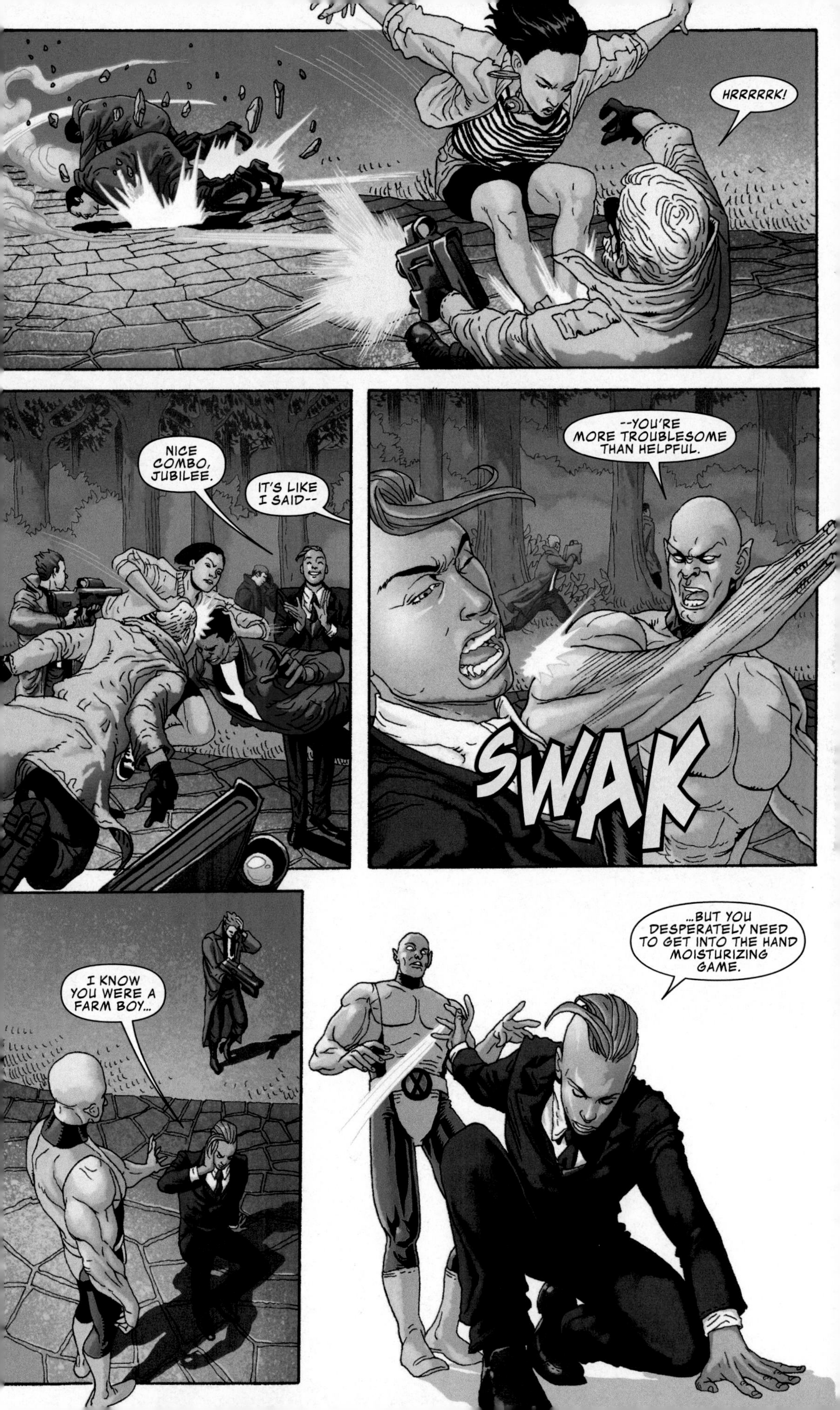
HRRRRRK!
NICE COMBO, JUBILEE.
IT'S LIKE I SAID--
--YOU'RE MORE TROUBLESOME THAN HELPFUL.
SWAK
I KNOW YOU WERE A FARM BOY...
...BUT YOU DESPERATELY NEED TO GET INTO THE HAND MOISTURIZING GAME.

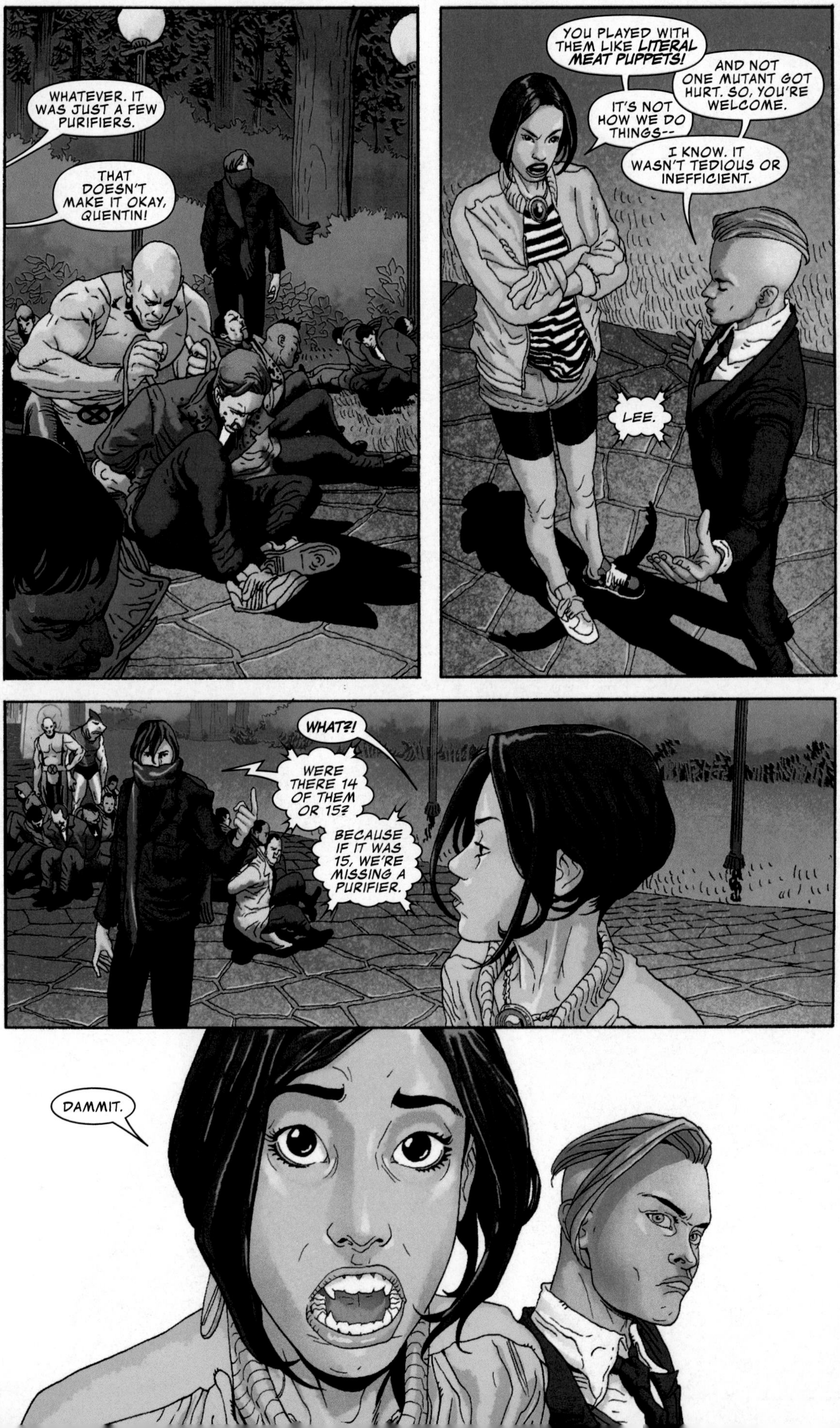
WHATEVER. IT WAS JUST A FEW PURIFIERS.
THAT DOESN'T MAKE IT OKAY, QUENTIN!
YOU PLAYED WITH THEM LIKE LITERAL MEAT PUPPETS!
IT'S NOT HOW WE DO THINGS--
AND NOT ONE MUTANT GOT HURT. SO, YOU'RE WELCOME.
I KNOW. IT WASN'T TEDIOUS OR INEFFICIENT.
LEE.
WHAT?!
WERE THERE 14 OF THEM OR 15?
BECAUSE IF IT WAS 15, WE'RE MISSING A PURIFIER.
DAMMIT.

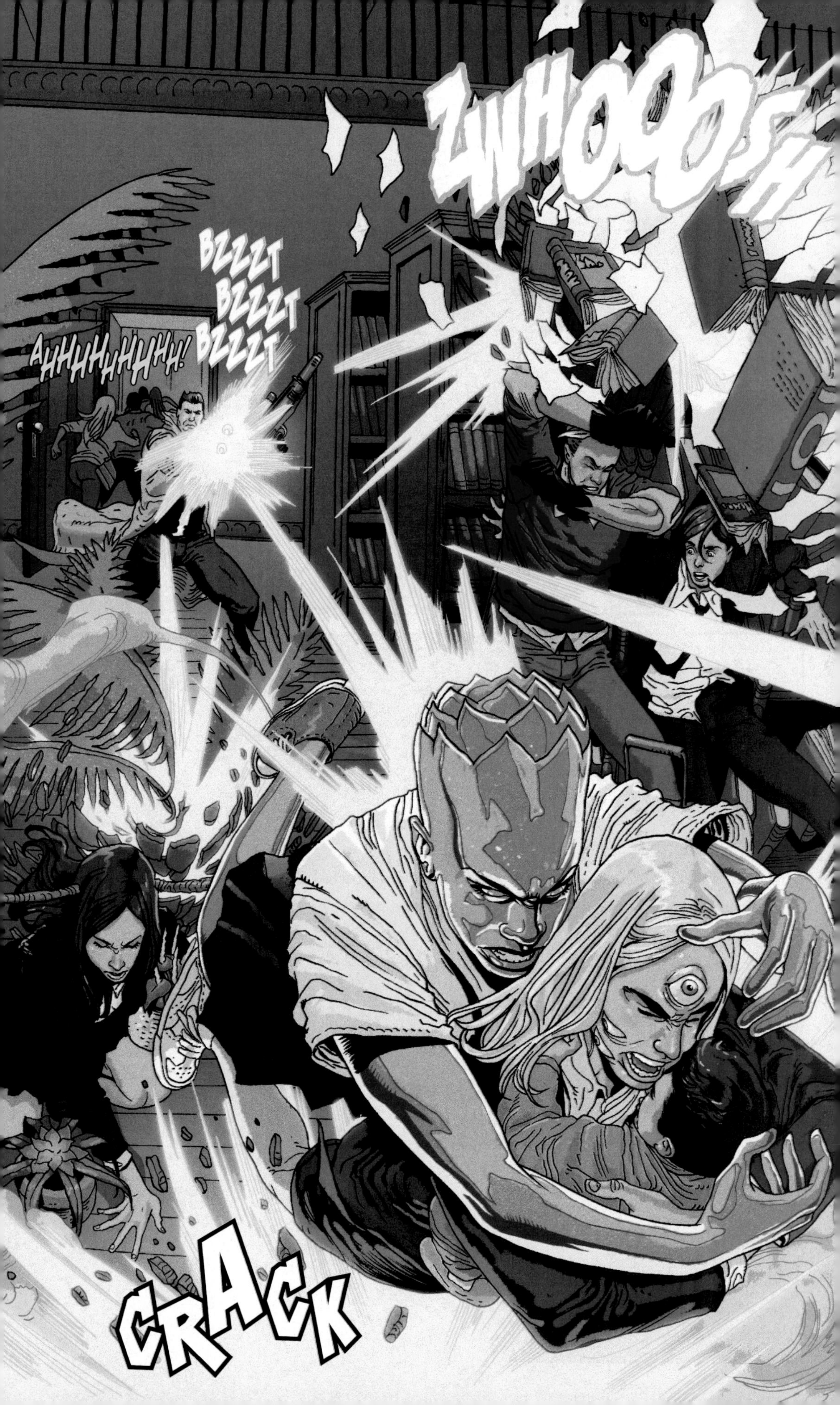

ZWHOOOOSH
AHHHHHHHHH!
BZZZZT
BZZZZT
BZZZZT
CRACK

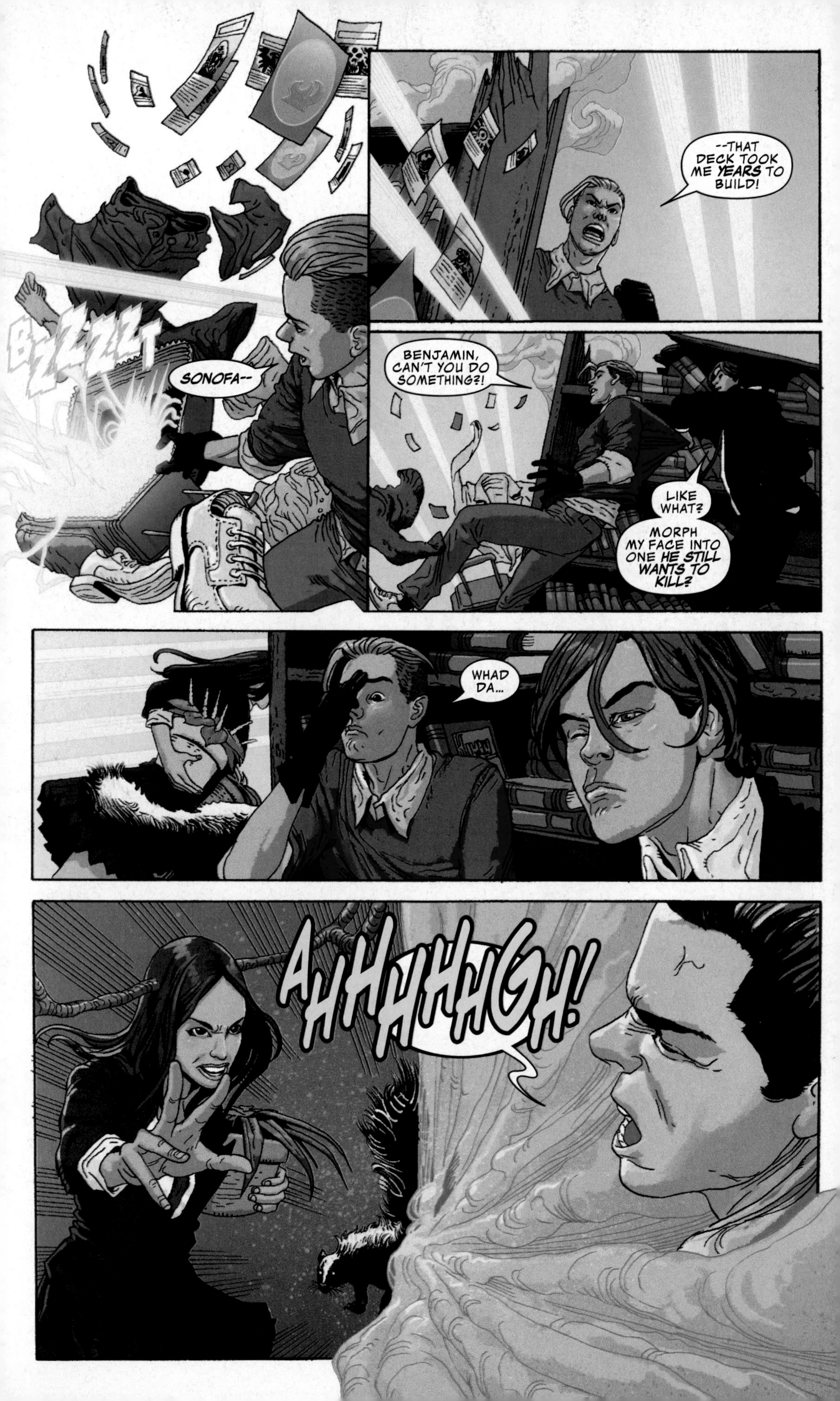
BZZZZZT
SONOFA--
--THAT DECK TOOK ME YEARS TO BUILD!
BENJAMIN, CAN'T YOU DO SOMETHING?!
LIKE WHAT?
MORPH MY FACE INTO ONE HE STILL WANTS TO KILL?
WHAD DA...
AHHHHHGH!

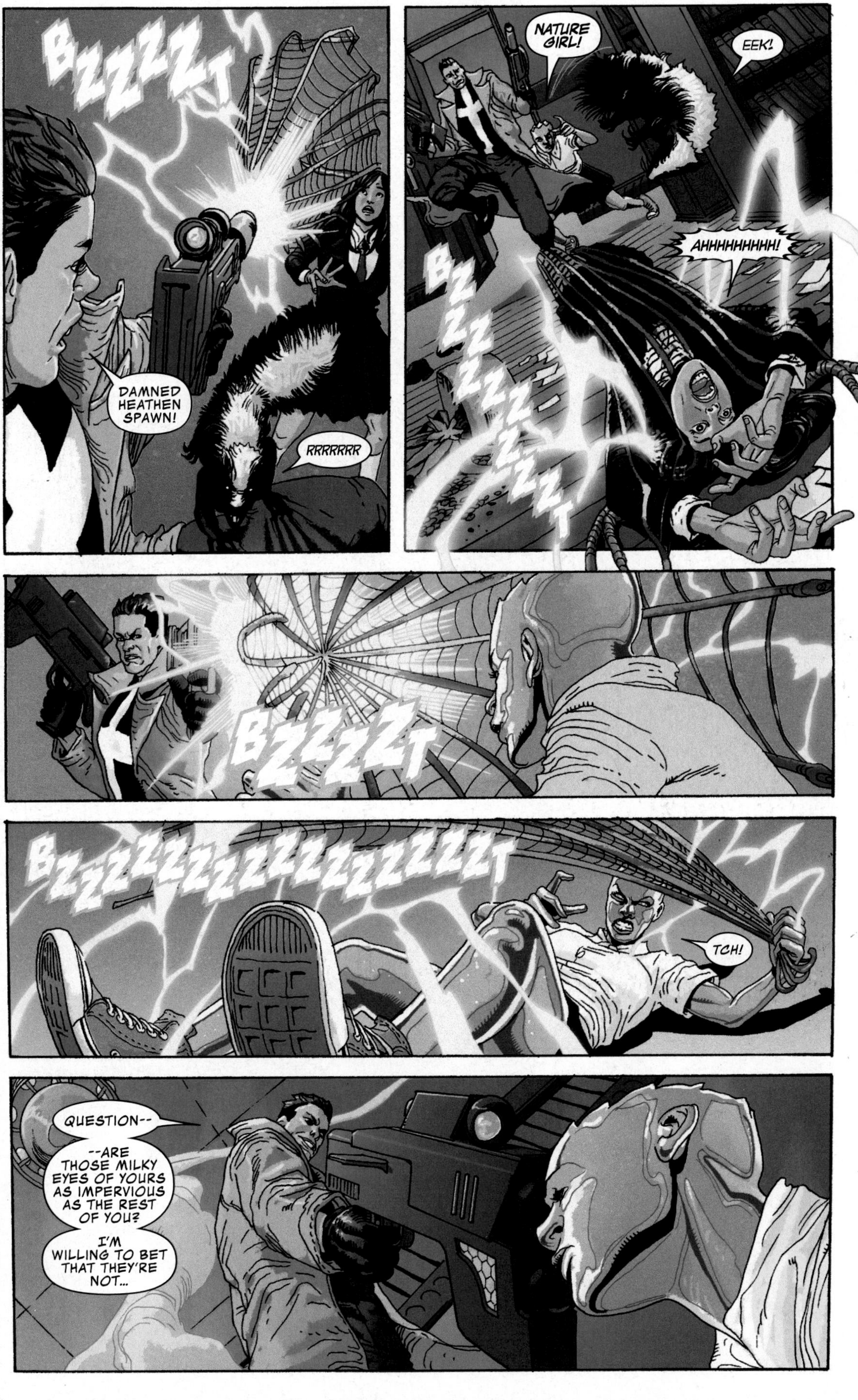
BZZZZZT
DAMNED HEATHEN SPAWN!
RRRRRRR
NATURE GIRL!
EEK!
AHHHHHHHHH!
BZZZZZZZZZZT
BZZZZZT
BZZZZZZZZZZZZZZZZZZT
TCH!
QUESTION--
--ARE THOSE MILKY EYES OF YOURS AS IMPERVIOUS AS THE REST OF YOU?
I'M WILLING TO BET THAT THEY'RE NOT...

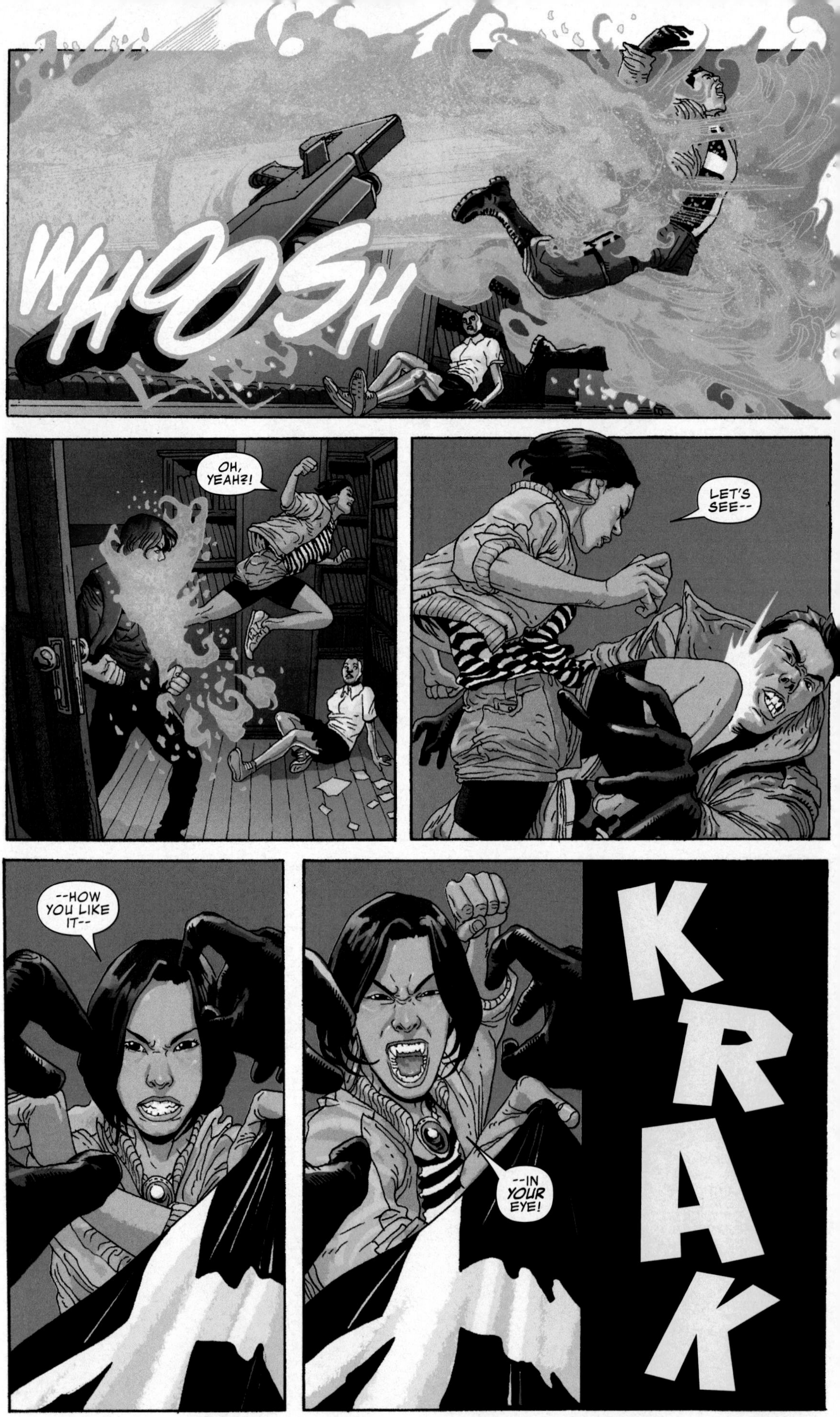
WHOOSH
OH, YEAH?!
LET'S SEE--
--HOW YOU LIKE IT--
--IN YOUR EYE!
KRAK

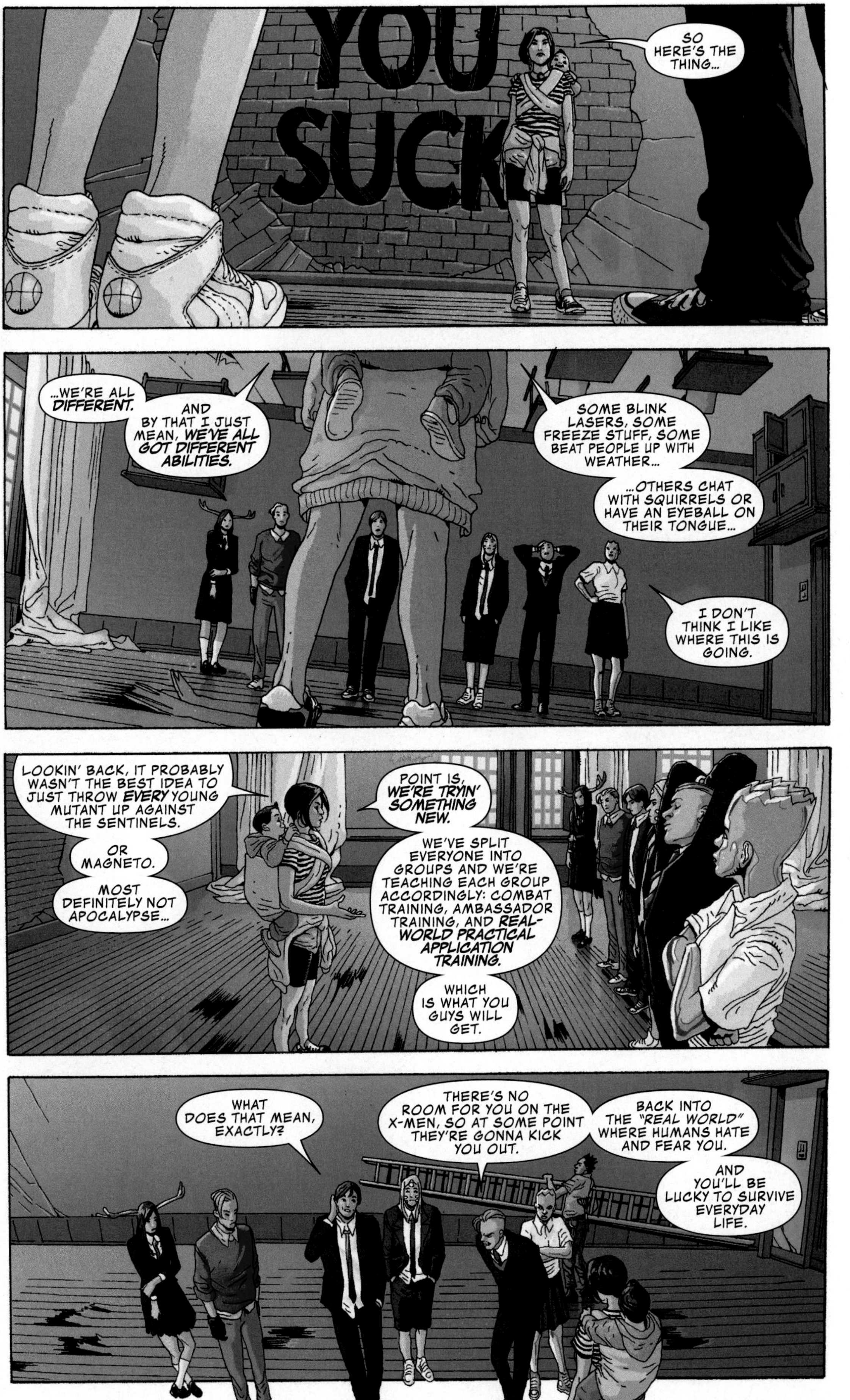
YOU SUCK
SO HERE'S THE THING...
...WE'RE ALL DIFFERENT.
AND BY THAT I JUST MEAN, WE'VE ALL GOT DIFFERENT ABILITIES.
SOME BLINK LASERS, SOME FREEZE STUFF, SOME BEAT PEOPLE UP WITH WEATHER...
...OTHERS CHAT WITH SQUIRRELS OR HAVE AN EYEBALL ON THEIR TONGUE...
I DON'T THINK I LIKE WHERE THIS IS GOING.
LOOKIN' BACK, IT PROBABLY WASN'T THE BEST IDEA TO JUST THROW EVERY YOUNG MUTANT UP AGAINST THE SENTINELS.
OR MAGNETO.
MOST DEFINITELY NOT APOCALYPSE...
POINT IS, WE'RE TRYIN' SOMETHING NEW.
WE'VE SPLIT EVERYONE INTO GROUPS AND WE'RE TEACHING EACH GROUP ACCORDINGLY: COMBAT TRAINING, AMBASSADOR TRAINING, AND REAL-WORLD PRACTICAL APPLICATION TRAINING.
WHICH IS WHAT YOU GUYS WILL GET.
WHAT DOES THAT MEAN, EXACTLY?
THERE'S NO ROOM FOR YOU ON THE X-MEN, SO AT SOME POINT THEY'RE GONNA KICK YOU OUT.
BACK INTO THE "REAL WORLD" WHERE HUMANS HATE AND FEAR YOU.
AND YOU'LL BE LUCKY TO SURVIVE EVERYDAY LIFE.

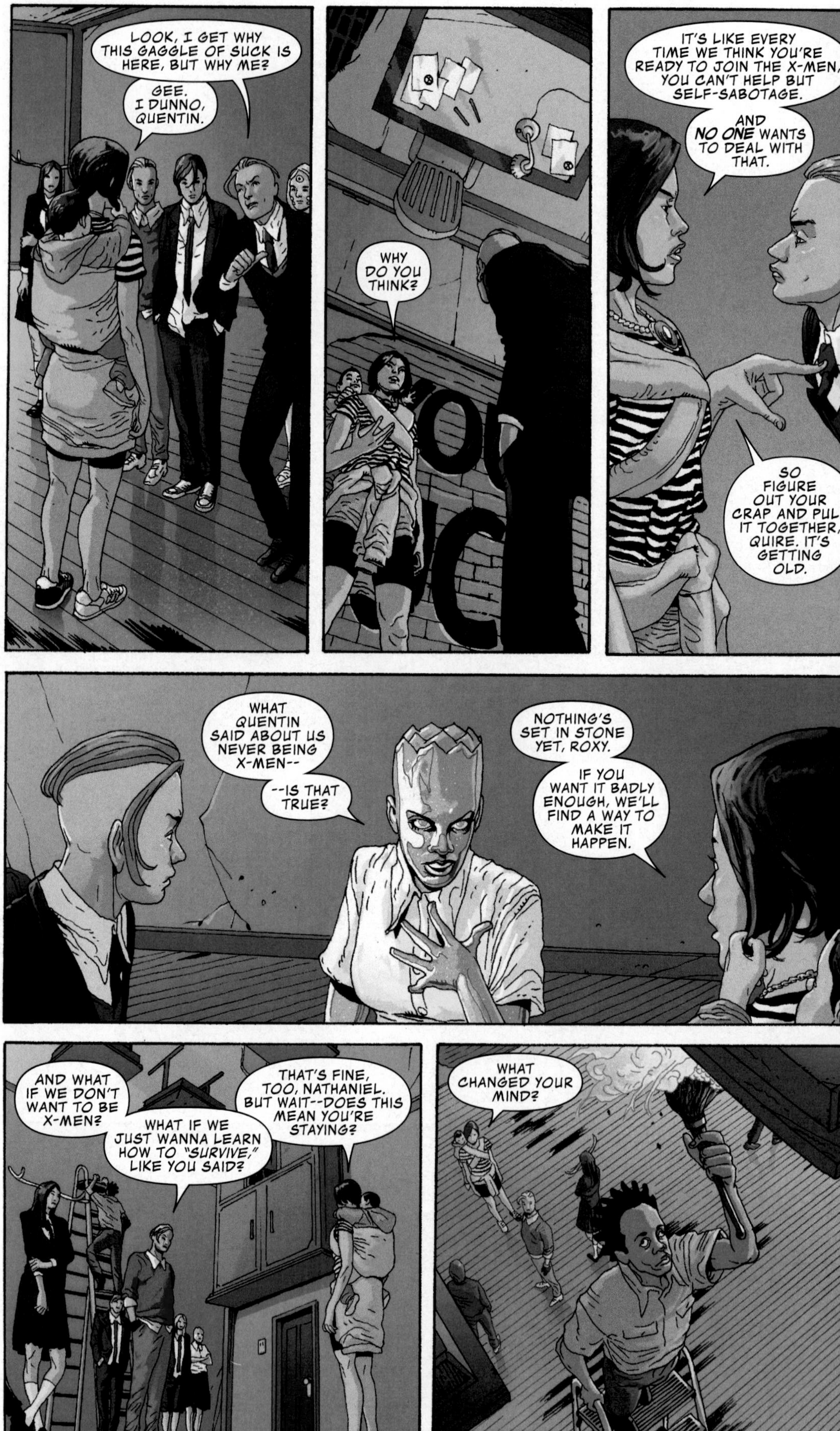
LOOK, I GET WHY THIS GAGGLE OF SUCK IS HERE, BUT WHY ME?
GEE. I DUNNO, QUENTIN.
WHY DO YOU THINK?
IT'S LIKE EVERY TIME WE THINK YOU'RE READY TO JOIN THE X-MEN, YOU CAN'T HELP BUT SELF-SABOTAGE.
AND NO ONE WANTS TO DEAL WITH THAT.
SO FIGURE OUT YOUR CRAP AND PULL IT TOGETHER, QUIRE. IT'S GETTING OLD.
WHAT QUENTIN SAID ABOUT US NEVER BEING X-MEN--
--IS THAT TRUE?
NOTHING'S SET IN STONE YET, ROXY.
IF YOU WANT IT BADLY ENOUGH, WE'LL FIND A WAY TO MAKE IT HAPPEN.
AND WHAT IF WE DON'T WANT TO BE X-MEN?
WHAT IF WE JUST WANNA LEARN HOW TO "SURVIVE," LIKE YOU SAID?
THAT'S FINE, TOO, NATHANIEL. BUT WAIT--DOES THIS MEAN YOU'RE STAYING?
WHAT CHANGED YOUR MIND?

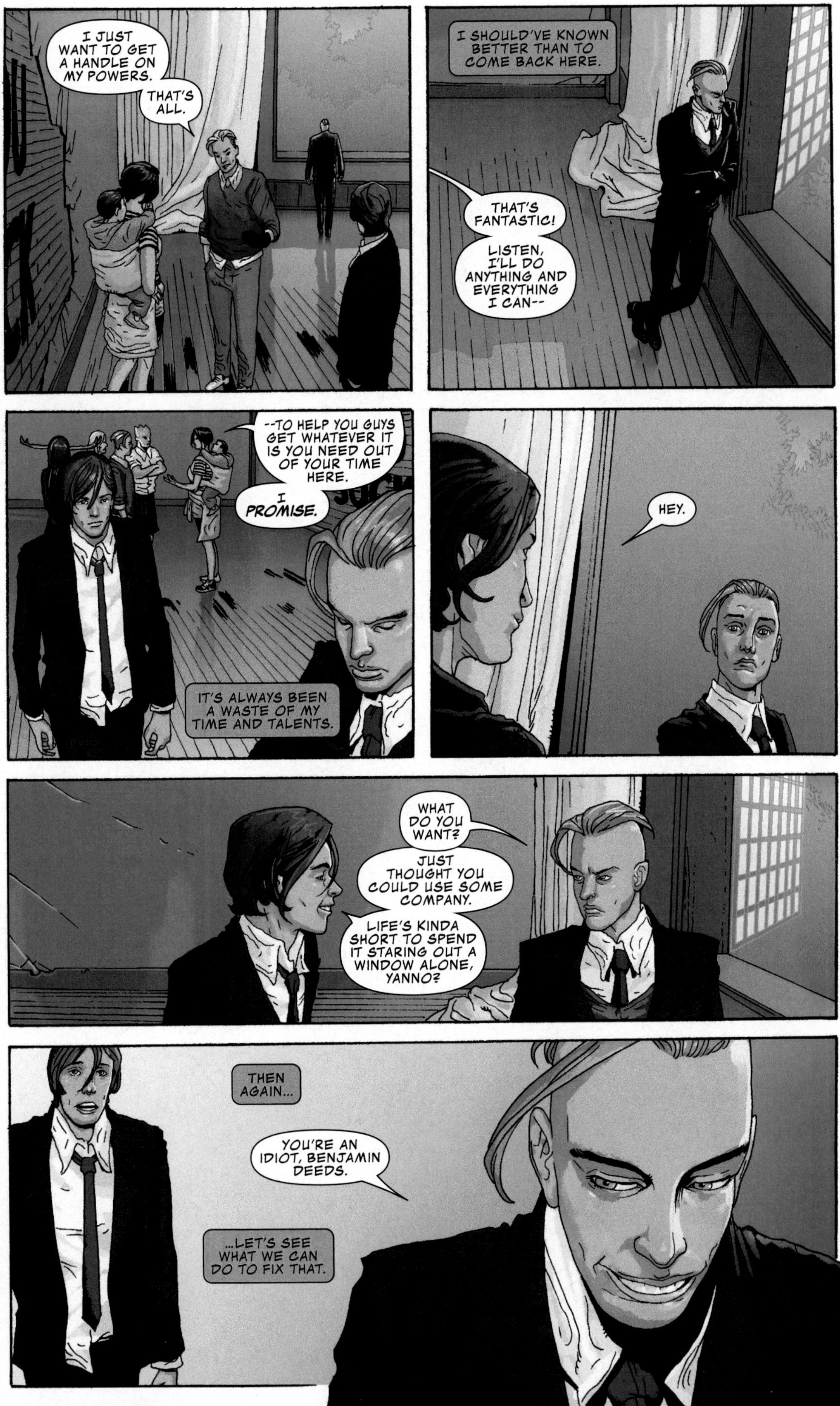
I JUST WANT TO GET A HANDLE ON MY POWERS.
THAT'S ALL.
I SHOULD'VE KNOWN BETTER THAN TO COME BACK HERE.
THAT'S FANTASTIC!
LISTEN, I'LL DO ANYTHING AND EVERYTHING I CAN--
--TO HELP YOU GUYS GET WHATEVER IT IS YOU NEED OUT OF YOUR TIME HERE.
I *PROMISE.*
IT'S ALWAYS BEEN A WASTE OF MY TIME AND TALENTS.
HEY.
WHAT DO YOU WANT?
JUST THOUGHT YOU COULD USE SOME COMPANY.
LIFE'S KINDA SHORT TO SPEND IT STARING OUT A WINDOW ALONE, YANNO?
THEN AGAIN...
YOU'RE AN IDIOT, BENJAMIN DEEDS.
...LET'S SEE WHAT WE CAN DO TO FIX THAT.

3

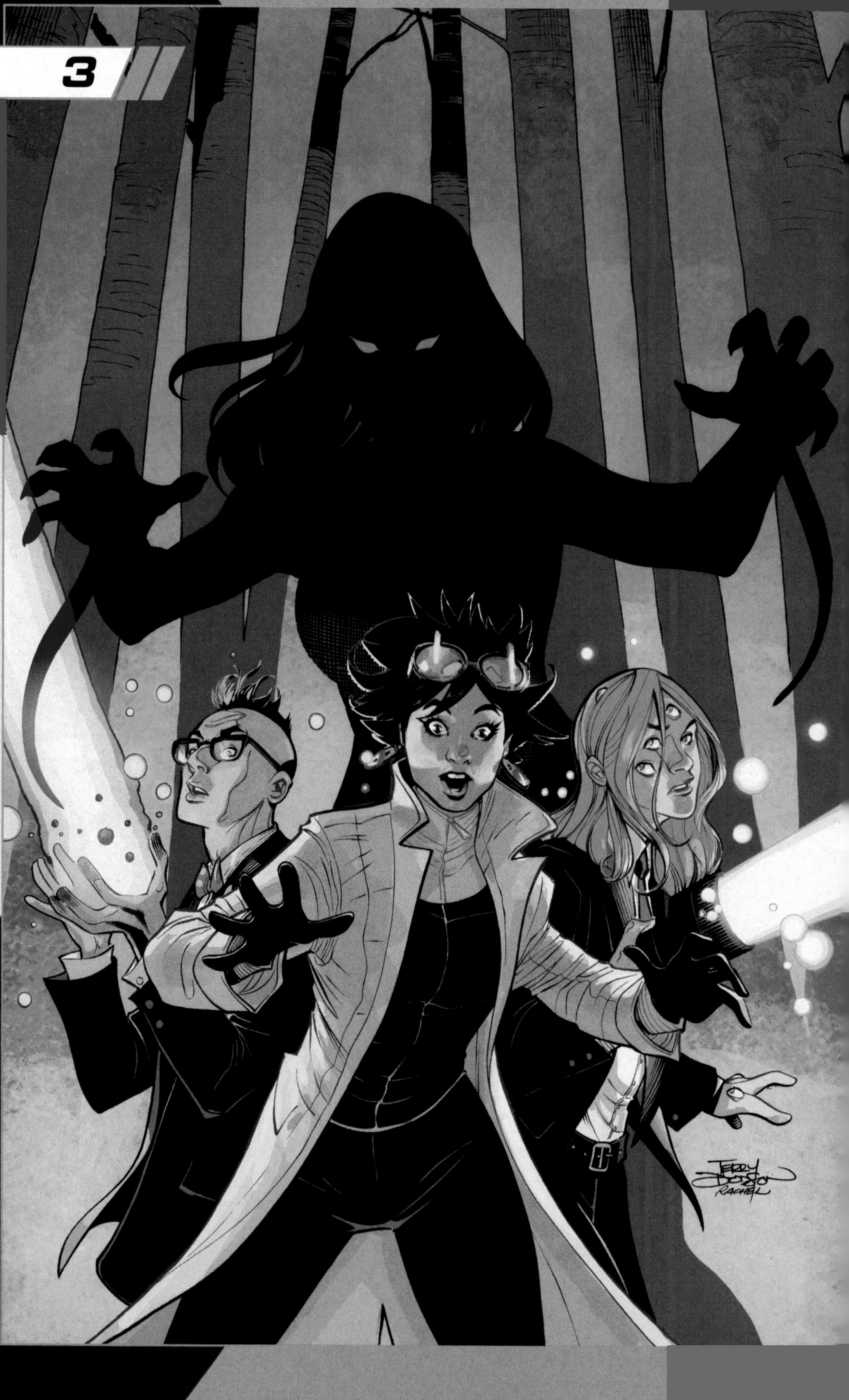
TERRY DODSON
RACHEL

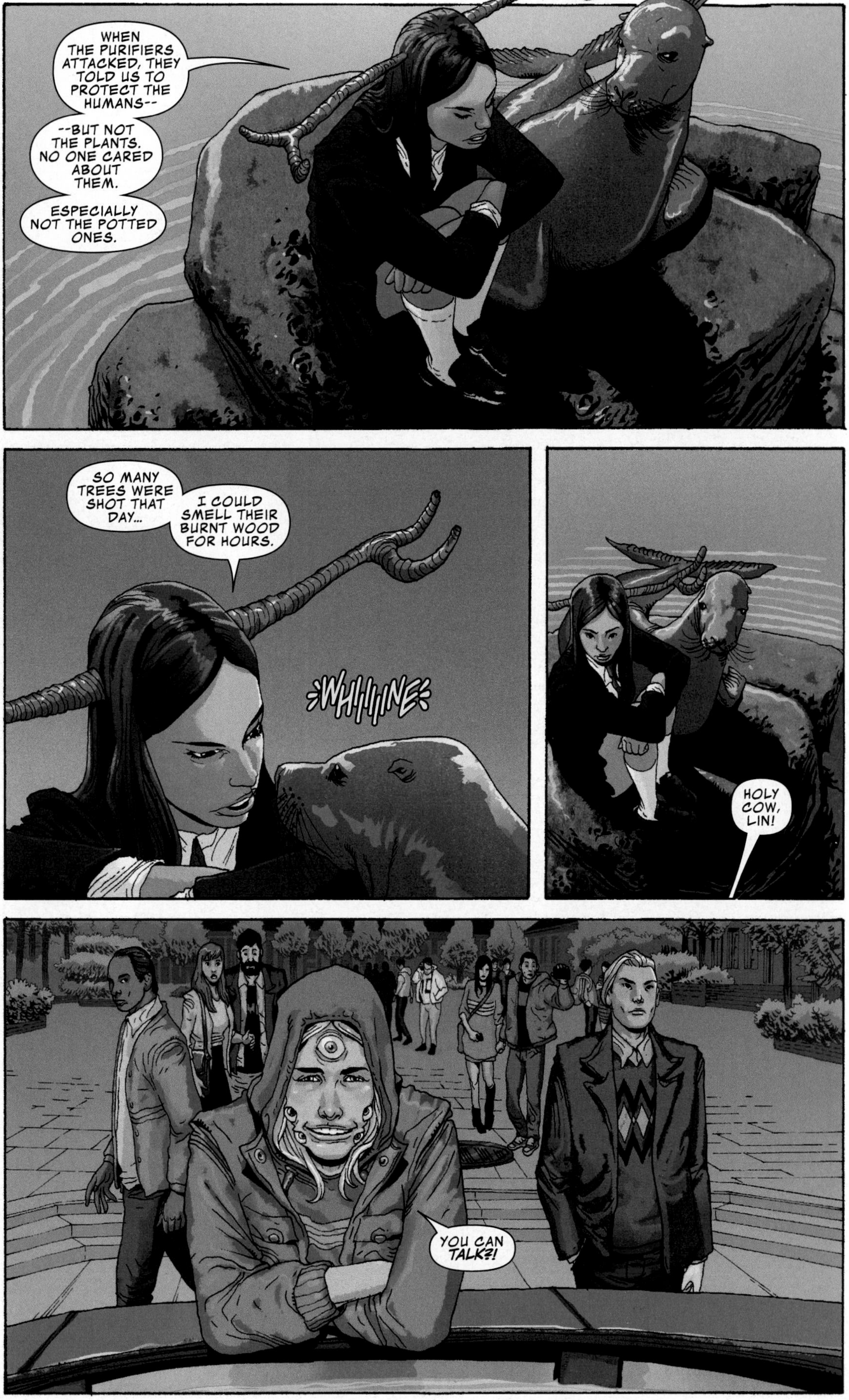
WHEN THE PURIFIERS ATTACKED, THEY TOLD US TO PROTECT THE HUMANS--
--BUT NOT THE PLANTS. NO ONE CARED ABOUT THEM.
ESPECIALLY NOT THE POTTED ONES.
SO MANY TREES WERE SHOT THAT DAY...
I COULD SMELL THEIR BURNT WOOD FOR HOURS.
WHIIIINE
HOLY COW, LIN!
YOU CAN TALK?!

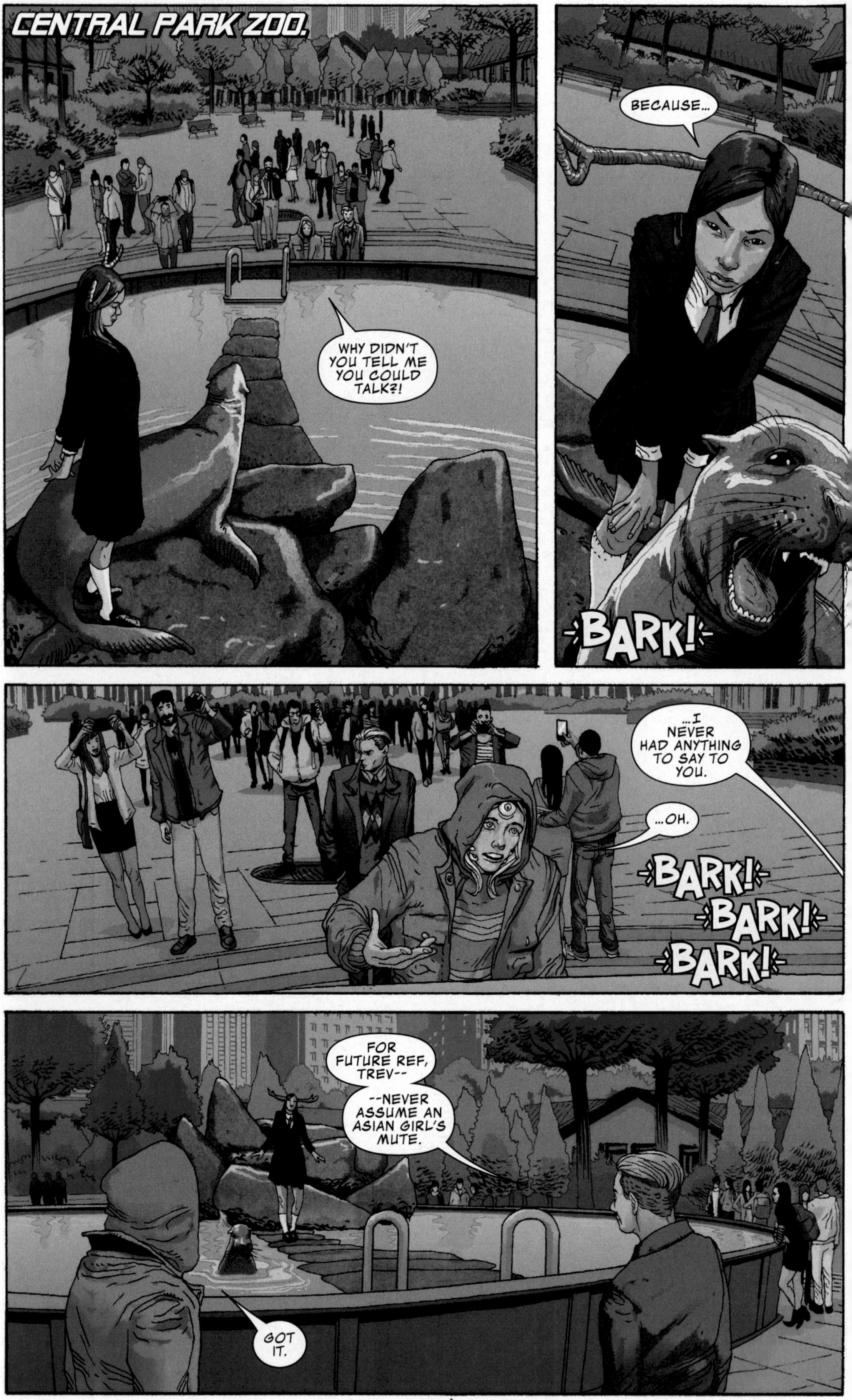
CENTRAL PARK ZOO.
WHY DIDN'T YOU TELL ME YOU COULD TALK?!
BECAUSE...
BARK!
...I NEVER HAD ANYTHING TO SAY TO YOU.
...OH.
BARK!
BARK!
BARK!
FOR FUTURE REF, TREV--
--NEVER ASSUME AN ASIAN GIRL'S MUTE.
GOT IT.

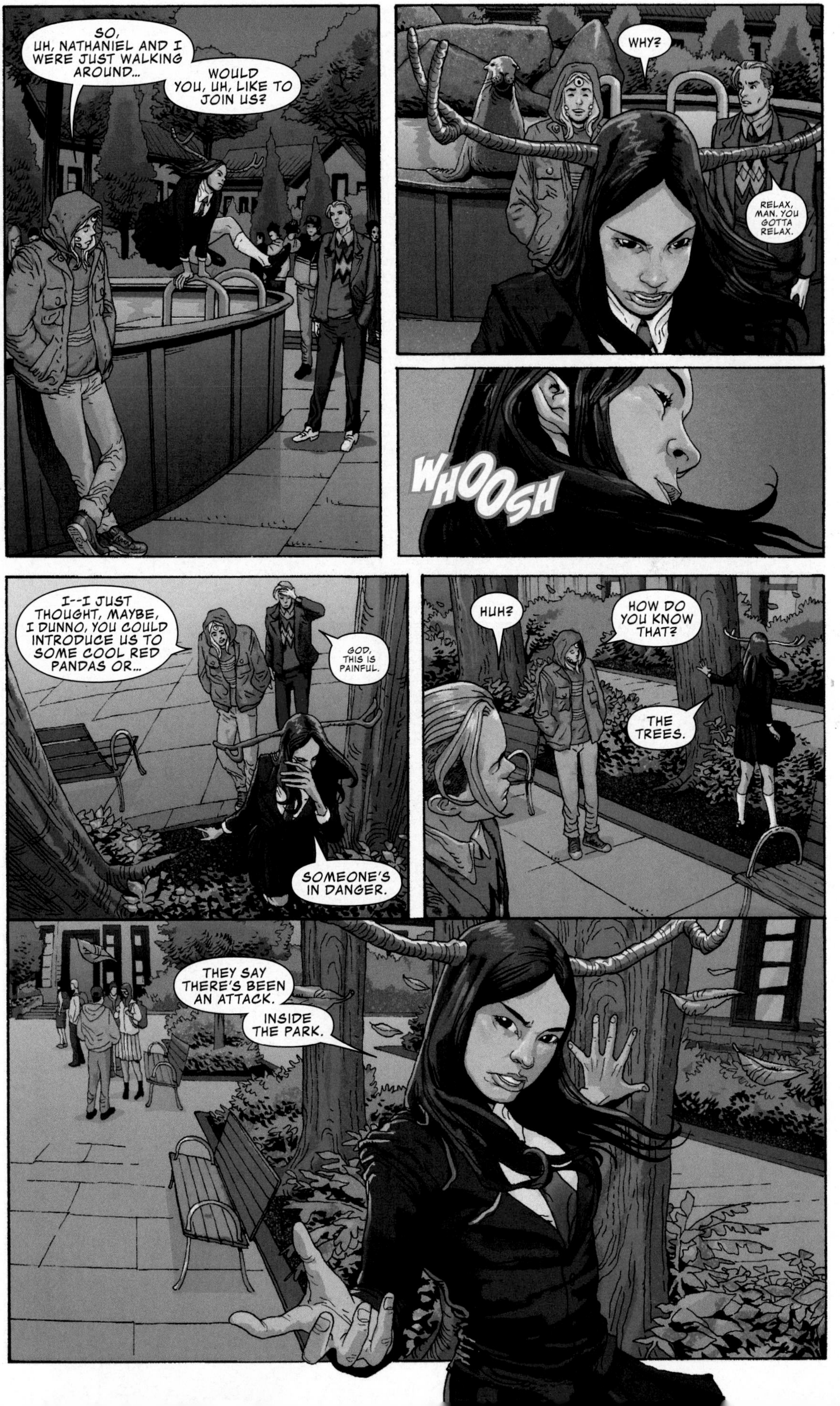
SO, UH, NATHANIEL AND I WERE JUST WALKING AROUND...
WOULD YOU, UH, LIKE TO JOIN US?
WHY?
RELAX, MAN. YOU GOTTA RELAX.
WHOOSH
I--I JUST THOUGHT, MAYBE, I DUNNO, YOU COULD INTRODUCE US TO SOME COOL RED PANDAS OR...
GOD, THIS IS PAINFUL.
SOMEONE'S IN DANGER.
HUH?
HOW DO YOU KNOW THAT?
THE TREES.
THEY SAY THERE'S BEEN AN ATTACK.
INSIDE THE PARK.

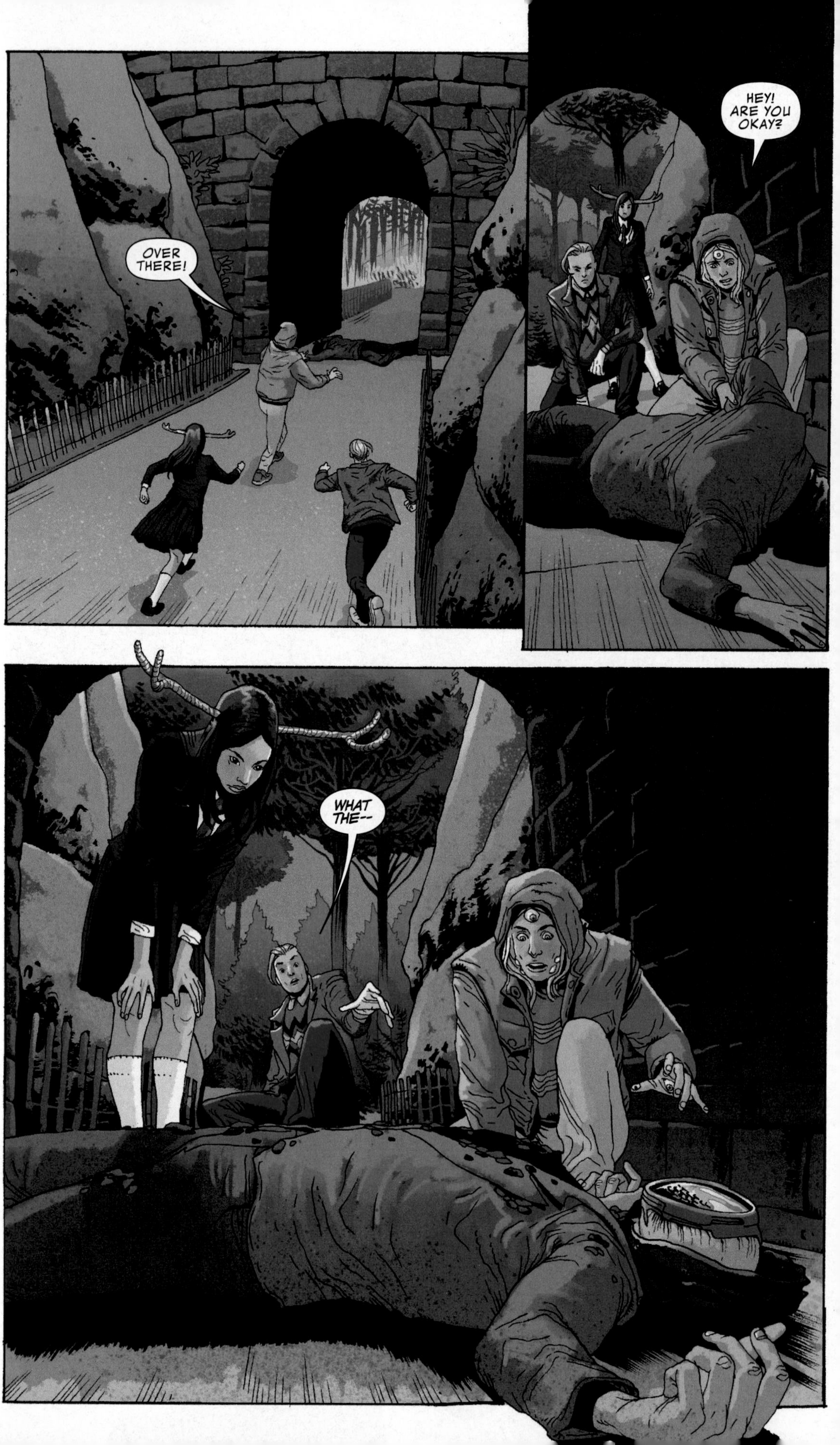
OVER THERE!
HEY! ARE YOU OKAY?
WHAT THE--

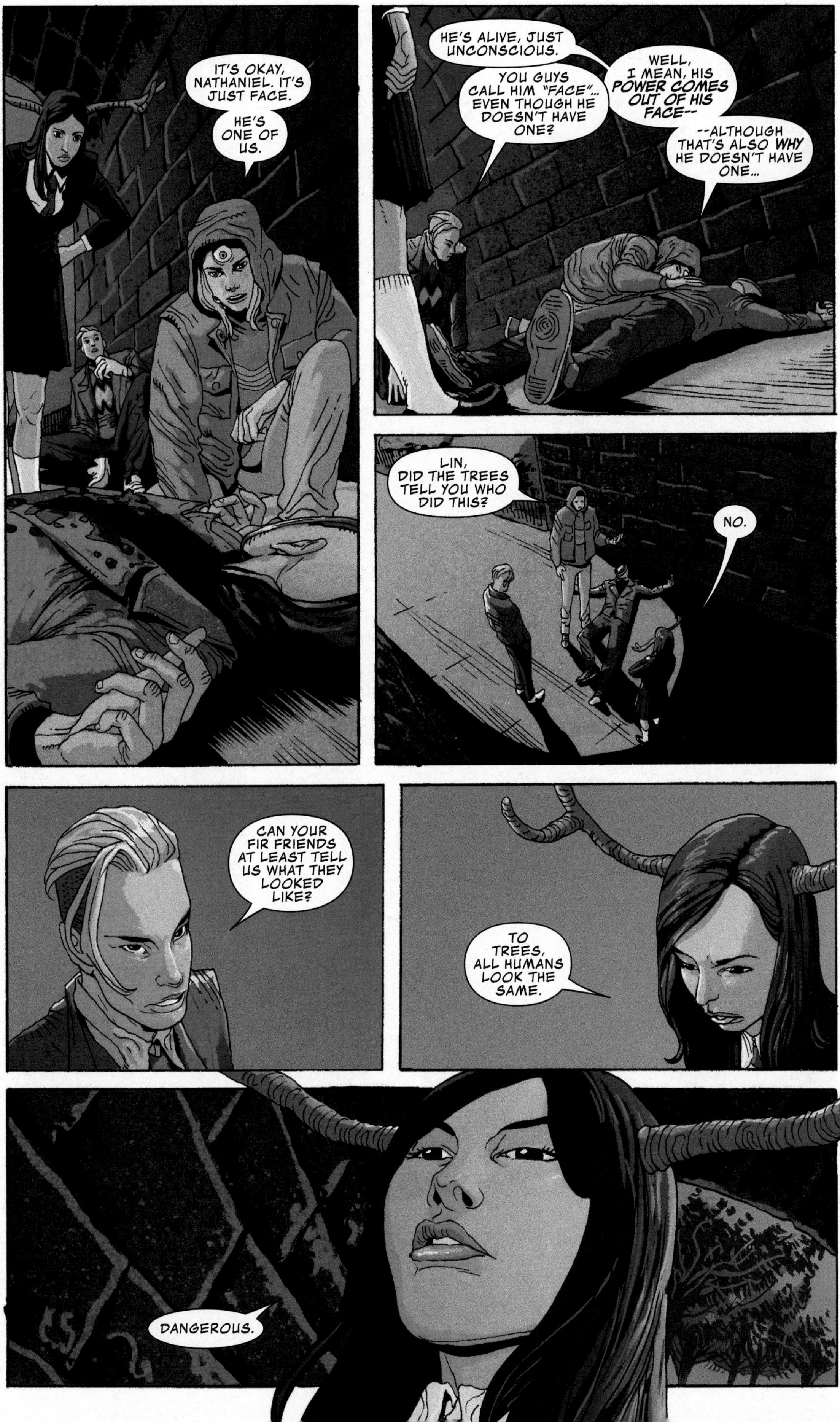
IT'S OKAY, NATHANIEL. IT'S JUST FACE.
HE'S ONE OF US.
HE'S ALIVE, JUST UNCONSCIOUS.
YOU GUYS CALL HIM "FACE"... EVEN THOUGH HE DOESN'T HAVE ONE?
WELL, I MEAN, HIS POWER COMES OUT OF HIS FACE--
--ALTHOUGH THAT'S ALSO WHY HE DOESN'T HAVE ONE...
LIN, DID THE TREES TELL YOU WHO DID THIS?
NO.
CAN YOUR FIR FRIENDS AT LEAST TELL US WHAT THEY LOOKED LIKE?
TO TREES, ALL HUMANS LOOK THE SAME.
DANGEROUS.

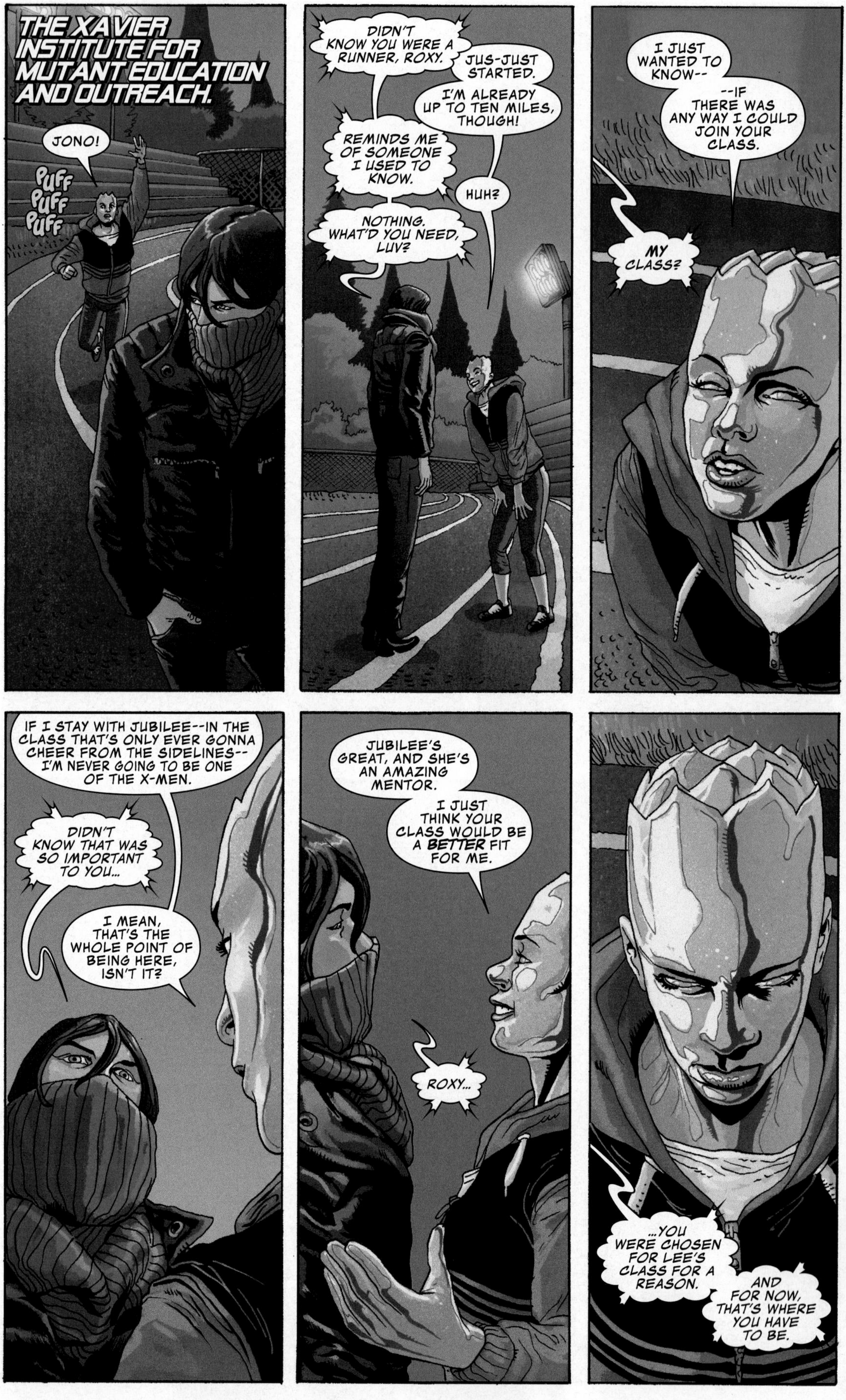
THE XAVIER INSTITUTE FOR MUTANT EDUCATION AND OUTREACH.
JONO!
PUFF PUFF PUFF
DIDN'T KNOW YOU WERE A RUNNER, ROXY.
JUS-JUST STARTED.
I'M ALREADY UP TO TEN MILES, THOUGH!
REMINDS ME OF SOMEONE I USED TO KNOW.
HUH?
NOTHING. WHAT'D YOU NEED, LUV?
I JUST WANTED TO KNOW--
--IF THERE WAS ANY WAY I COULD JOIN YOUR CLASS.
MY CLASS?
IF I STAY WITH JUBILEE--IN THE CLASS THAT'S ONLY EVER GONNA CHEER FROM THE SIDELINES--I'M NEVER GOING TO BE ONE OF THE X-MEN.
DIDN'T KNOW THAT WAS SO IMPORTANT TO YOU...
I MEAN, THAT'S THE WHOLE POINT OF BEING HERE, ISN'T IT?
JUBILEE'S GREAT, AND SHE'S AN AMAZING MENTOR.
I JUST THINK YOUR CLASS WOULD BE A BETTER FIT FOR ME.
ROXY...
...YOU WERE CHOSEN FOR LEE'S CLASS FOR A REASON.
AND FOR NOW, THAT'S WHERE YOU HAVE TO BE.

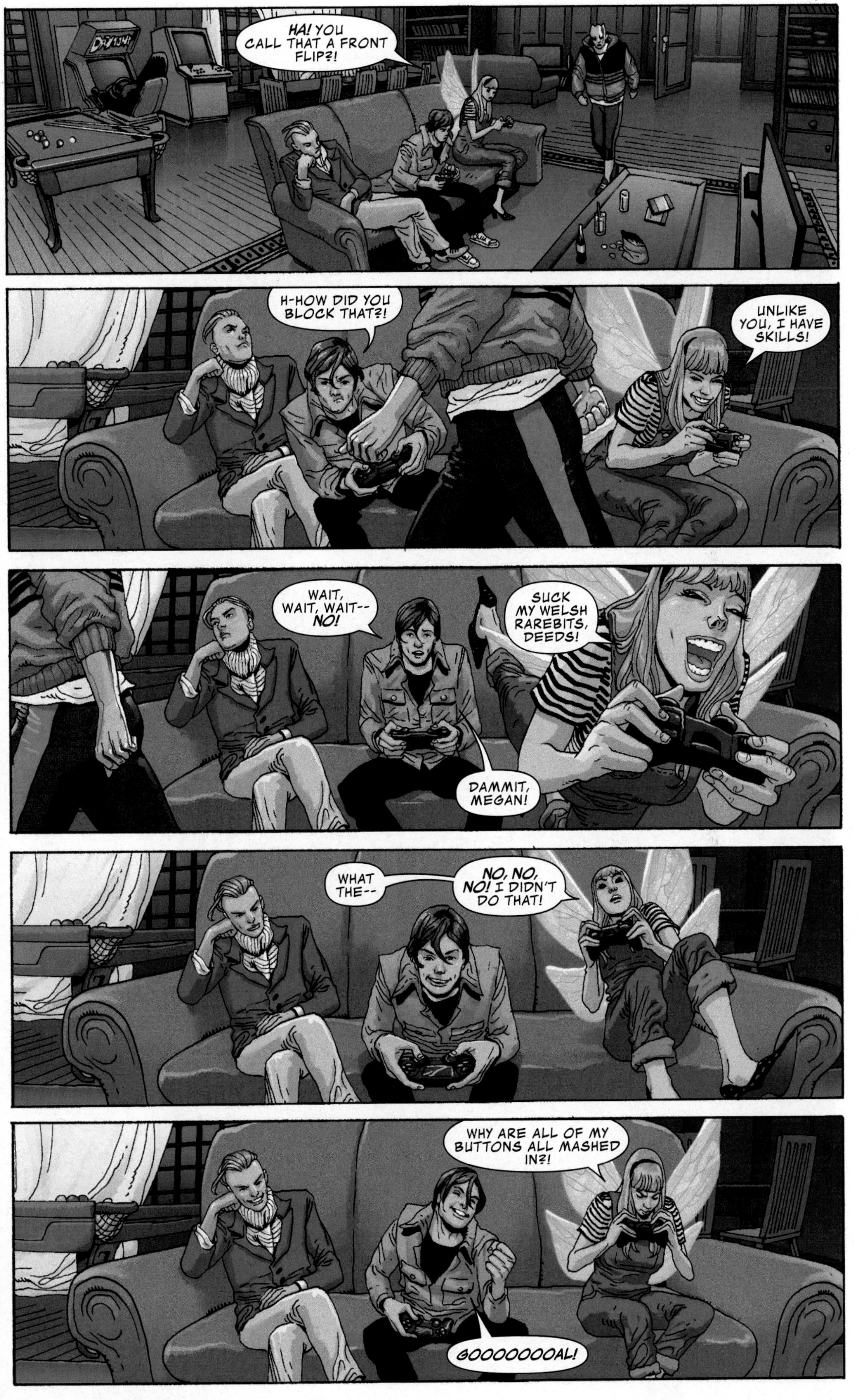
HA! YOU CALL THAT A FRONT FLIP?!
H-HOW DID YOU BLOCK THAT?!
UNLIKE YOU, I HAVE SKILLS!
WAIT, WAIT, WAIT-- NO!
SUCK MY WELSH RAREBITS, DEEDS!
DAMMIT, MEGAN!
WHAT THE--
NO, NO, NO! I DIDN'T DO THAT!
WHY ARE ALL OF MY BUTTONS ALL MASHED IN?!
GOOOOOOOAL!

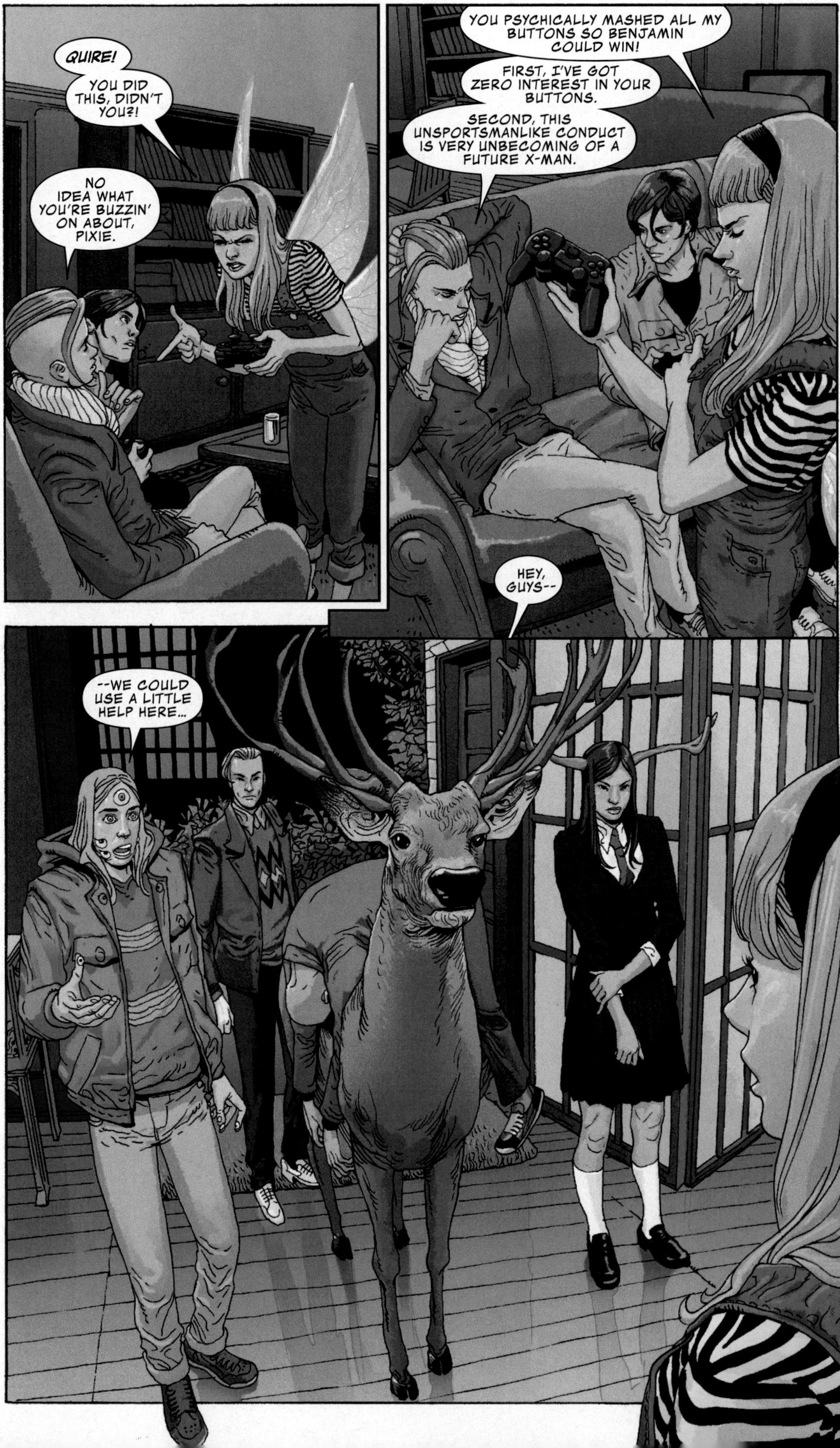
QUIRE!
YOU DID THIS, DIDN'T YOU?!
NO IDEA WHAT YOU'RE BUZZIN' ON ABOUT, PIXIE.
YOU PSYCHICALLY MASHED ALL MY BUTTONS SO BENJAMIN COULD WIN!
FIRST, I'VE GOT ZERO INTEREST IN YOUR BUTTONS.
SECOND, THIS UNSPORTSMANLIKE CONDUCT IS VERY UNBECOMING OF A FUTURE X-MAN.
HEY, GUYS--
--WE COULD USE A LITTLE HELP HERE...

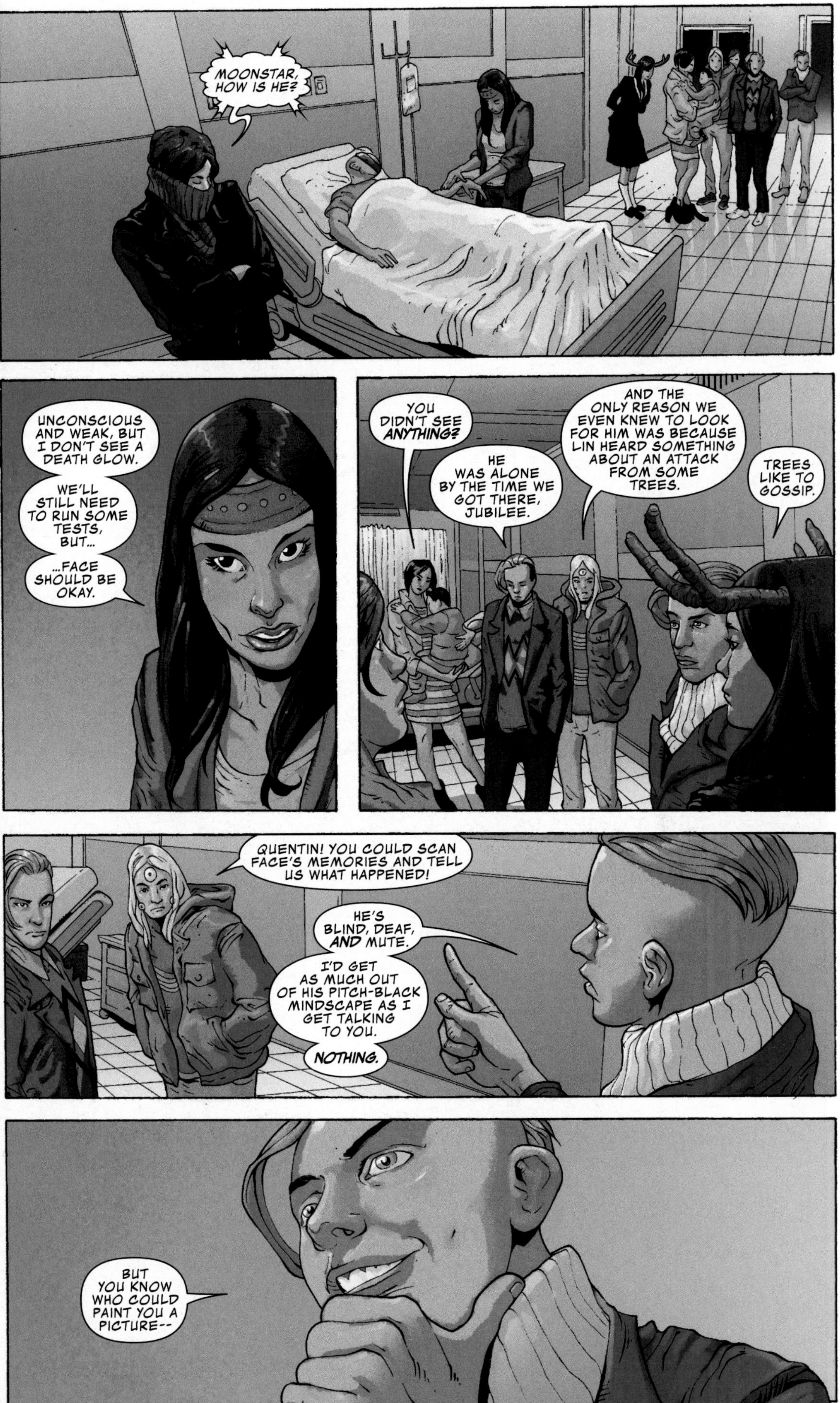

MOONSTAR, HOW IS HE?
UNCONSCIOUS AND WEAK, BUT I DON'T SEE A DEATH GLOW.
WE'LL STILL NEED TO RUN SOME TESTS, BUT...
...FACE SHOULD BE OKAY.
YOU DIDN'T SEE ANYTHING?
HE WAS ALONE BY THE TIME WE GOT THERE, JUBILEE.
AND THE ONLY REASON WE EVEN KNEW TO LOOK FOR HIM WAS BECAUSE LIN HEARD SOMETHING ABOUT AN ATTACK FROM SOME TREES.
TREES LIKE TO GOSSIP.
QUENTIN! YOU COULD SCAN FACE'S MEMORIES AND TELL US WHAT HAPPENED!
HE'S BLIND, DEAF, AND MUTE.
I'D GET AS MUCH OUT OF HIS PITCH-BLACK MINDSCAPE AS I GET TALKING TO YOU.
NOTHING.
BUT YOU KNOW WHO COULD PAINT YOU A PICTURE--

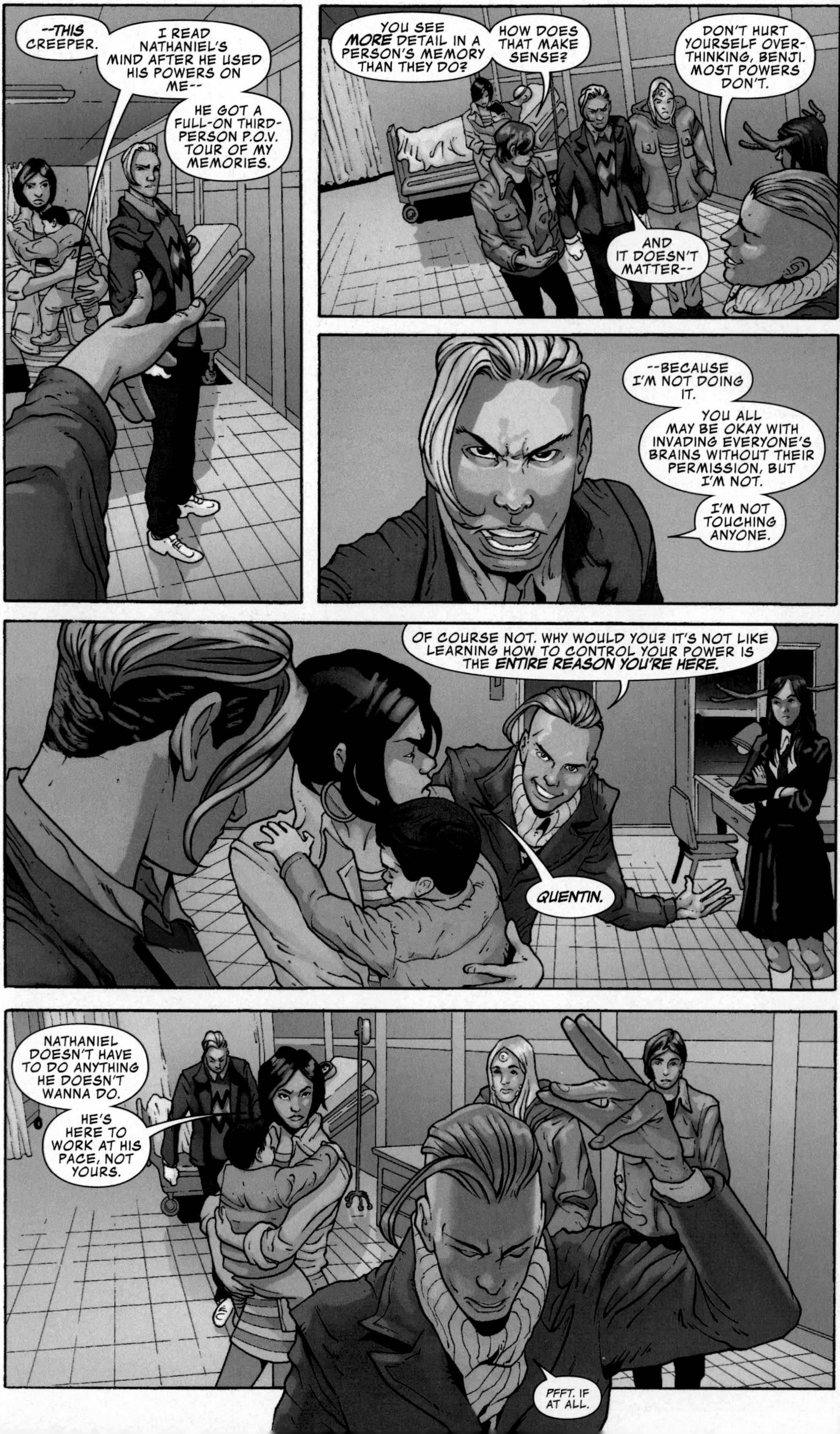

--THIS CREEPER.
I READ NATHANIEL'S MIND AFTER HE USED HIS POWERS ON ME--
HE GOT A FULL-ON THIRD-PERSON P.O.V. TOUR OF MY MEMORIES.
YOU SEE MORE DETAIL IN A PERSON'S MEMORY THAN THEY DO?
HOW DOES THAT MAKE SENSE?
DON'T HURT YOURSELF OVER-THINKING, BENJI. MOST POWERS DON'T.
AND IT DOESN'T MATTER--
--BECAUSE I'M NOT DOING IT.
YOU ALL MAY BE OKAY WITH INVADING EVERYONE'S BRAINS WITHOUT THEIR PERMISSION, BUT I'M NOT.
I'M NOT TOUCHING ANYONE.
OF COURSE NOT. WHY WOULD YOU? IT'S NOT LIKE LEARNING HOW TO CONTROL YOUR POWER IS THE ENTIRE REASON YOU'RE HERE.
QUENTIN.
NATHANIEL DOESN'T HAVE TO DO ANYTHING HE DOESN'T WANNA DO.
HE'S HERE TO WORK AT HIS PACE, NOT YOURS.
PFFT. IF AT ALL.

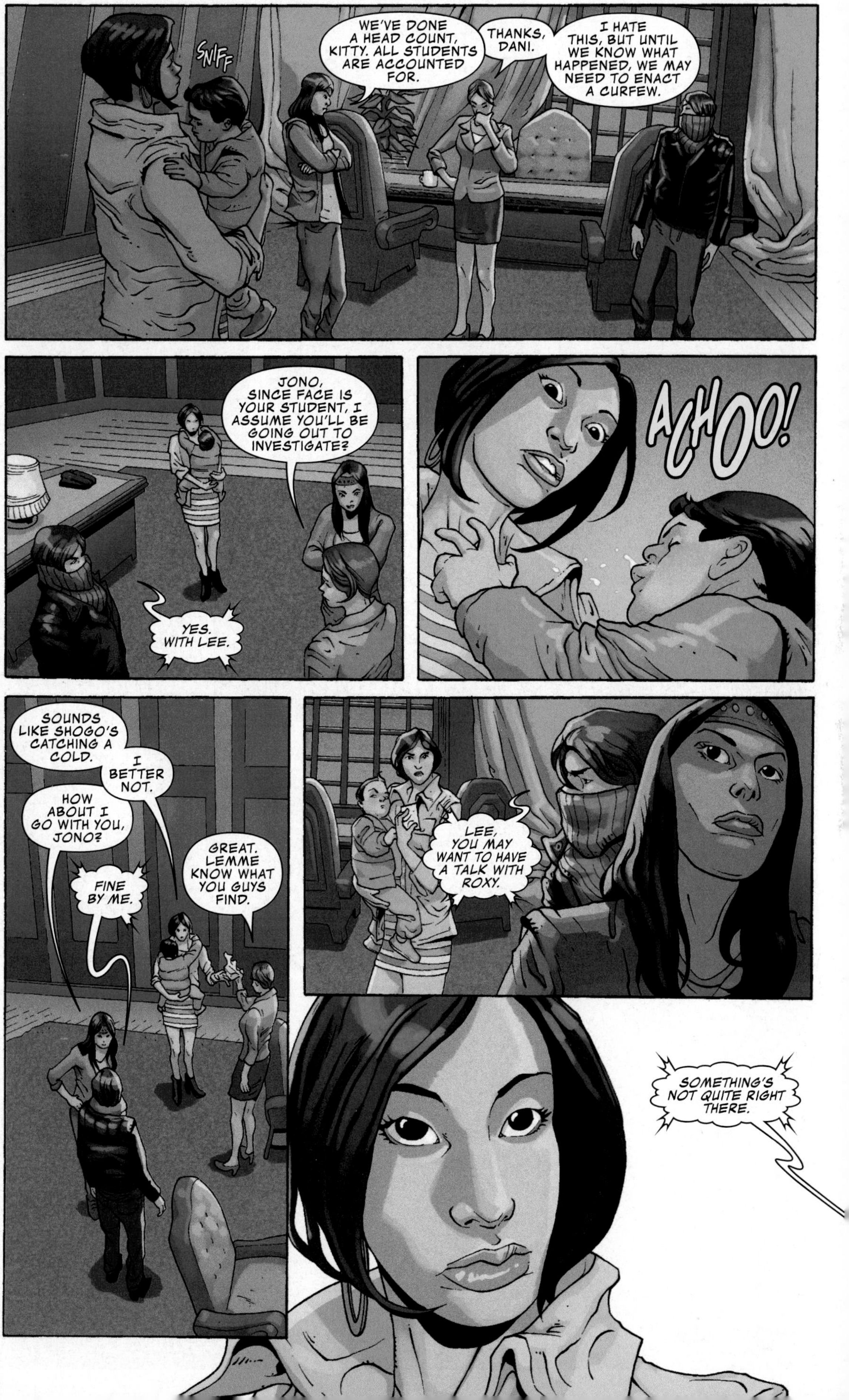
SNIFF
WE'VE DONE A HEAD COUNT, KITTY. ALL STUDENTS ARE ACCOUNTED FOR.
THANKS, DANI.
I HATE THIS, BUT UNTIL WE KNOW WHAT HAPPENED, WE MAY NEED TO ENACT A CURFEW.
JONO, SINCE FACE IS YOUR STUDENT, I ASSUME YOU'LL BE GOING OUT TO INVESTIGATE?
YES. WITH LEE.
ACHOO!
SOUNDS LIKE SHOGO'S CATCHING A COLD.
I BETTER NOT.
HOW ABOUT I GO WITH YOU, JONO?
FINE BY ME.
GREAT. LEMME KNOW WHAT YOU GUYS FIND.
LEE, YOU MAY WANT TO HAVE A TALK WITH ROXY.
SOMETHING'S NOT QUITE RIGHT THERE.

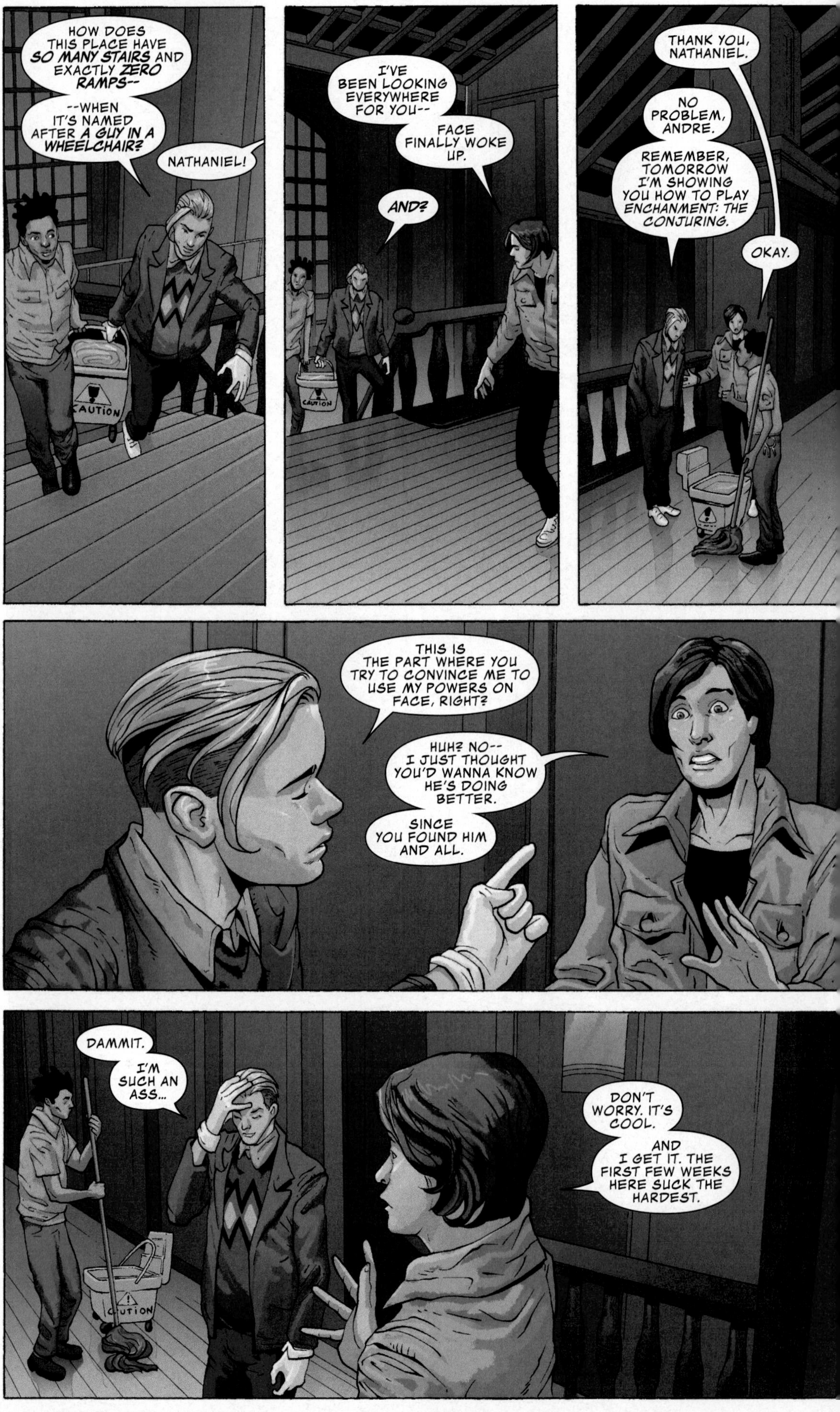
HOW DOES THIS PLACE HAVE SO MANY STAIRS AND EXACTLY ZERO RAMPS--
--WHEN IT'S NAMED AFTER A GUY IN A WHEELCHAIR?
NATHANIEL!
CAUTION
I'VE BEEN LOOKING EVERYWHERE FOR YOU--
FACE FINALLY WOKE UP.
AND?
CAUTION
THANK YOU, NATHANIEL.
NO PROBLEM, ANDRE.
REMEMBER, TOMORROW I'M SHOWING YOU HOW TO PLAY ENCHANMENT: THE CONJURING.
OKAY.
THIS IS THE PART WHERE YOU TRY TO CONVINCE ME TO USE MY POWERS ON FACE, RIGHT?
HUH? NO-- I JUST THOUGHT YOU'D WANNA KNOW HE'S DOING BETTER.
SINCE YOU FOUND HIM AND ALL.
DAMMIT.
I'M SUCH AN ASS...
DON'T WORRY. IT'S COOL.
AND I GET IT. THE FIRST FEW WEEKS HERE SUCK THE HARDEST.
CAUTION

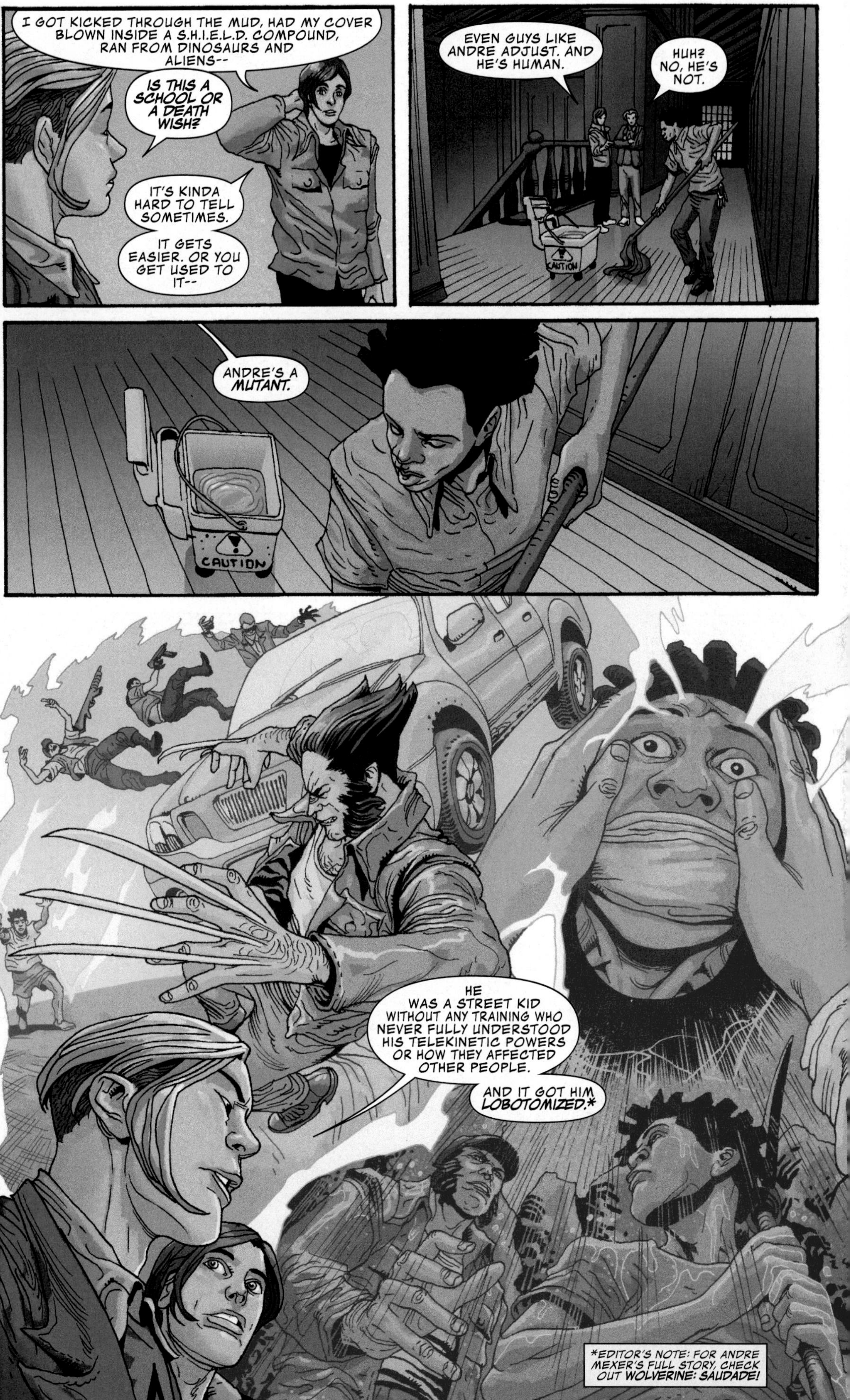
I GOT KICKED THROUGH THE MUD, HAD MY COVER BLOWN INSIDE A S.H.I.E.L.D. COMPOUND, RAN FROM DINOSAURS AND ALIENS--
IS THIS A SCHOOL OR A DEATH WISH?
IT'S KINDA HARD TO TELL SOMETIMES.
IT GETS EASIER. OR YOU GET USED TO IT--
EVEN GUYS LIKE ANDRE ADJUST. AND HE'S HUMAN.
HUH? NO, HE'S NOT.
CAUTION
ANDRE'S A MUTANT.
CAUTION
HE WAS A STREET KID WITHOUT ANY TRAINING WHO NEVER FULLY UNDERSTOOD HIS TELEKINETIC POWERS OR HOW THEY AFFECTED OTHER PEOPLE.
AND IT GOT HIM LOBOTOMIZED.*
*EDITOR'S NOTE: FOR ANDRE MEXER'S FULL STORY, CHECK OUT WOLVERINE: SAUDADE!

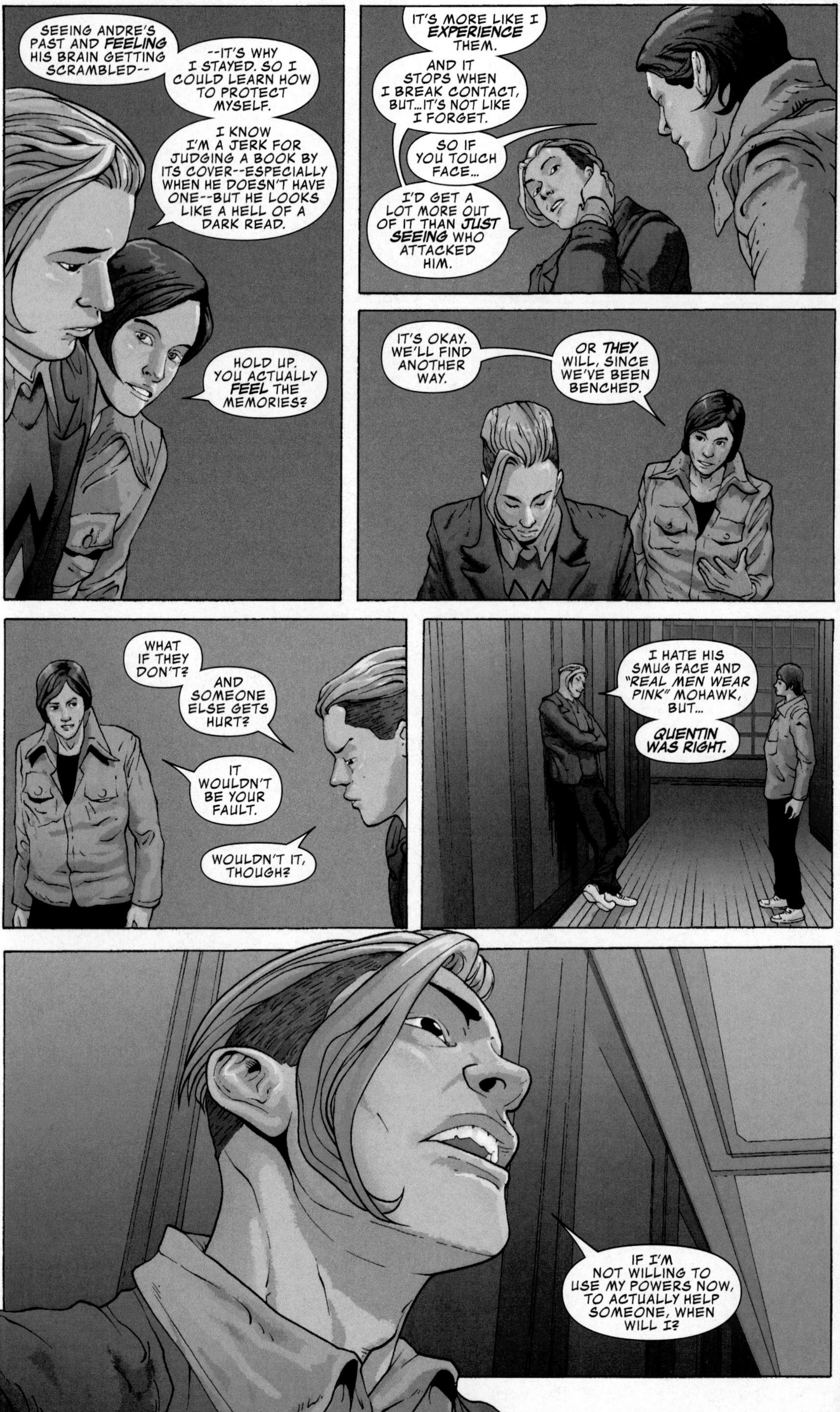
SEEING ANDRE'S PAST AND FEELING HIS BRAIN GETTING SCRAMBLED--
--IT'S WHY I STAYED. SO I COULD LEARN HOW TO PROTECT MYSELF.
I KNOW I'M A JERK FOR JUDGING A BOOK BY ITS COVER--ESPECIALLY WHEN HE DOESN'T HAVE ONE--BUT HE LOOKS LIKE A HELL OF A DARK READ.
HOLD UP. YOU ACTUALLY FEEL THE MEMORIES?
IT'S MORE LIKE I EXPERIENCE THEM.
AND IT STOPS WHEN I BREAK CONTACT, BUT...IT'S NOT LIKE I FORGET.
SO IF YOU TOUCH FACE...
I'D GET A LOT MORE OUT OF IT THAN JUST SEEING WHO ATTACKED HIM.
IT'S OKAY. WE'LL FIND ANOTHER WAY.
OR THEY WILL, SINCE WE'VE BEEN BENCHED.
WHAT IF THEY DON'T?
AND SOMEONE ELSE GETS HURT?
IT WOULDN'T BE YOUR FAULT.
WOULDN'T IT, THOUGH?
I HATE HIS SMUG FACE AND "REAL MEN WEAR PINK" MOHAWK, BUT...
QUENTIN WAS RIGHT.
IF I'M NOT WILLING TO USE MY POWERS NOW, TO ACTUALLY HELP SOMEONE, WHEN WILL I?

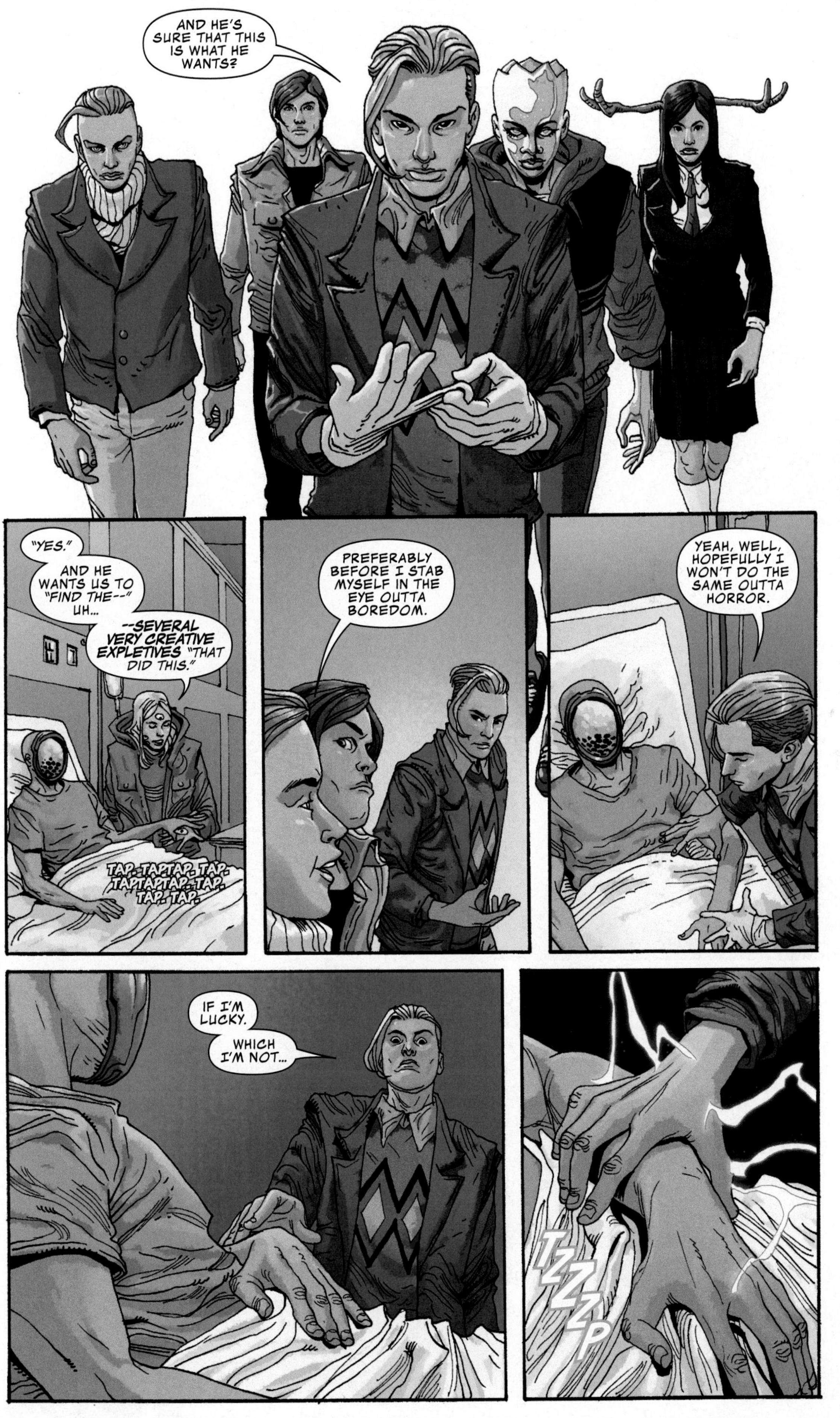
AND HE'S SURE THAT THIS IS WHAT HE WANTS?
"YES."
AND HE WANTS US TO "FIND THE--" UH...
--SEVERAL VERY CREATIVE EXPLETIVES "THAT DID THIS."
TAP. TAPTAP. TAP. TAPTAPTAP. TAP. TAP. TAP.
PREFERABLY BEFORE I STAB MYSELF IN THE EYE OUTTA BOREDOM.
YEAH, WELL, HOPEFULLY I WON'T DO THE SAME OUTTA HORROR.
IF I'M LUCKY.
WHICH I'M NOT...
TZZZP

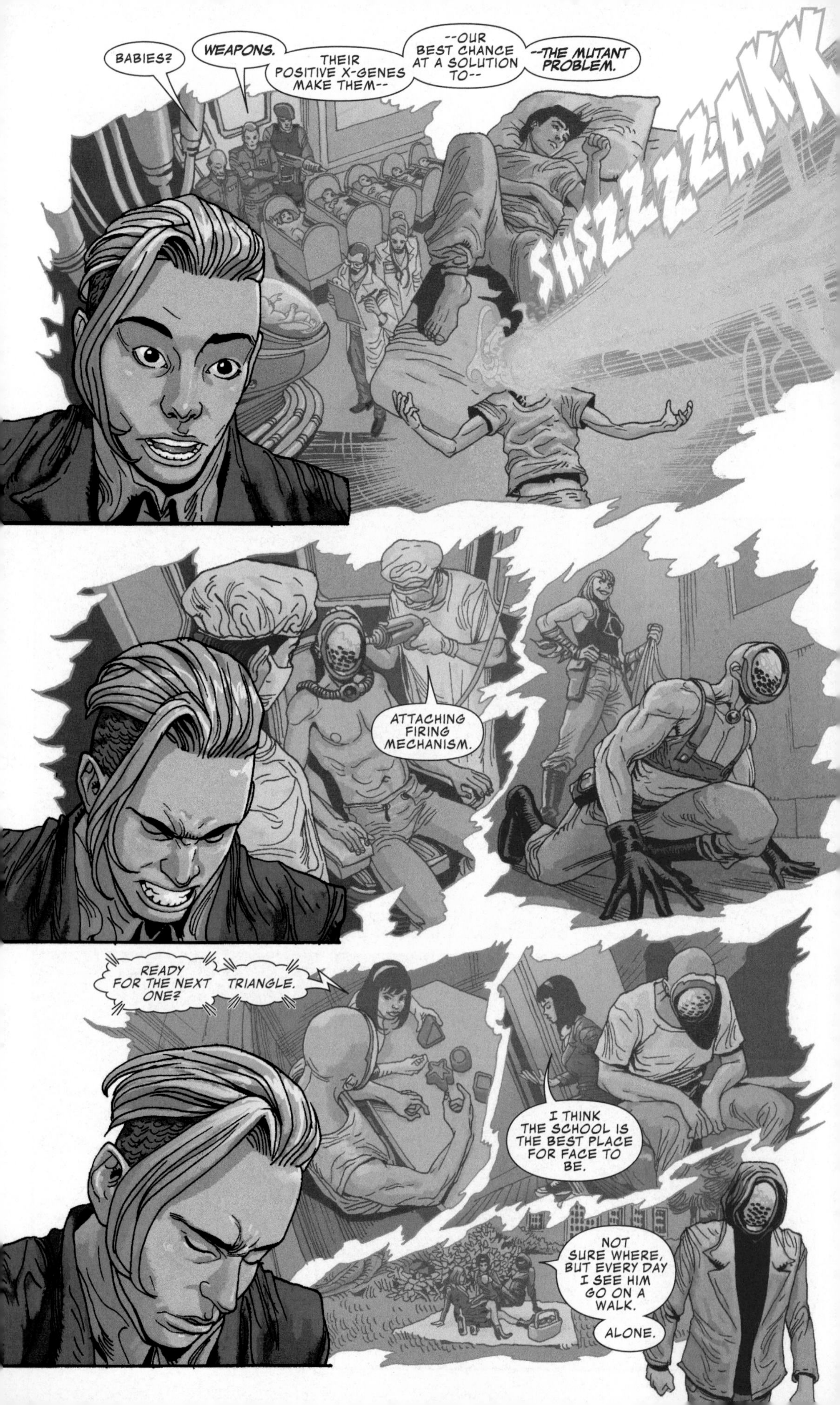
BABIES?
WEAPONS.
THEIR POSITIVE X-GENES MAKE THEM--
--OUR BEST CHANCE AT A SOLUTION TO--
--THE MUTANT PROBLEM.
SHSZZZZAK
ATTACHING FIRING MECHANISM.
READY FOR THE NEXT ONE?
TRIANGLE.
I THINK THE SCHOOL IS THE BEST PLACE FOR FACE TO BE.
NOT SURE WHERE, BUT EVERY DAY I SEE HIM GO ON A WALK.
ALONE.

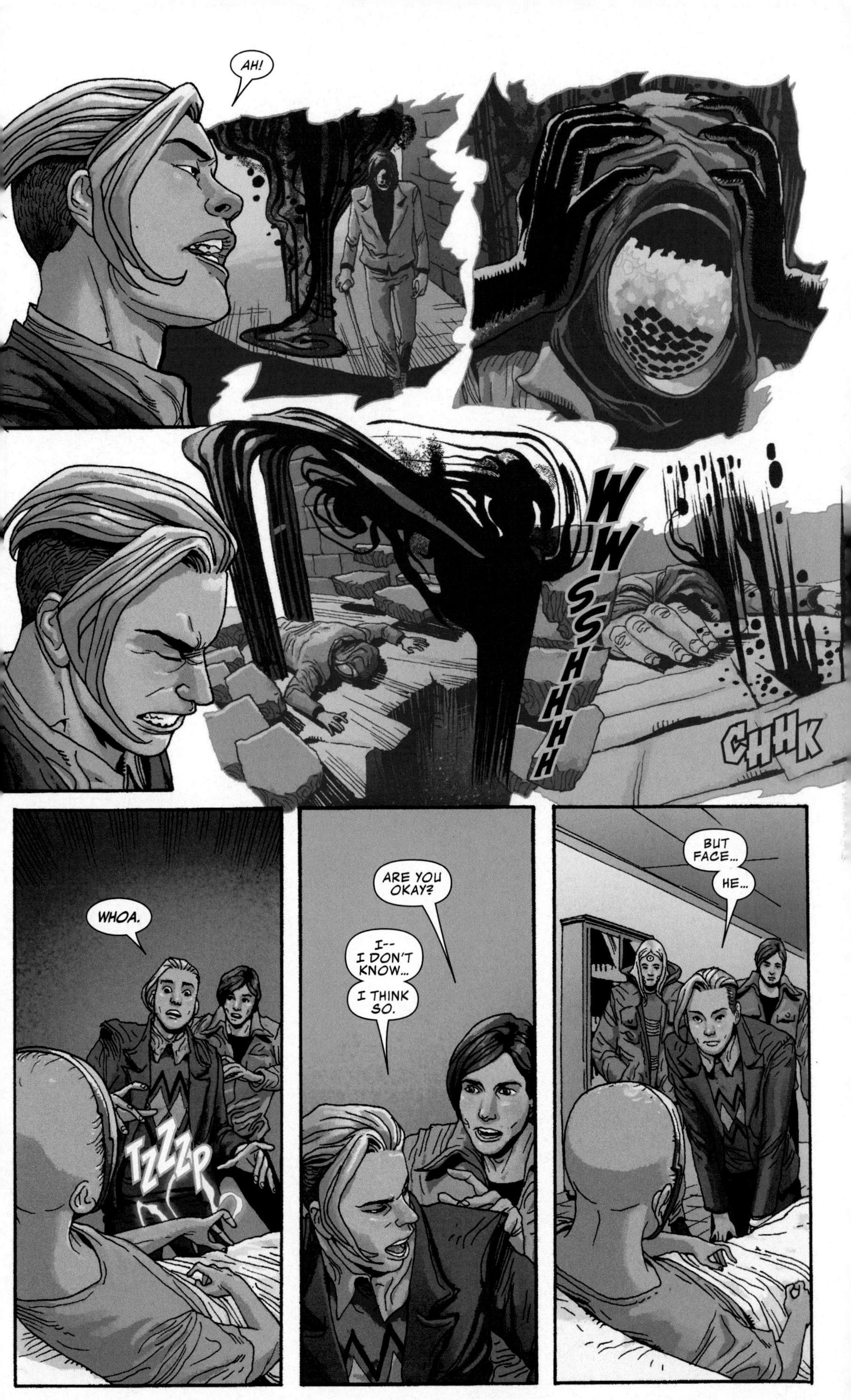

AH!
WWSSHHHH
CHHK
WHOA.
TZZZP
ARE YOU OKAY?
I-- I DON'T KNOW...
I THINK SO.
BUT FACE...
HE...

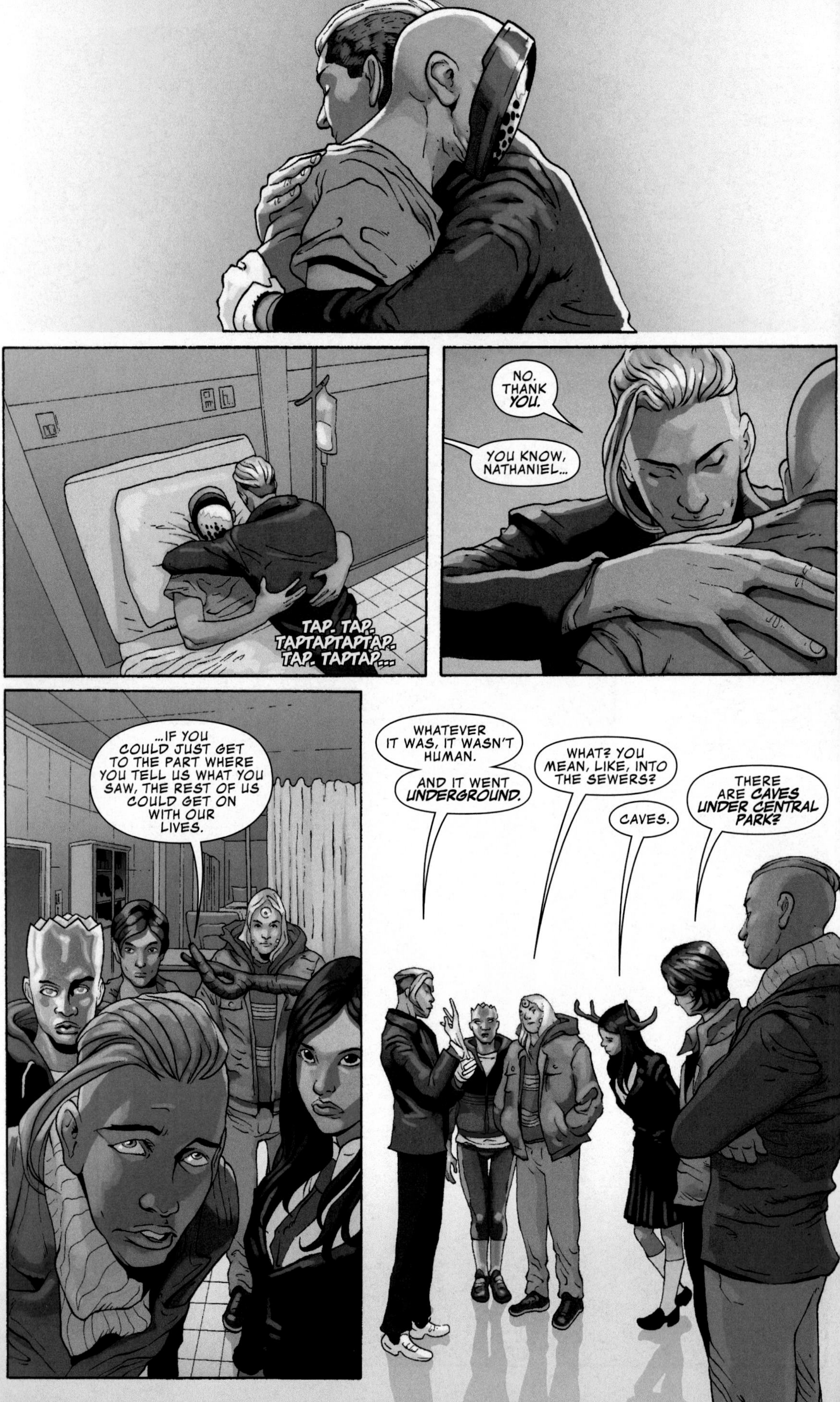

TAP. TAP. TAPTAPTAPTAP. TAP. TAPTAP...
NO. THANK YOU.
YOU KNOW, NATHANIEL...
...IF YOU COULD JUST GET TO THE PART WHERE YOU TELL US WHAT YOU SAW, THE REST OF US COULD GET ON WITH OUR LIVES.
WHATEVER IT WAS, IT WASN'T HUMAN.
AND IT WENT UNDERGROUND.
WHAT? YOU MEAN, LIKE, INTO THE SEWERS?
CAVES.
THERE ARE CAVES UNDER CENTRAL PARK?

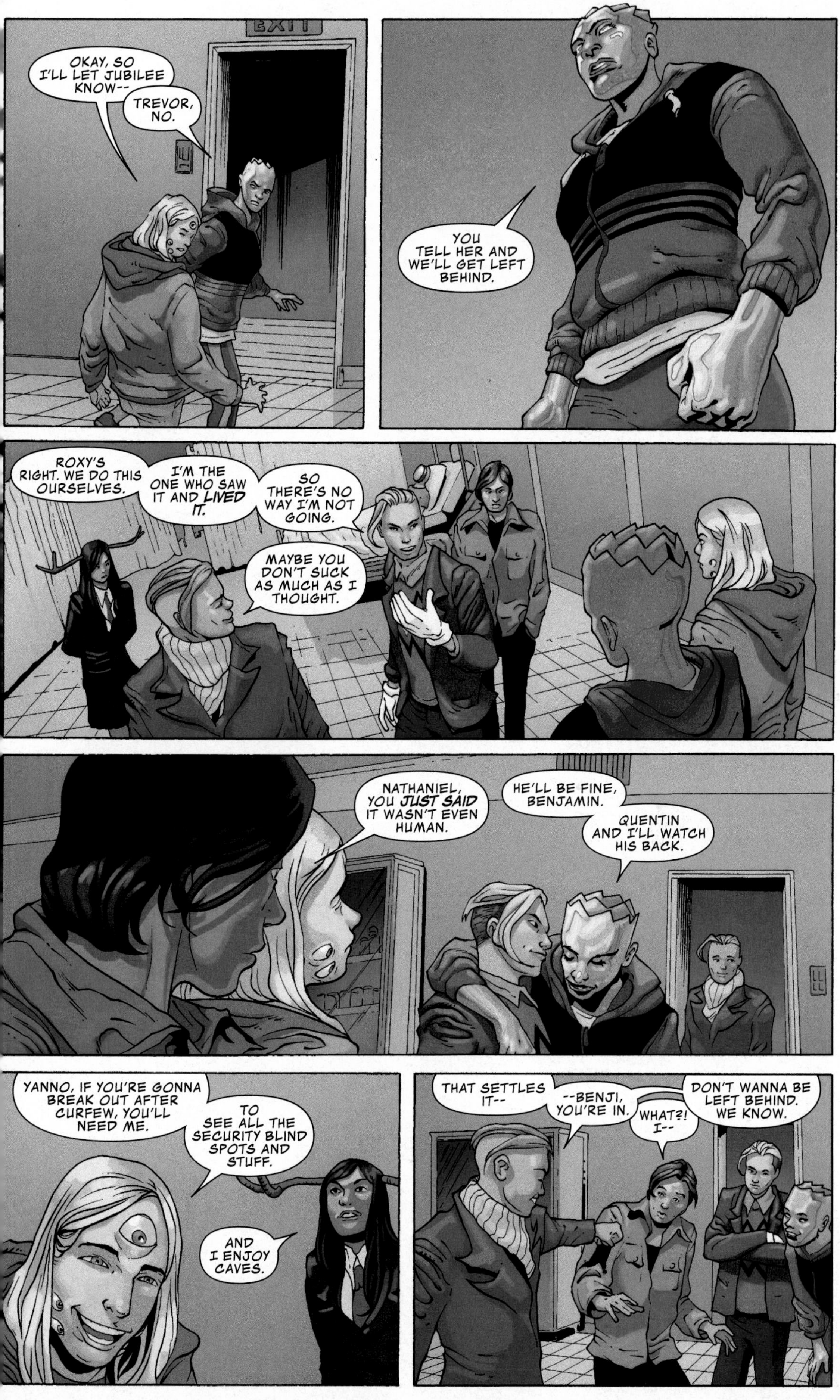
EXIT
OKAY, SO I'LL LET JUBILEE KNOW--
TREVOR, NO.
YOU TELL HER AND WE'LL GET LEFT BEHIND.
ROXY'S RIGHT. WE DO THIS OURSELVES.
I'M THE ONE WHO SAW IT AND LIVED IT.
SO THERE'S NO WAY I'M NOT GOING.
MAYBE YOU DON'T SUCK AS MUCH AS I THOUGHT.
NATHANIEL, YOU JUST SAID IT WASN'T EVEN HUMAN.
HE'LL BE FINE, BENJAMIN.
QUENTIN AND I'LL WATCH HIS BACK.
YANNO, IF YOU'RE GONNA BREAK OUT AFTER CURFEW, YOU'LL NEED ME.
TO SEE ALL THE SECURITY BLIND SPOTS AND STUFF.
AND I ENJOY CAVES.
THAT SETTLES IT--
--BENJI, YOU'RE IN.
WHAT?! I--
DON'T WANNA BE LEFT BEHIND. WE KNOW.

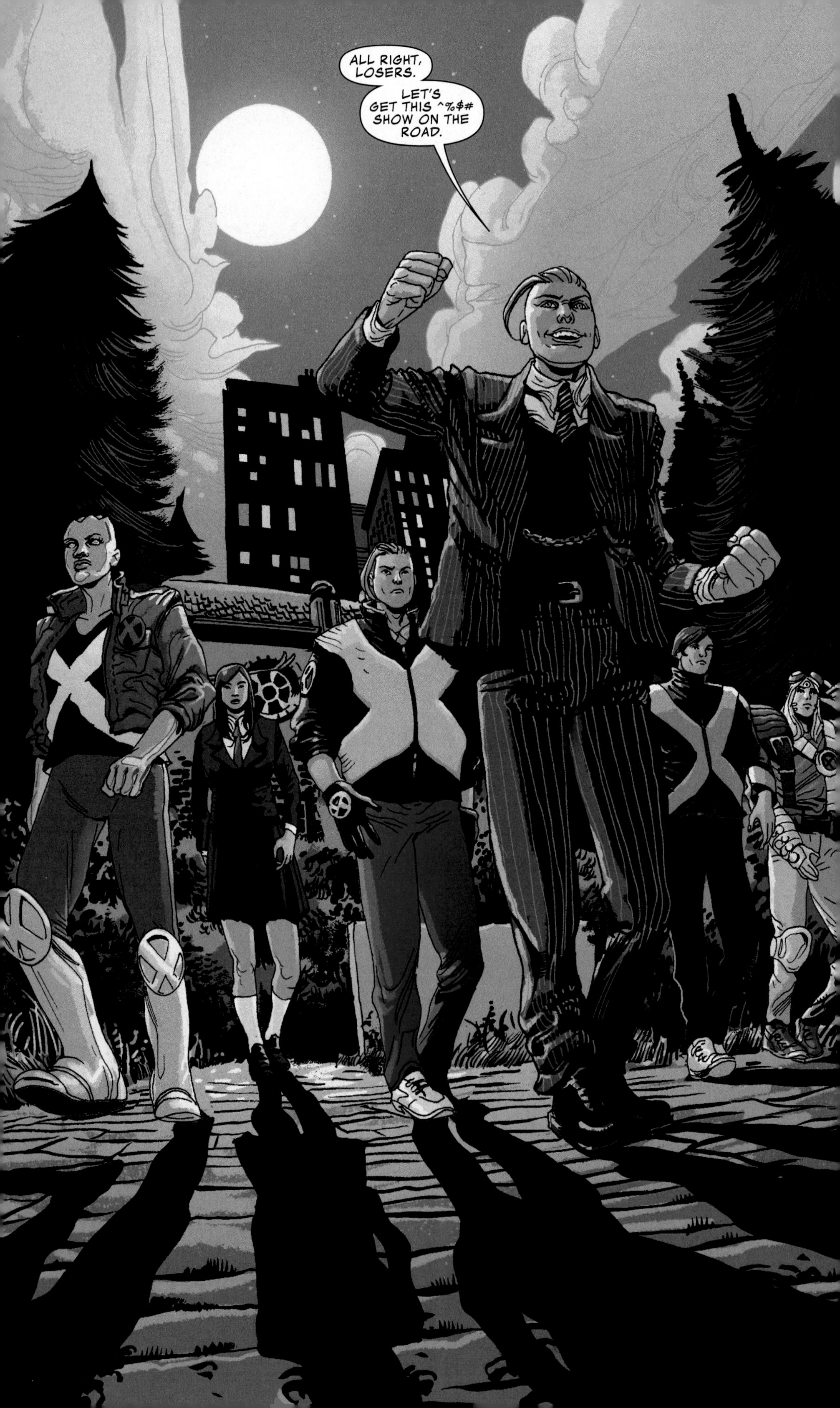
ALL RIGHT, LOSERS.
LET'S GET THIS ^%$# SHOW ON THE ROAD.

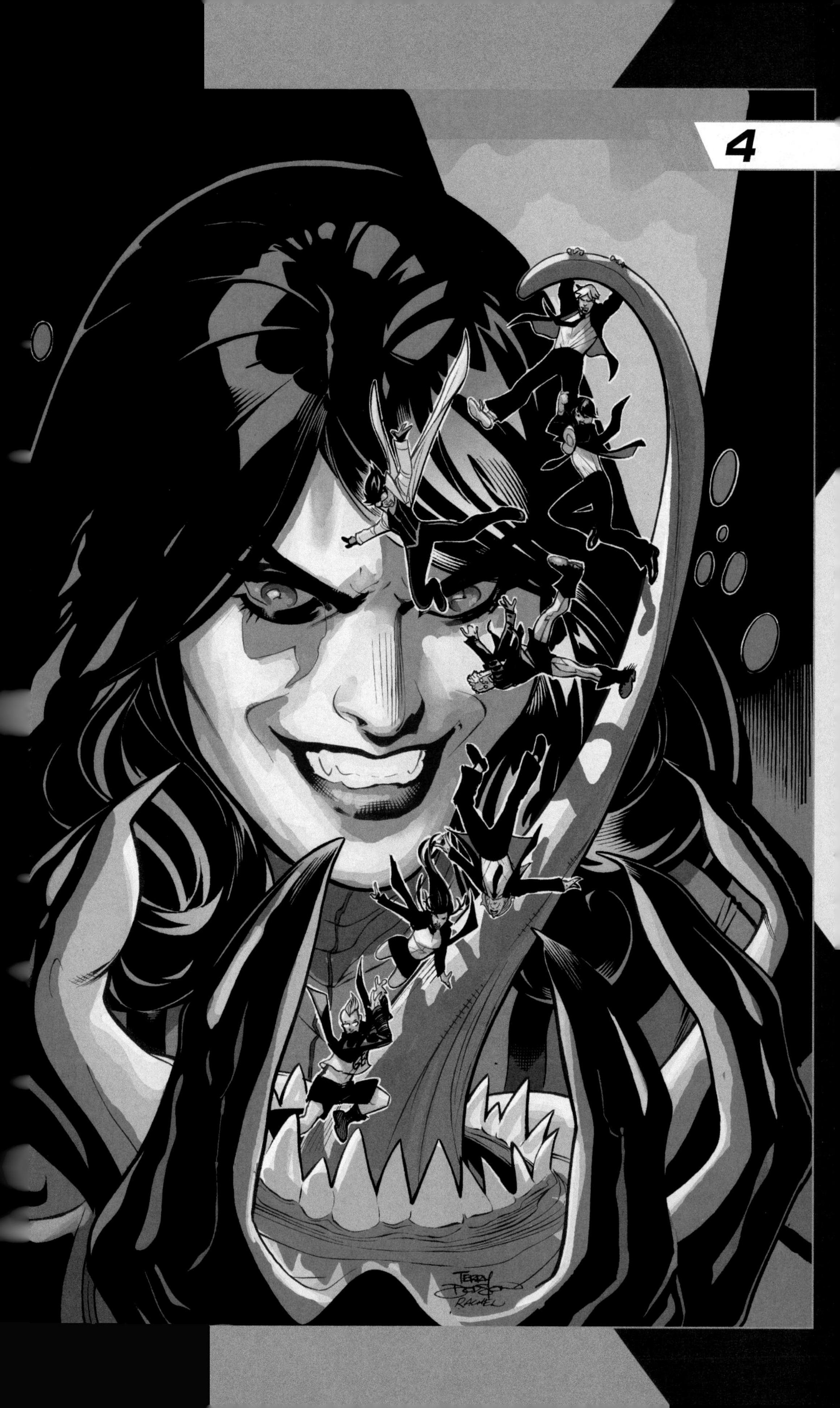
4

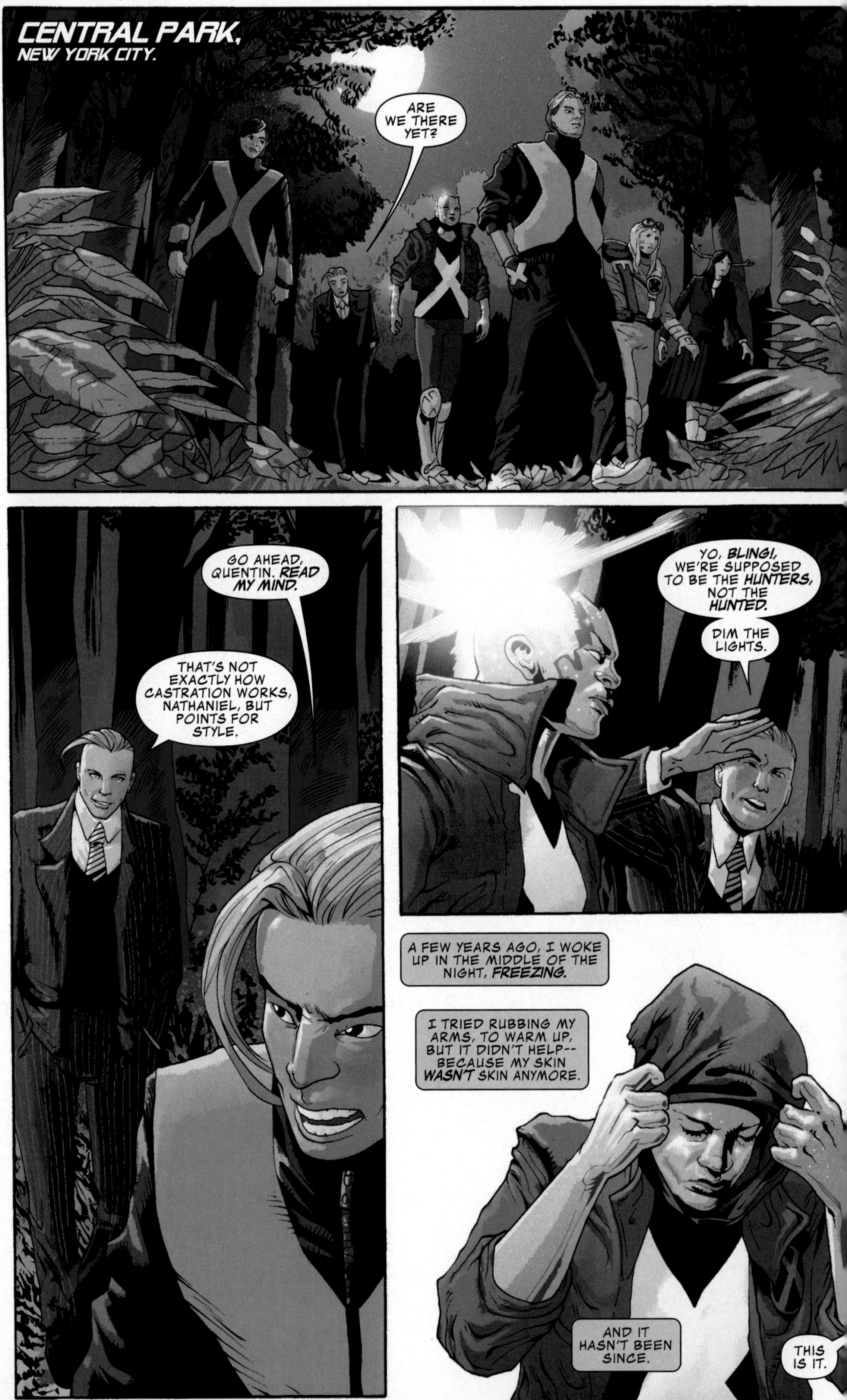
CENTRAL PARK, NEW YORK CITY.
ARE WE THERE YET?
GO AHEAD, QUENTIN. READ MY MIND.
THAT'S NOT EXACTLY HOW CASTRATION WORKS, NATHANIEL, BUT POINTS FOR STYLE.
YO, BLING!, WE'RE SUPPOSED TO BE THE HUNTERS, NOT THE HUNTED.
DIM THE LIGHTS.
A FEW YEARS AGO, I WOKE UP IN THE MIDDLE OF THE NIGHT, FREEZING.
I TRIED RUBBING MY ARMS, TO WARM UP, BUT IT DIDN'T HELP-- BECAUSE MY SKIN WASN'T SKIN ANYMORE.
AND IT HASN'T BEEN SINCE.
THIS IS IT.

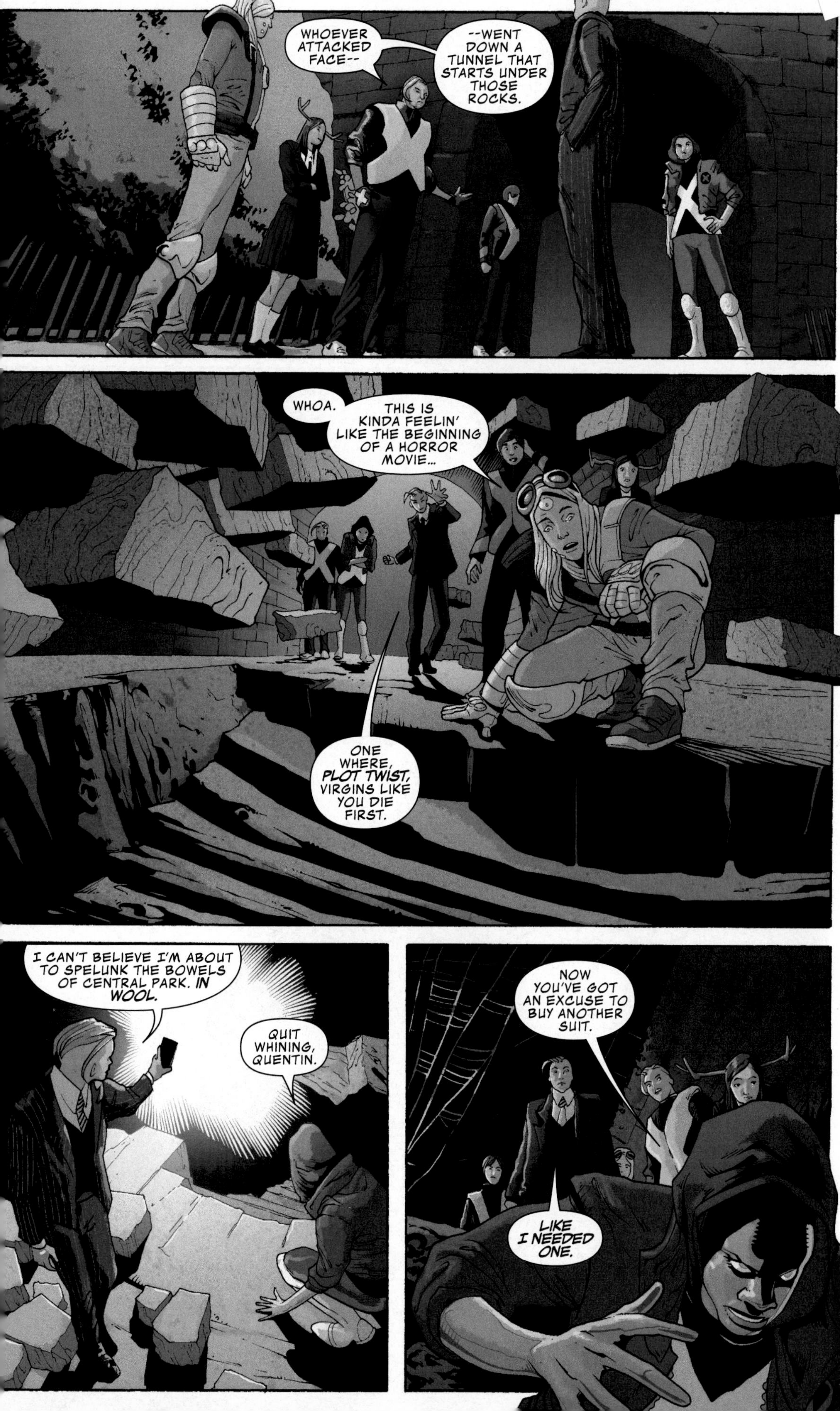

WHOEVER ATTACKED FACE--
--WENT DOWN A TUNNEL THAT STARTS UNDER THOSE ROCKS.
WHOA.
THIS IS KINDA FEELIN' LIKE THE BEGINNING OF A HORROR MOVIE...
ONE WHERE, PLOT TWIST, VIRGINS LIKE YOU DIE FIRST.
I CAN'T BELIEVE I'M ABOUT TO SPELUNK THE BOWELS OF CENTRAL PARK. IN WOOL.
QUIT WHINING, QUENTIN.
NOW YOU'VE GOT AN EXCUSE TO BUY ANOTHER SUIT.
LIKE I NEEDED ONE.

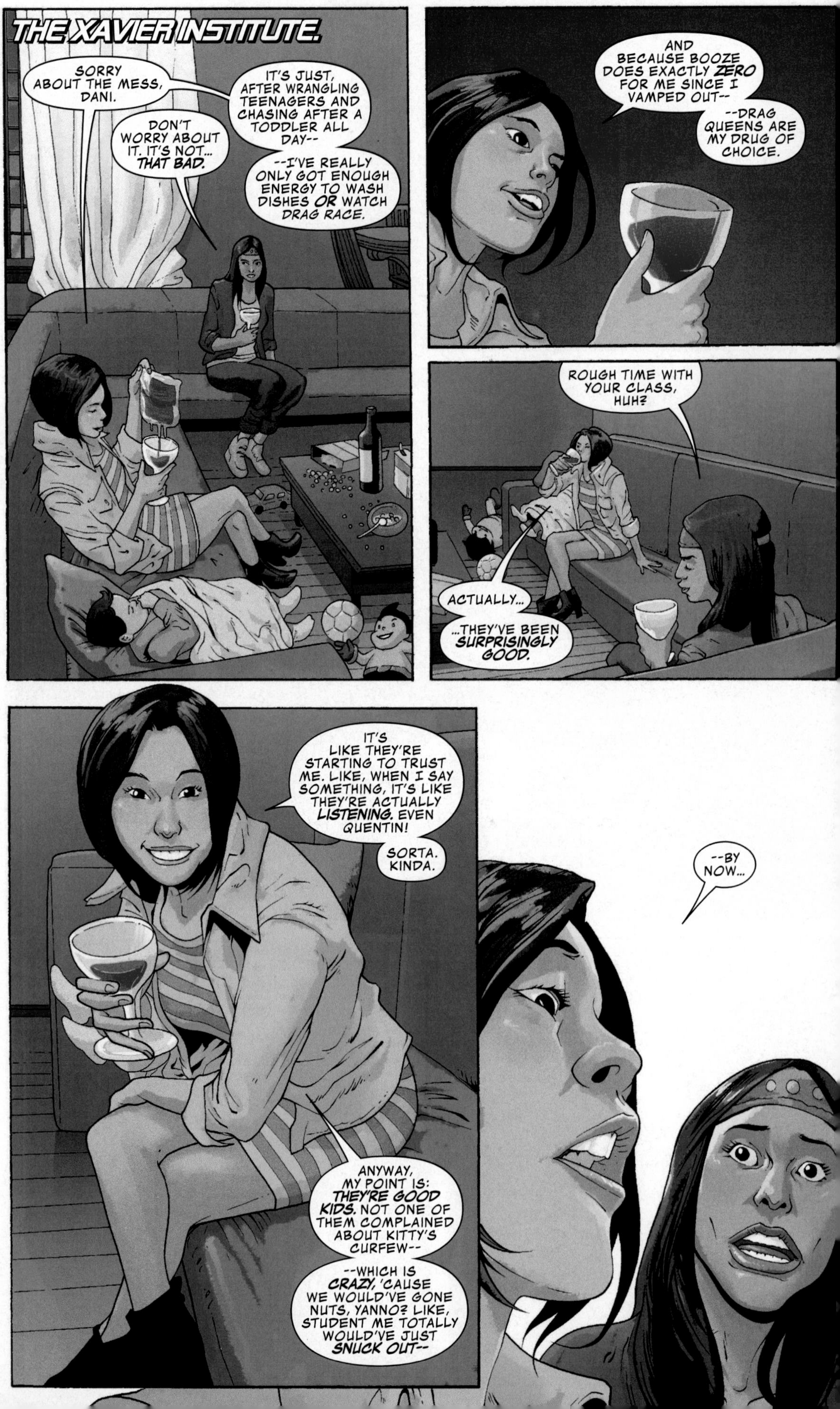
THE XAVIER INSTITUTE.
SORRY ABOUT THE MESS, DANI.
IT'S JUST, AFTER WRANGLING TEENAGERS AND CHASING AFTER A TODDLER ALL DAY--
DON'T WORRY ABOUT IT. IT'S NOT... THAT BAD.
--I'VE REALLY ONLY GOT ENOUGH ENERGY TO WASH DISHES OR WATCH DRAG RACE.
AND BECAUSE BOOZE DOES EXACTLY ZERO FOR ME SINCE I VAMPED OUT--
--DRAG QUEENS ARE MY DRUG OF CHOICE.
ROUGH TIME WITH YOUR CLASS, HUH?
ACTUALLY...
...THEY'VE BEEN SURPRISINGLY GOOD.
IT'S LIKE THEY'RE STARTING TO TRUST ME. LIKE, WHEN I SAY SOMETHING, IT'S LIKE THEY'RE ACTUALLY LISTENING. EVEN QUENTIN!
SORTA. KINDA.
ANYWAY, MY POINT IS: THEY'RE GOOD KIDS. NOT ONE OF THEM COMPLAINED ABOUT KITTY'S CURFEW--
--WHICH IS CRAZY, 'CAUSE WE WOULD'VE GONE NUTS, YANNO? LIKE, STUDENT ME TOTALLY WOULD'VE JUST SNUCK OUT--
--BY NOW...

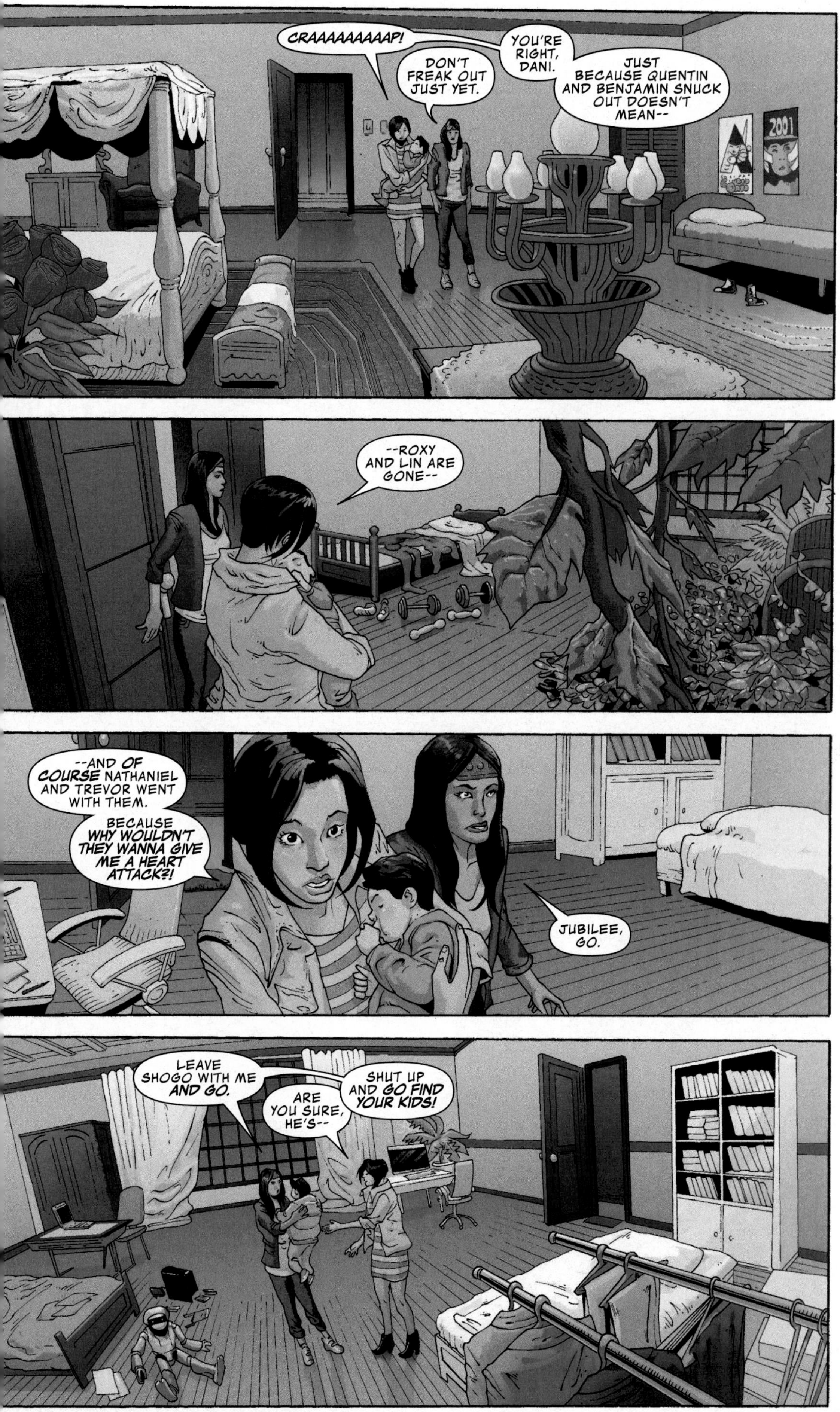
CRAAAAAAAAAP!
DON'T FREAK OUT JUST YET.
YOU'RE RIGHT, DANI.
JUST BECAUSE QUENTIN AND BENJAMIN SNUCK OUT DOESN'T MEAN--
2001
--ROXY AND LIN ARE GONE--
--AND OF COURSE NATHANIEL AND TREVOR WENT WITH THEM.
BECAUSE WHY WOULDN'T THEY WANNA GIVE ME A HEART ATTACK?!
JUBILEE, GO.
LEAVE SHOGO WITH ME AND GO.
ARE YOU SURE, HE'S--
SHUT UP AND GO FIND YOUR KIDS!

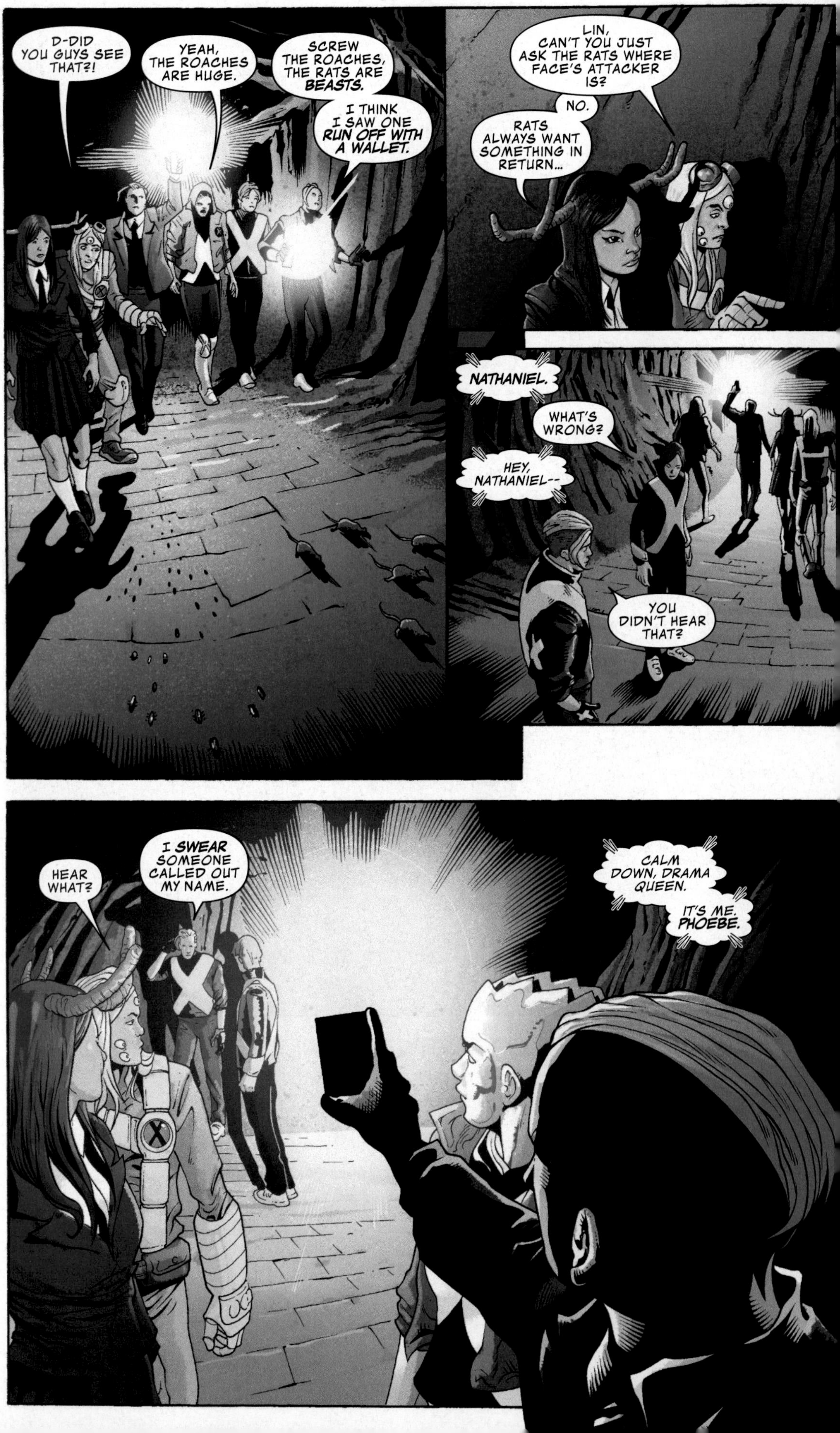
D-DID YOU GUYS SEE THAT?!
YEAH, THE ROACHES ARE HUGE.
SCREW THE ROACHES, THE RATS ARE BEASTS.
I THINK I SAW ONE RUN OFF WITH A WALLET.
LIN, CAN'T YOU JUST ASK THE RATS WHERE FACE'S ATTACKER IS?
NO.
RATS ALWAYS WANT SOMETHING IN RETURN...
NATHANIEL.
WHAT'S WRONG?
HEY, NATHANIEL--
YOU DIDN'T HEAR THAT?
HEAR WHAT?
I SWEAR SOMEONE CALLED OUT MY NAME.
CALM DOWN, DRAMA QUEEN.
IT'S ME. PHOEBE.

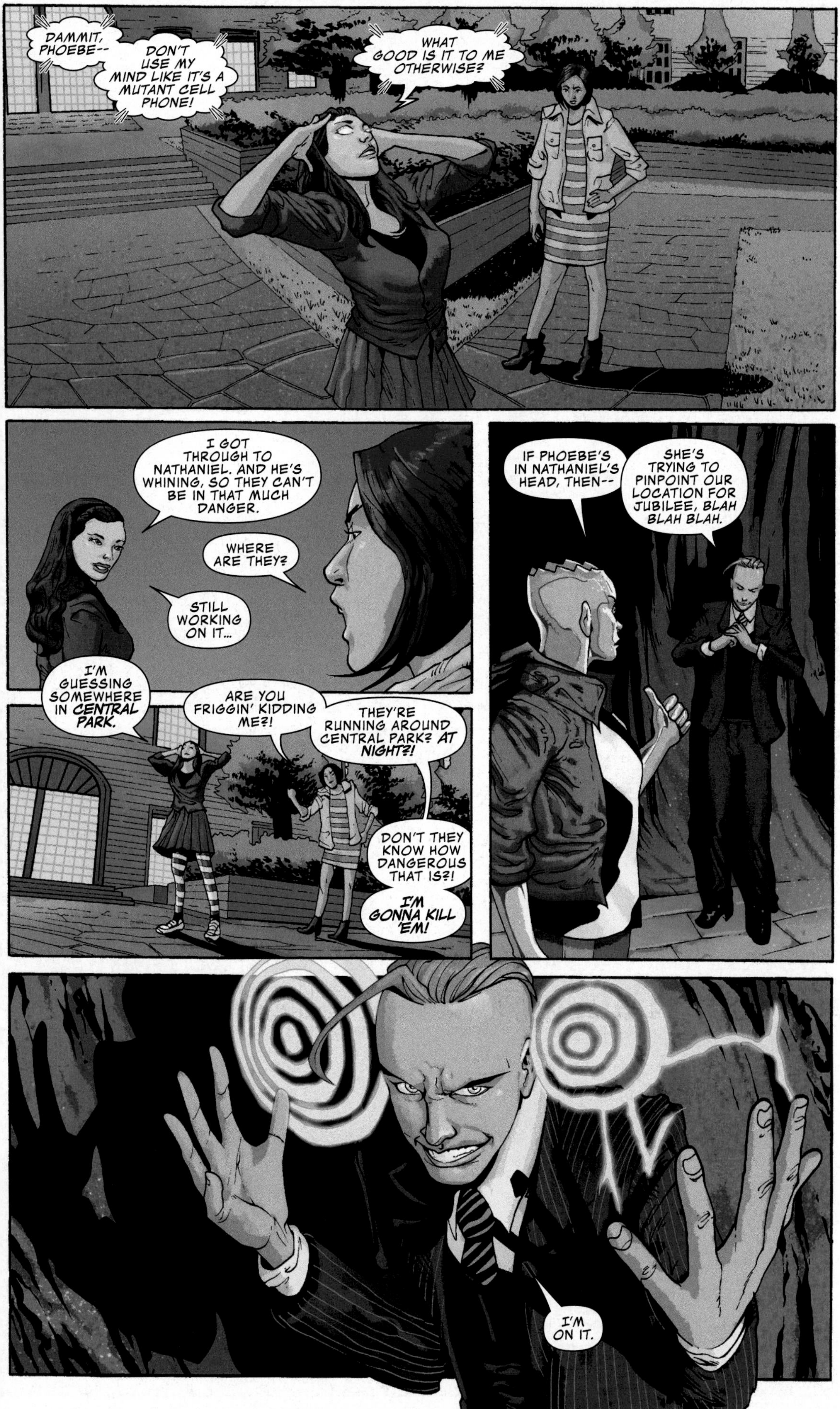
DAMMIT, PHOEBE--
DON'T USE MY MIND LIKE IT'S A MUTANT CELL PHONE!
WHAT GOOD IS IT TO ME OTHERWISE?
I GOT THROUGH TO NATHANIEL. AND HE'S WHINING, SO THEY CAN'T BE IN THAT MUCH DANGER.
WHERE ARE THEY?
STILL WORKING ON IT...
I'M GUESSING SOMEWHERE IN CENTRAL PARK.
ARE YOU FRIGGIN' KIDDING ME?!
THEY'RE RUNNING AROUND CENTRAL PARK? AT NIGHT?!
DON'T THEY KNOW HOW DANGEROUS THAT IS?!
I'M GONNA KILL 'EM!
IF PHOEBE'S IN NATHANIEL'S HEAD, THEN--
SHE'S TRYING TO PINPOINT OUR LOCATION FOR JUBILEE, BLAH BLAH BLAH.
I'M ON IT.

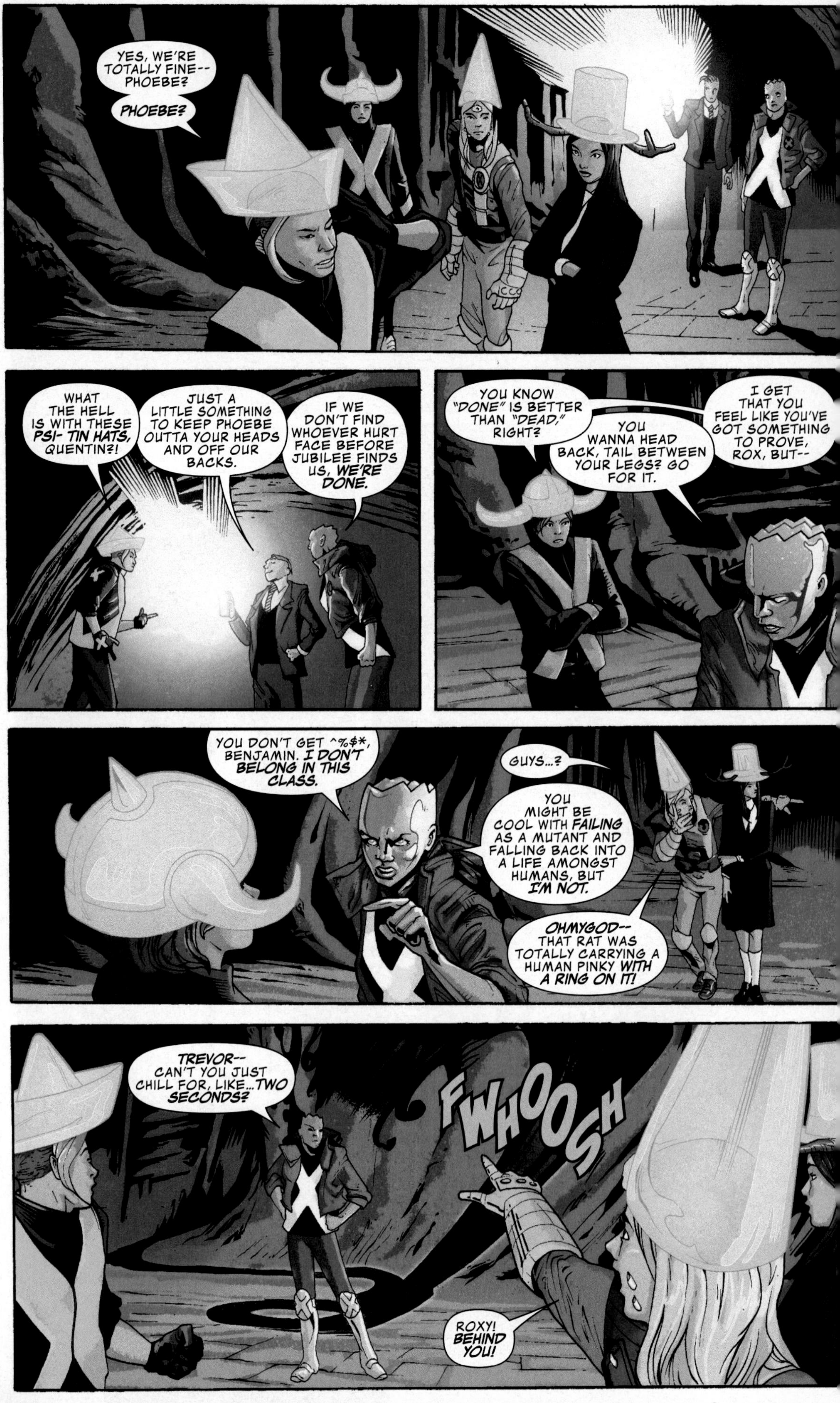
YES, WE'RE TOTALLY FINE-- PHOEBE?
PHOEBE?
WHAT THE HELL IS WITH THESE PSI- TIN HATS, QUENTIN?!
JUST A LITTLE SOMETHING TO KEEP PHOEBE OUTTA YOUR HEADS AND OFF OUR BACKS.
IF WE DON'T FIND WHOEVER HURT FACE BEFORE JUBILEE FINDS US, WE'RE DONE.
YOU KNOW "DONE" IS BETTER THAN "DEAD," RIGHT?
YOU WANNA HEAD BACK, TAIL BETWEEN YOUR LEGS? GO FOR IT.
I GET THAT YOU FEEL LIKE YOU'VE GOT SOMETHING TO PROVE, ROX, BUT--
YOU DON'T GET ^%$*, BENJAMIN. I DON'T BELONG IN THIS CLASS.
GUYS...?
YOU MIGHT BE COOL WITH FAILING AS A MUTANT AND FALLING BACK INTO A LIFE AMONGST HUMANS, BUT I'M NOT.
OHMYGOD-- THAT RAT WAS TOTALLY CARRYING A HUMAN PINKY WITH A RING ON IT!
TREVOR-- CAN'T YOU JUST CHILL FOR, LIKE...TWO SECONDS?
FWHOOSH
ROXY! BEHIND YOU!

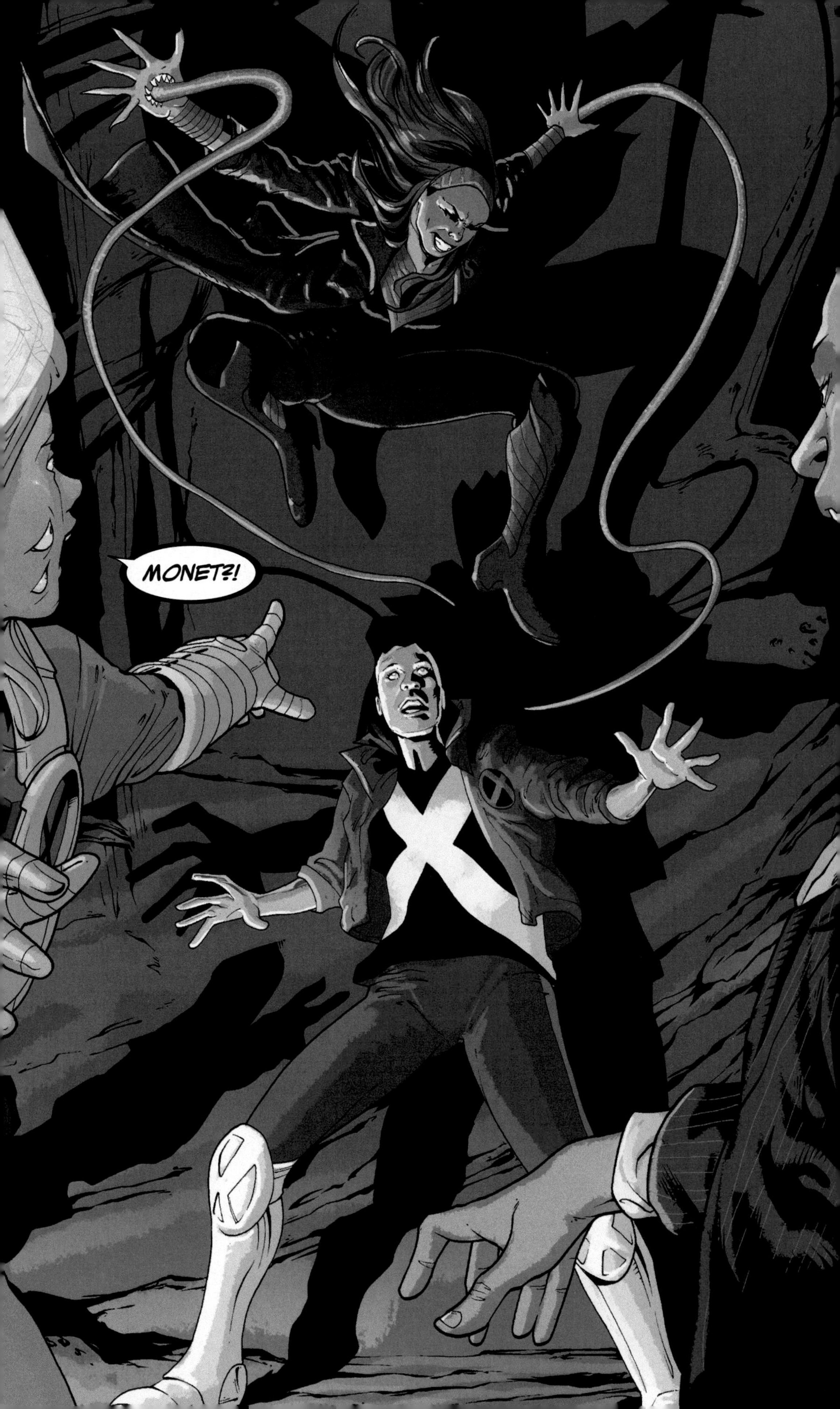
MONET?!

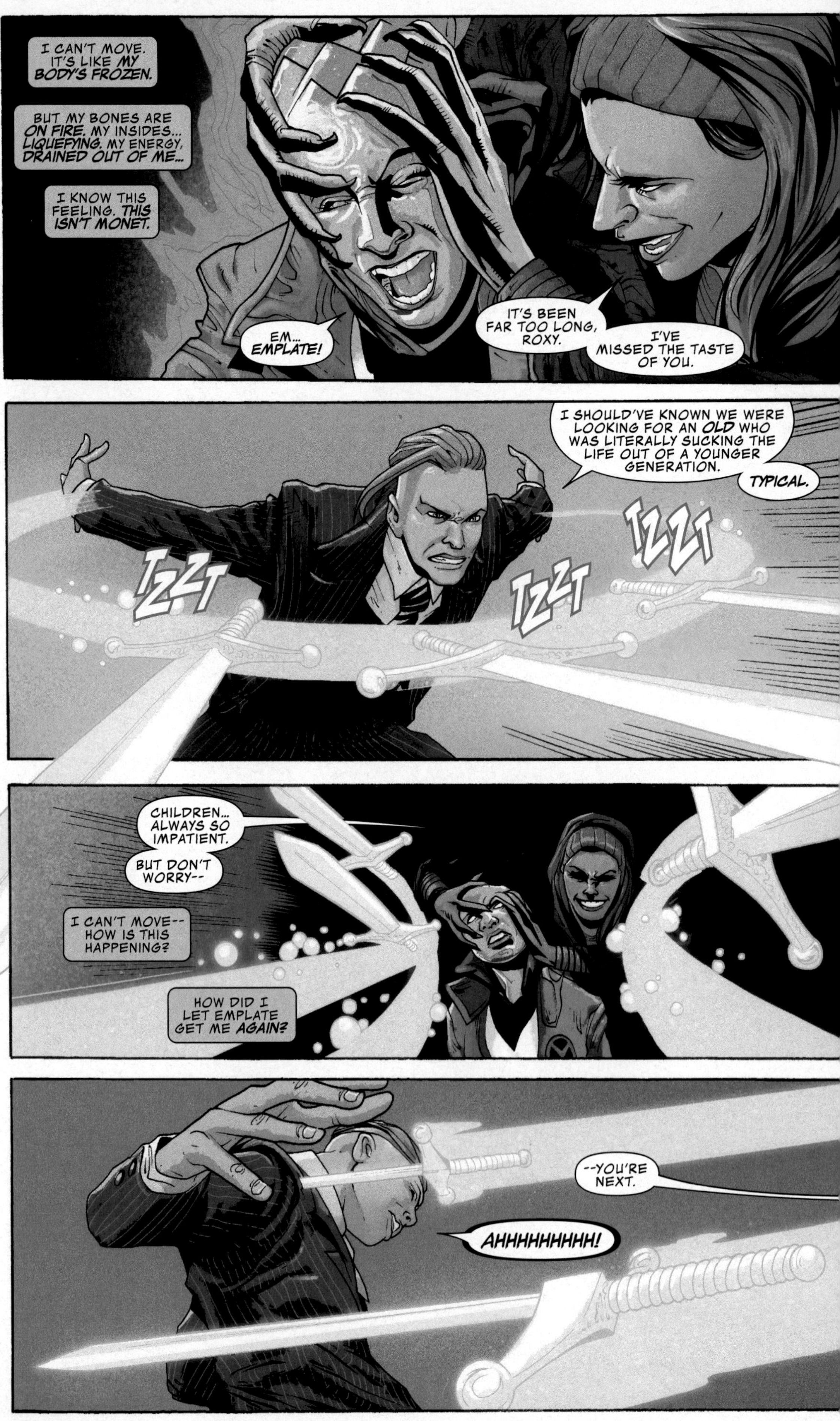
I CAN'T MOVE. IT'S LIKE MY BODY'S FROZEN.
BUT MY BONES ARE ON FIRE. MY INSIDES... LIQUEFYING. MY ENERGY, DRAINED OUT OF ME...
I KNOW THIS FEELING. THIS ISN'T MONET.
EM... EMPLATE!
IT'S BEEN FAR TOO LONG, ROXY.
I'VE MISSED THE TASTE OF YOU.
I SHOULD'VE KNOWN WE WERE LOOKING FOR AN OLD WHO WAS LITERALLY SUCKING THE LIFE OUT OF A YOUNGER GENERATION.
TYPICAL.
TZZT
TZZT
TZZT
CHILDREN... ALWAYS SO IMPATIENT.
BUT DON'T WORRY--
I CAN'T MOVE-- HOW IS THIS HAPPENING?
HOW DID I LET EMPLATE GET ME AGAIN?
--YOU'RE NEXT.
AHHHHHHHHH!

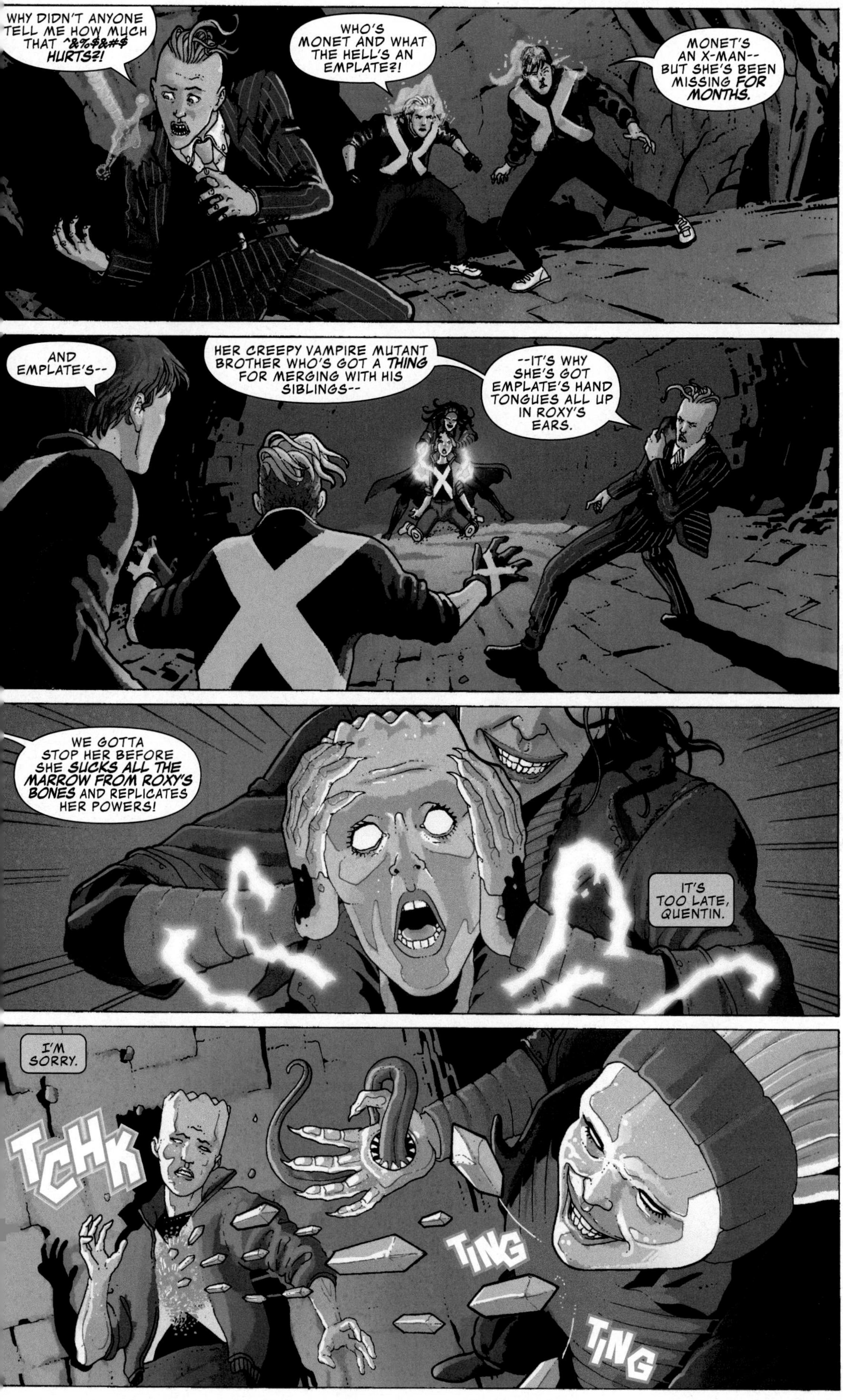
WHY DIDN'T ANYONE TELL ME HOW MUCH THAT ^&%$&#$ HURTS?!
WHO'S MONET AND WHAT THE HELL'S AN EMPLATE?!
MONET'S AN X-MAN-- BUT SHE'S BEEN MISSING FOR MONTHS.
AND EMPLATE'S--
HER CREEPY VAMPIRE MUTANT BROTHER WHO'S GOT A THING FOR MERGING WITH HIS SIBLINGS--
--IT'S WHY SHE'S GOT EMPLATE'S HAND TONGUES ALL UP IN ROXY'S EARS.
WE GOTTA STOP HER BEFORE SHE SUCKS ALL THE MARROW FROM ROXY'S BONES AND REPLICATES HER POWERS!
IT'S TOO LATE, QUENTIN.
I'M SORRY.
TCHK
TING
TING

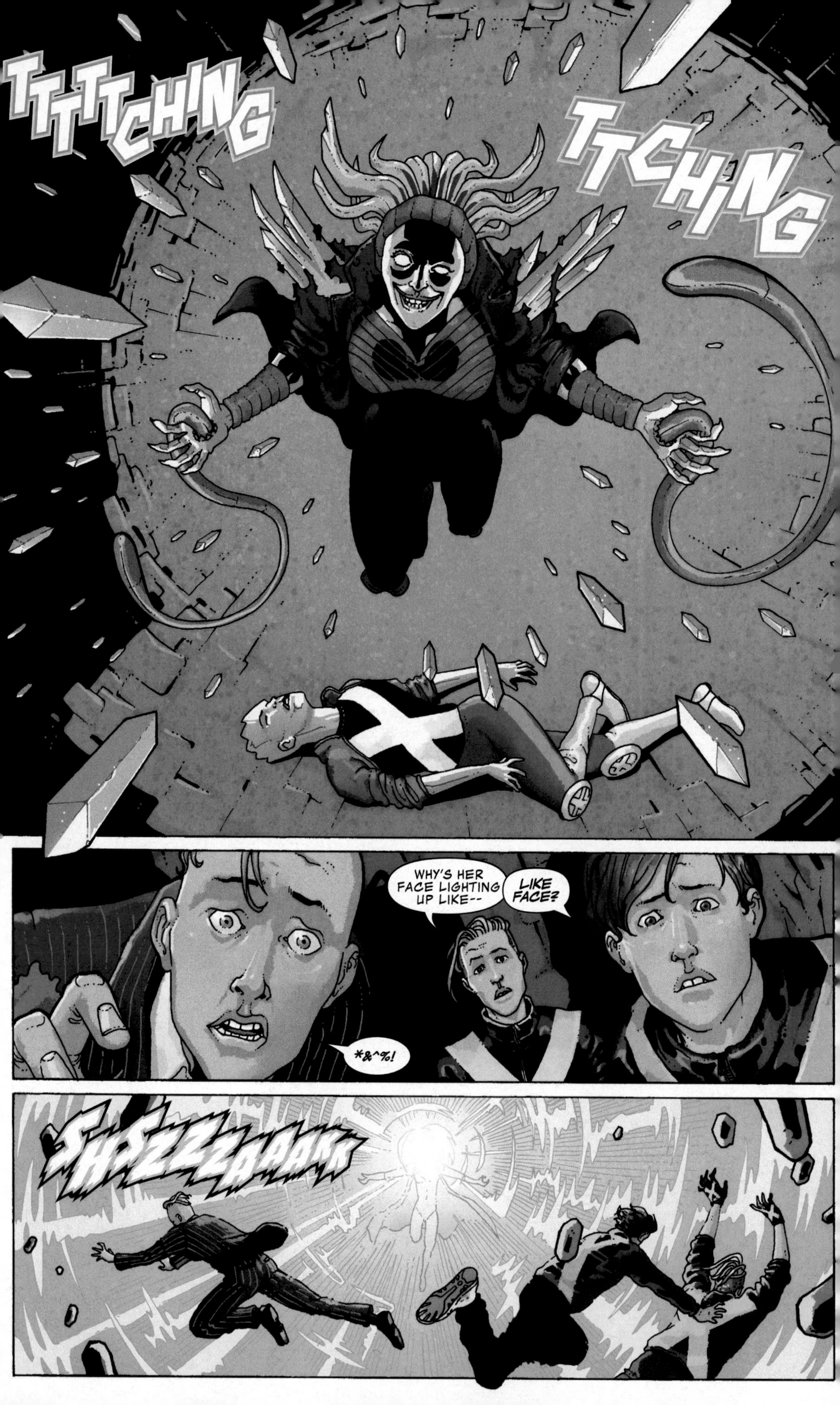
TTTTCHING
TTCHING
WHY'S HER FACE LIGHTING UP LIKE--
LIKE FACE?
*&^%!
SHZZZZAAAK

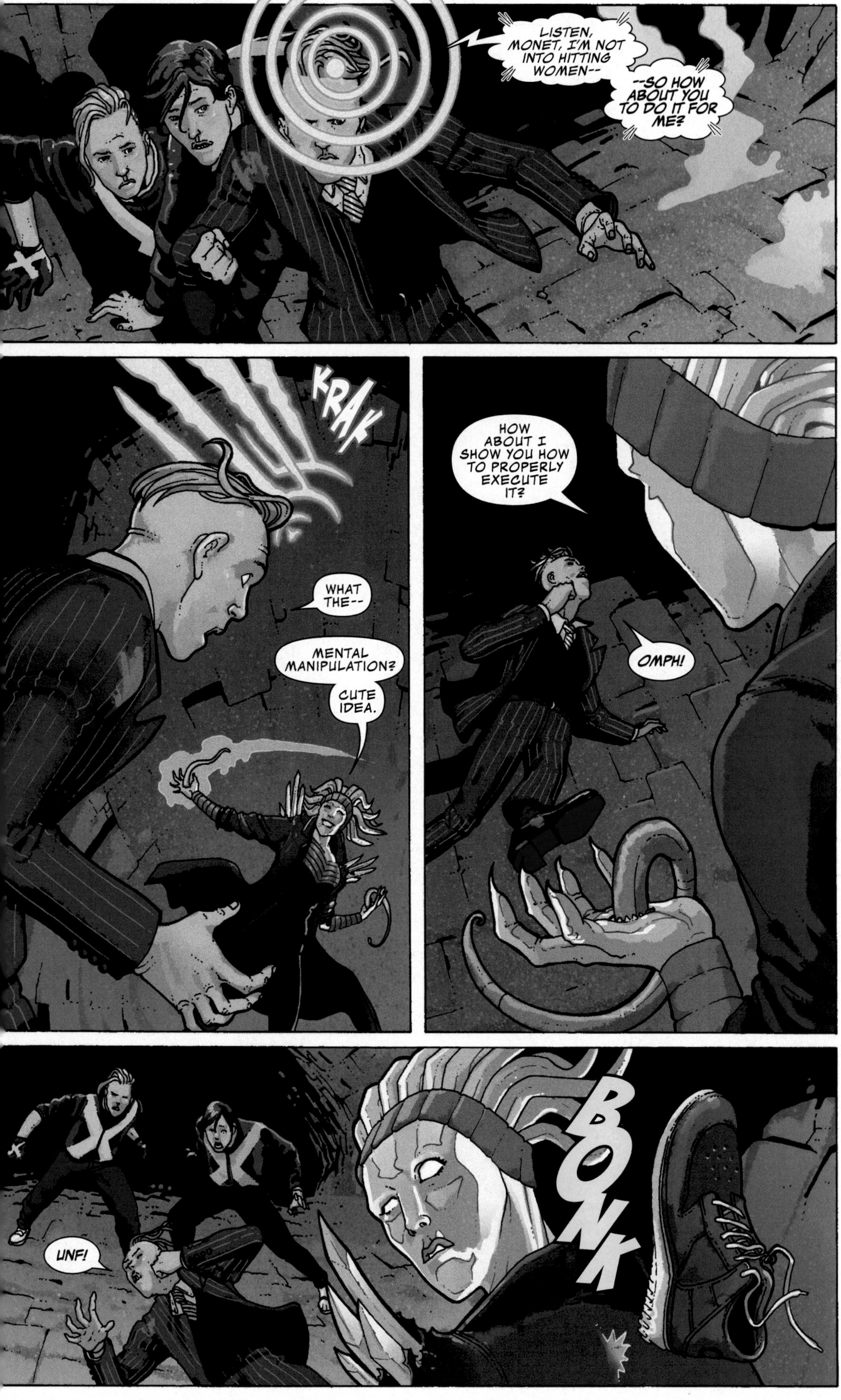

LISTEN, MONET, I'M NOT INTO HITTING WOMEN--
--SO HOW ABOUT YOU TO DO IT FOR ME?
KRAK
WHAT THE--
MENTAL MANIPULATION?
CUTE IDEA.
HOW ABOUT I SHOW YOU HOW TO PROPERLY EXECUTE IT?
OMPH!
UNF!
BONK

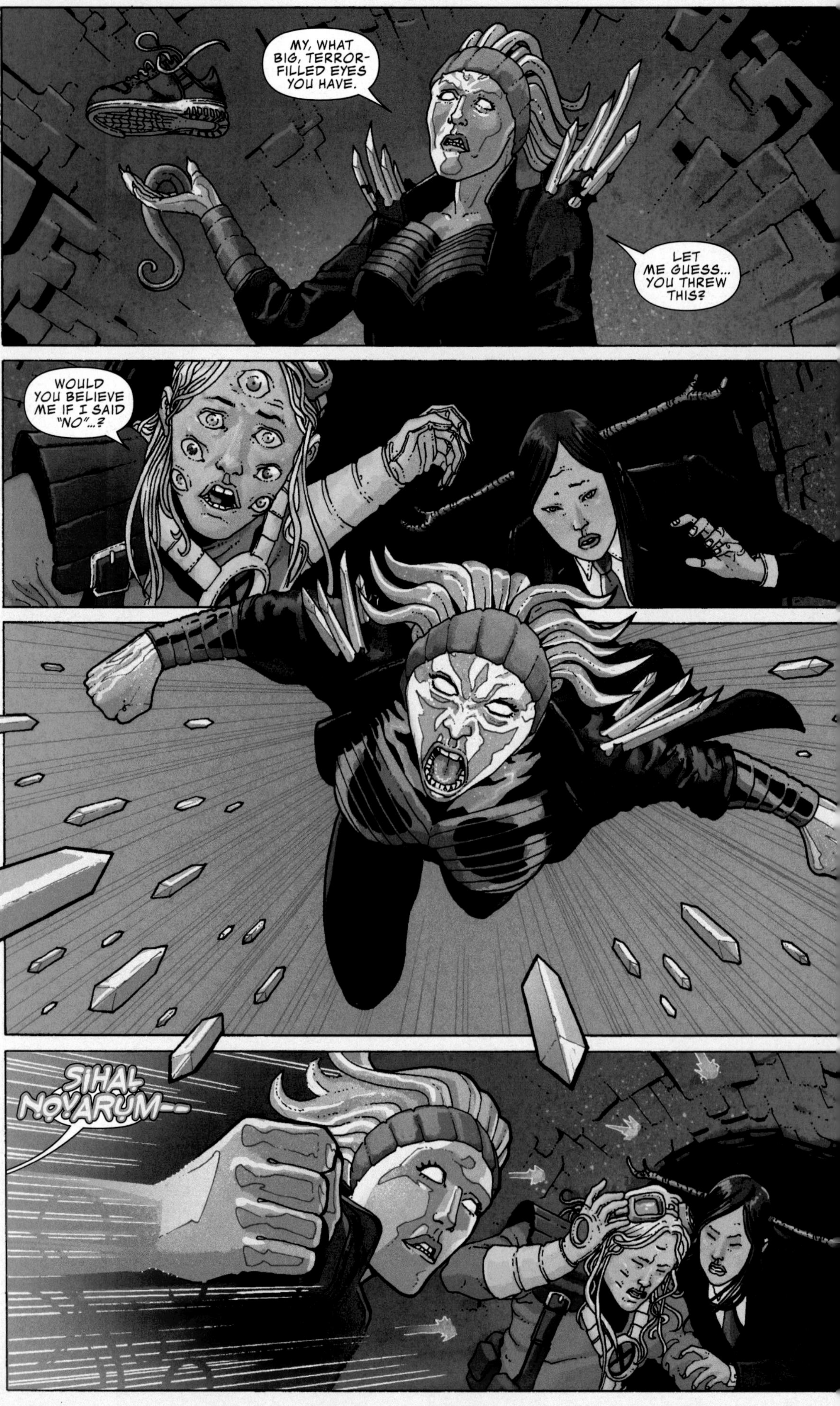
MY, WHAT BIG, TERROR-FILLED EYES YOU HAVE.
LET ME GUESS... YOU THREW THIS?
WOULD YOU BELIEVE ME IF I SAID "NO"...?
SIHAL NOYARUM--

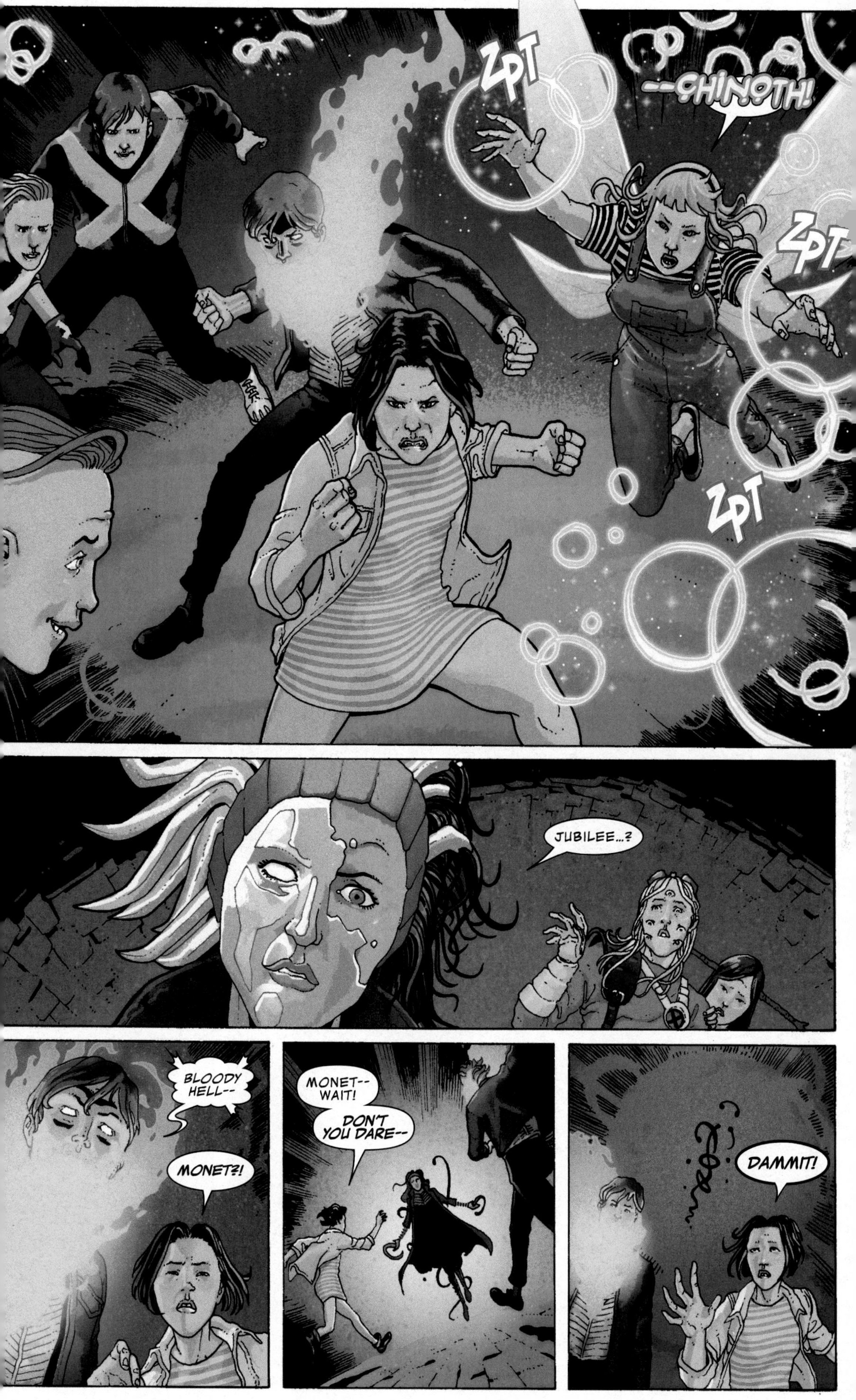

ZPT
--CHINOTH!
ZPT
ZPT
JUBILEE...?
BLOODY HELL--
MONET?!
MONET--WAIT!
DON'T YOU DARE--
DAMMIT!

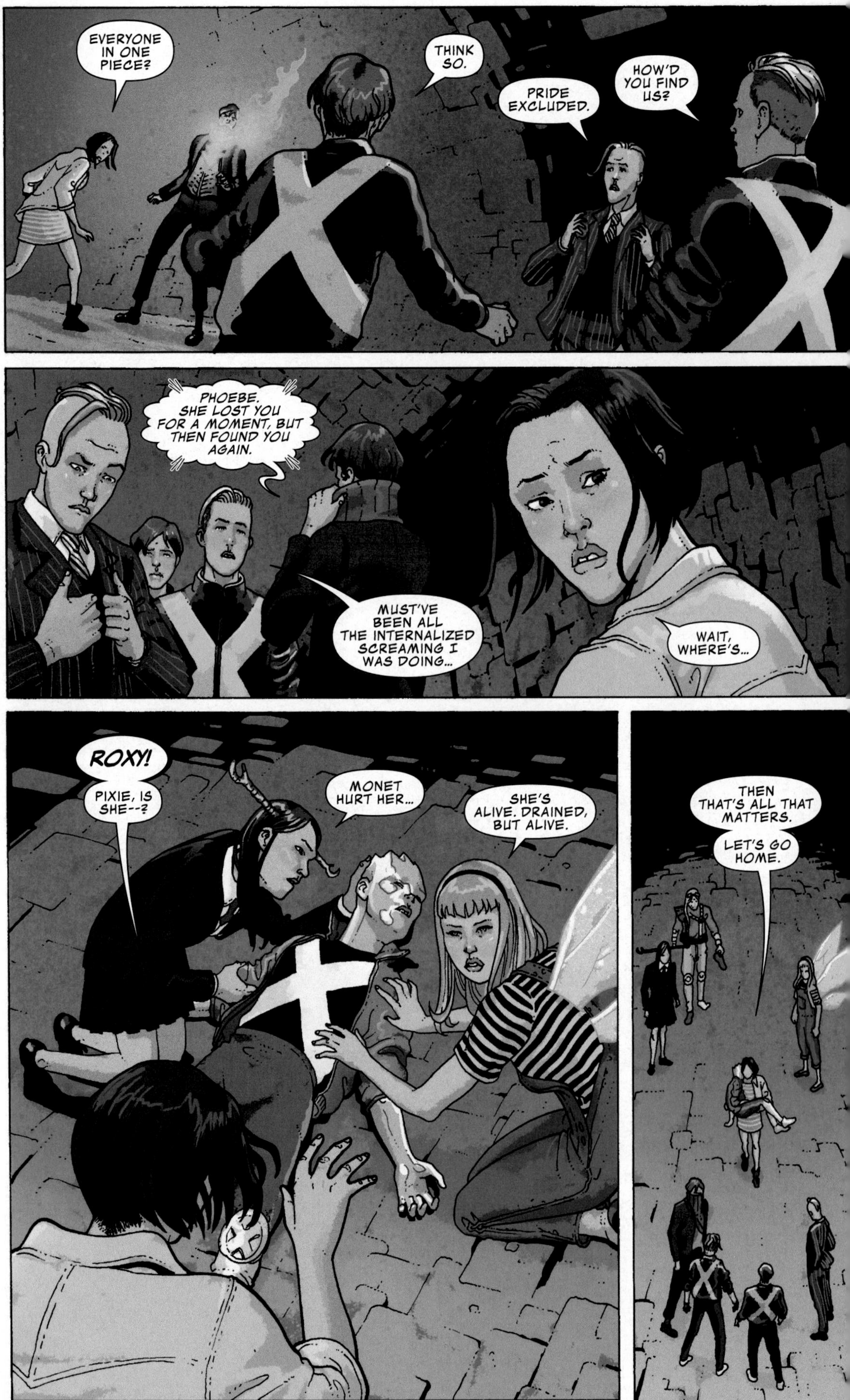
EVERYONE IN ONE PIECE?
THINK SO.
PRIDE EXCLUDED.
HOW'D YOU FIND US?
PHOEBE. SHE LOST YOU FOR A MOMENT, BUT THEN FOUND YOU AGAIN.
MUST'VE BEEN ALL THE INTERNALIZED SCREAMING I WAS DOING...
WAIT, WHERE'S...
ROXY!
PIXIE, IS SHE--?
MONET HURT HER...
SHE'S ALIVE. DRAINED, BUT ALIVE.
THEN THAT'S ALL THAT MATTERS.
LET'S GO HOME.

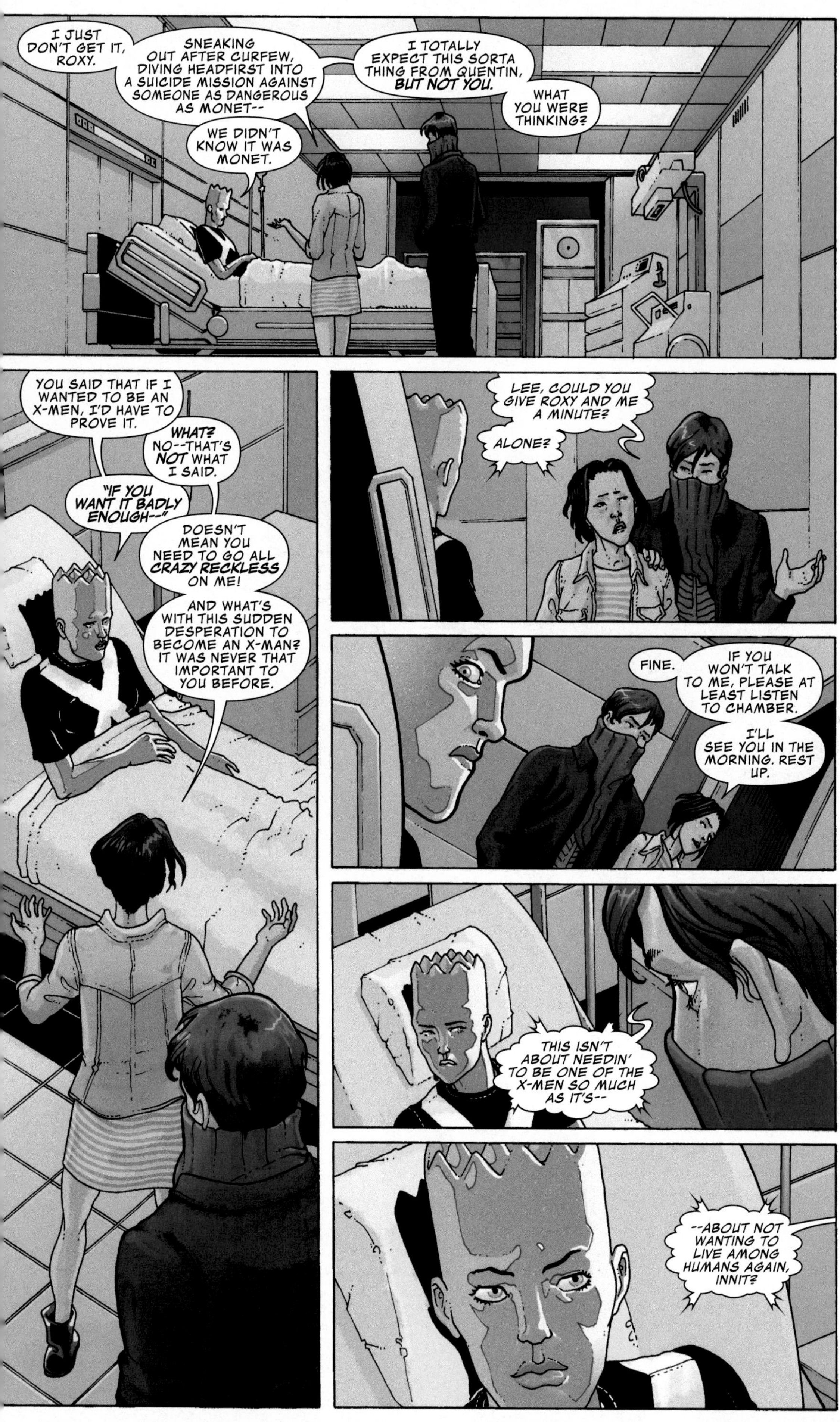
I JUST DON'T GET IT, ROXY.
SNEAKING OUT AFTER CURFEW, DIVING HEADFIRST INTO A SUICIDE MISSION AGAINST SOMEONE AS DANGEROUS AS MONET--
I TOTALLY EXPECT THIS SORTA THING FROM QUENTIN, BUT NOT YOU.
WHAT YOU WERE THINKING?
WE DIDN'T KNOW IT WAS MONET.
YOU SAID THAT IF I WANTED TO BE AN X-MEN, I'D HAVE TO PROVE IT.
WHAT? NO--THAT'S NOT WHAT I SAID.
"IF YOU WANT IT BADLY ENOUGH--"
DOESN'T MEAN YOU NEED TO GO ALL CRAZY RECKLESS ON ME!
AND WHAT'S WITH THIS SUDDEN DESPERATION TO BECOME AN X-MAN? IT WAS NEVER THAT IMPORTANT TO YOU BEFORE.
LEE, COULD YOU GIVE ROXY AND ME A MINUTE?
ALONE?
FINE.
IF YOU WON'T TALK TO ME, PLEASE AT LEAST LISTEN TO CHAMBER.
I'LL SEE YOU IN THE MORNING. REST UP.
THIS ISN'T ABOUT NEEDIN' TO BE ONE OF THE X-MEN SO MUCH AS IT'S--
--ABOUT NOT WANTING TO LIVE AMONG HUMANS AGAIN, INNIT?

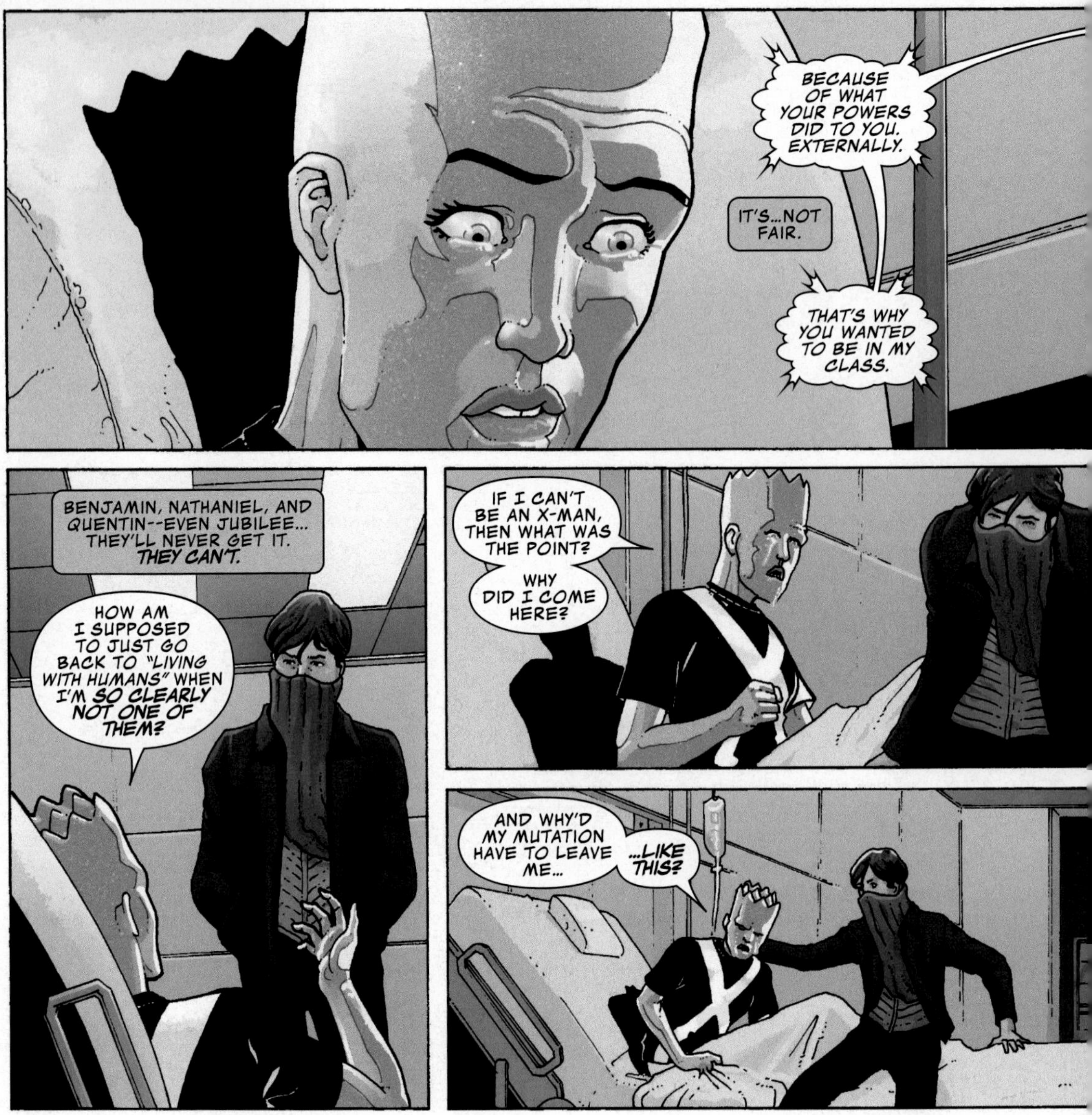
BECAUSE OF WHAT YOUR POWERS DID TO YOU. EXTERNALLY.
IT'S...NOT FAIR.
THAT'S WHY YOU WANTED TO BE IN MY CLASS.
BENJAMIN, NATHANIEL, AND QUENTIN--EVEN JUBILEE... THEY'LL NEVER GET IT. THEY CAN'T.
HOW AM I SUPPOSED TO JUST GO BACK TO "LIVING WITH HUMANS" WHEN I'M SO CLEARLY NOT ONE OF THEM?
IF I CAN'T BE AN X-MAN, THEN WHAT WAS THE POINT?
WHY DID I COME HERE?
AND WHY'D MY MUTATION HAVE TO LEAVE ME...
...LIKE THIS?

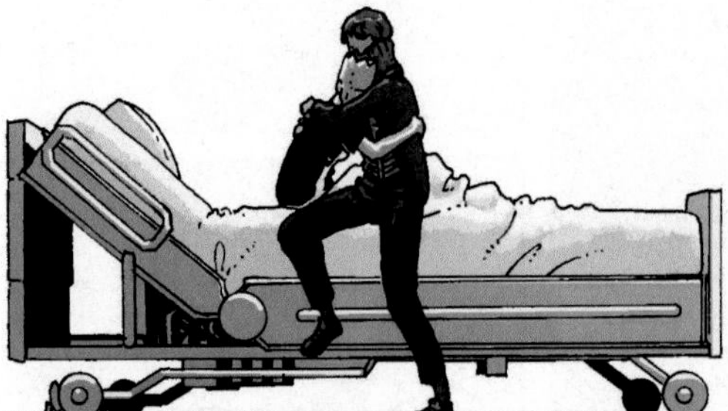

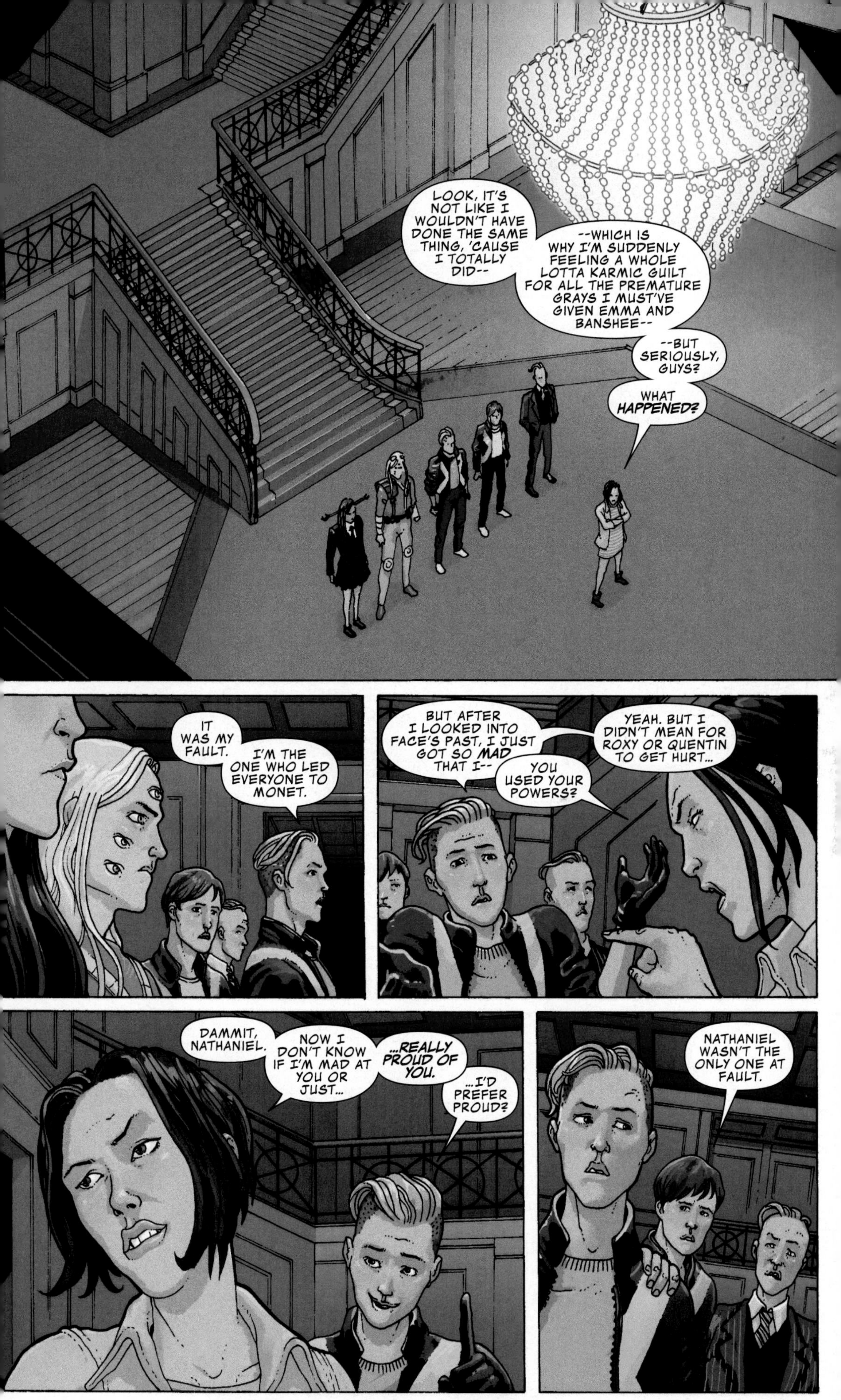

LOOK, IT'S NOT LIKE I WOULDN'T HAVE DONE THE SAME THING, 'CAUSE I TOTALLY DID--
--WHICH IS WHY I'M SUDDENLY FEELING A WHOLE LOTTA KARMIC GUILT FOR ALL THE PREMATURE GRAYS I MUST'VE GIVEN EMMA AND BANSHEE--
--BUT SERIOUSLY, GUYS?
WHAT HAPPENED?
IT WAS MY FAULT.
I'M THE ONE WHO LED EVERYONE TO MONET.
BUT AFTER I LOOKED INTO FACE'S PAST, I JUST GOT SO MAD THAT I--
YOU USED YOUR POWERS?
YEAH. BUT I DIDN'T MEAN FOR ROXY OR QUENTIN TO GET HURT...
DAMMIT, NATHANIEL.
NOW I DON'T KNOW IF I'M MAD AT YOU OR JUST...
...REALLY PROUD OF YOU.
...I'D PREFER PROUD?
NATHANIEL WASN'T THE ONLY ONE AT FAULT.

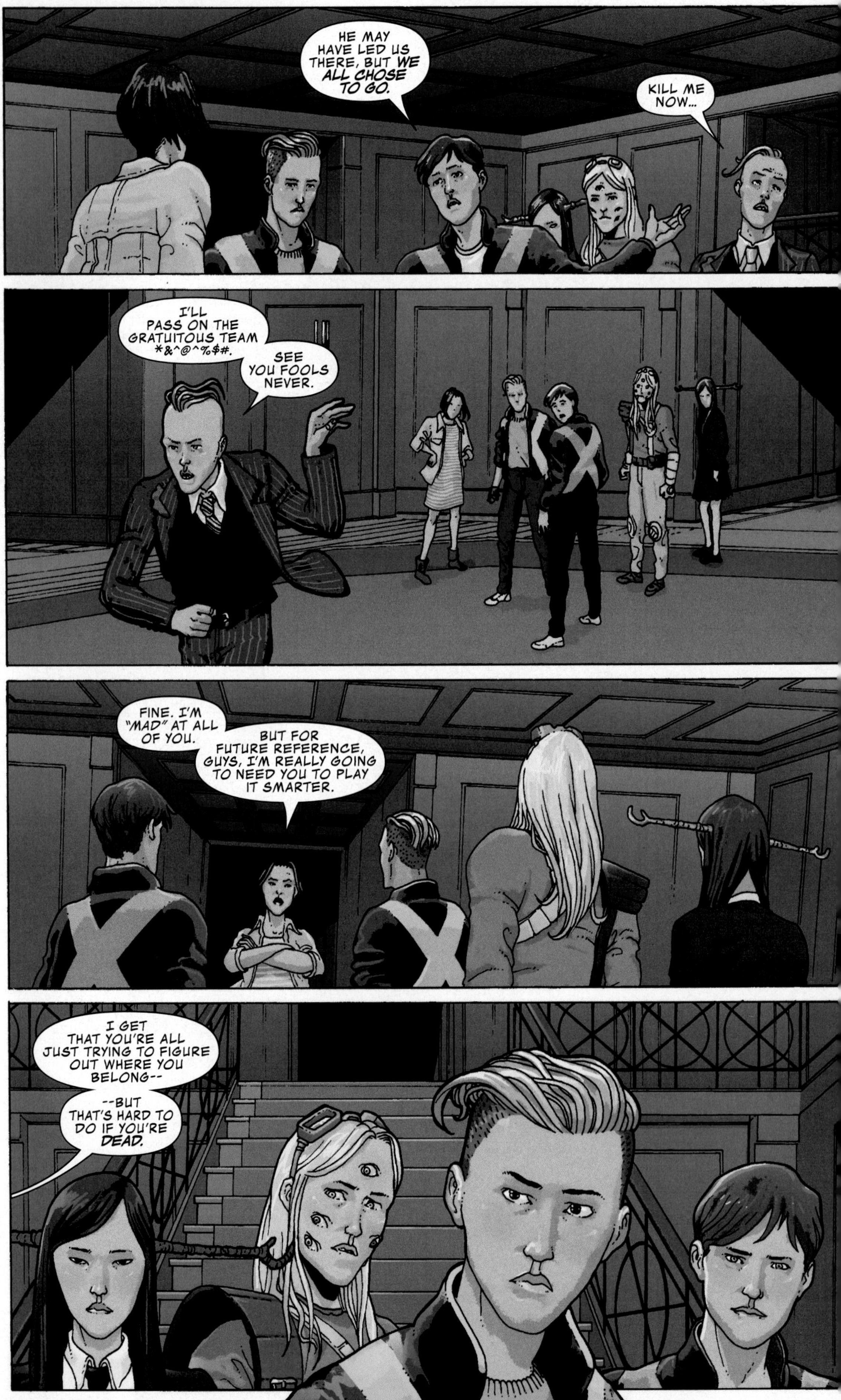
HE MAY HAVE LED US THERE, BUT WE ALL CHOSE TO GO.
KILL ME NOW...
I'LL PASS ON THE GRATUITOUS TEAM *&^@^%$#.
SEE YOU FOOLS NEVER.
FINE. I'M "MAD" AT ALL OF YOU.
BUT FOR FUTURE REFERENCE, GUYS, I'M REALLY GOING TO NEED YOU TO PLAY IT SMARTER.
I GET THAT YOU'RE ALL JUST TRYING TO FIGURE OUT WHERE YOU BELONG--
--BUT THAT'S HARD TO DO IF YOU'RE DEAD.

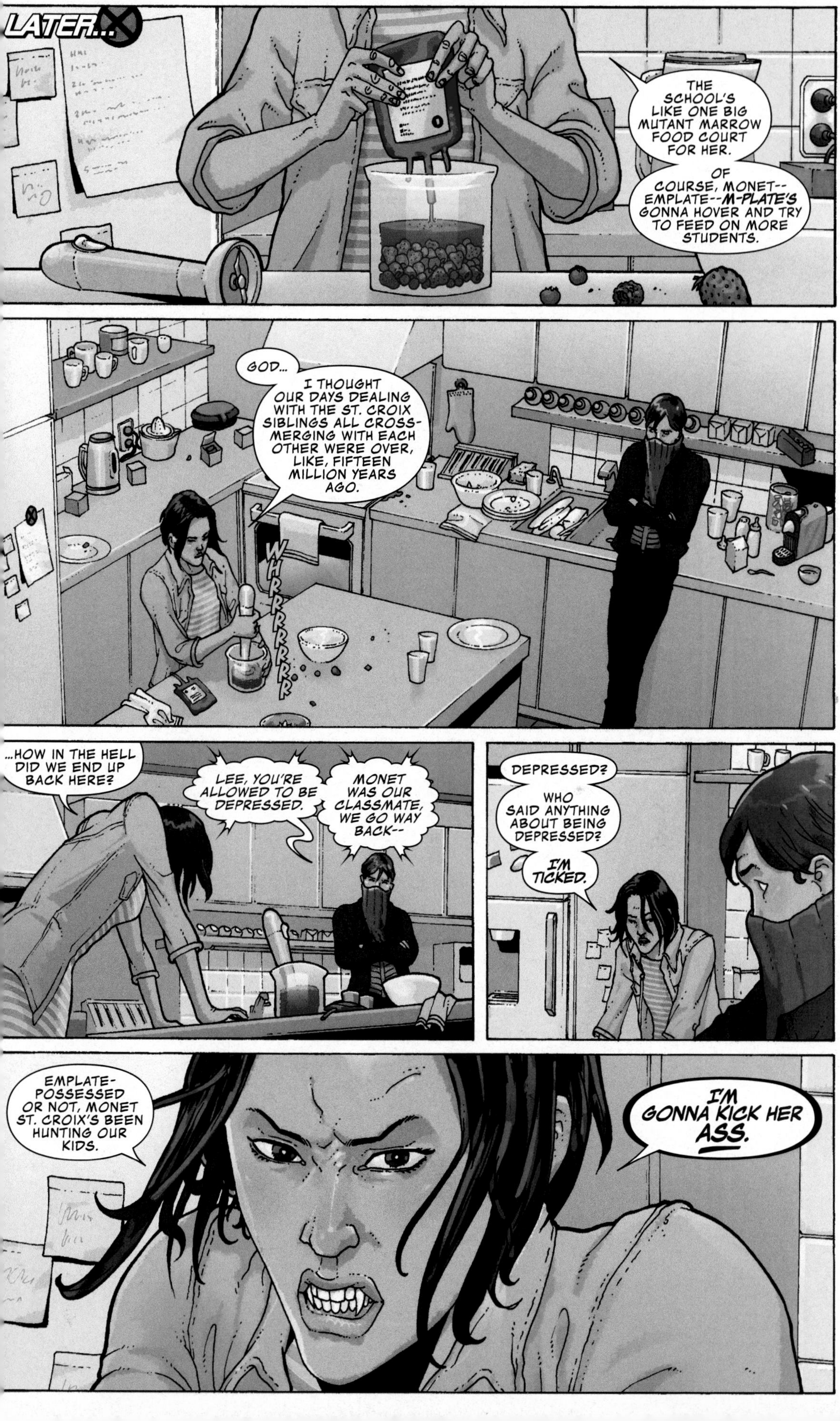
LATER...
THE SCHOOL'S LIKE ONE BIG MUTANT MARROW FOOD COURT FOR HER.
OF COURSE, MONET--EMPLATE--M-PLATE'S GONNA HOVER AND TRY TO FEED ON MORE STUDENTS.
GOD...
I THOUGHT OUR DAYS DEALING WITH THE ST. CROIX SIBLINGS ALL CROSS-MERGING WITH EACH OTHER WERE OVER, LIKE, FIFTEEN MILLION YEARS AGO.
WHRRRRRRRR
...HOW IN THE HELL DID WE END UP BACK HERE?
LEE, YOU'RE ALLOWED TO BE DEPRESSED.
MONET WAS OUR CLASSMATE, WE GO WAY BACK--
DEPRESSED?
WHO SAID ANYTHING ABOUT BEING DEPRESSED?
I'M TICKED.
EMPLATE-POSSESSED OR NOT, MONET ST. CROIX'S BEEN HUNTING OUR KIDS.
I'M GONNA KICK HER ASS.

5

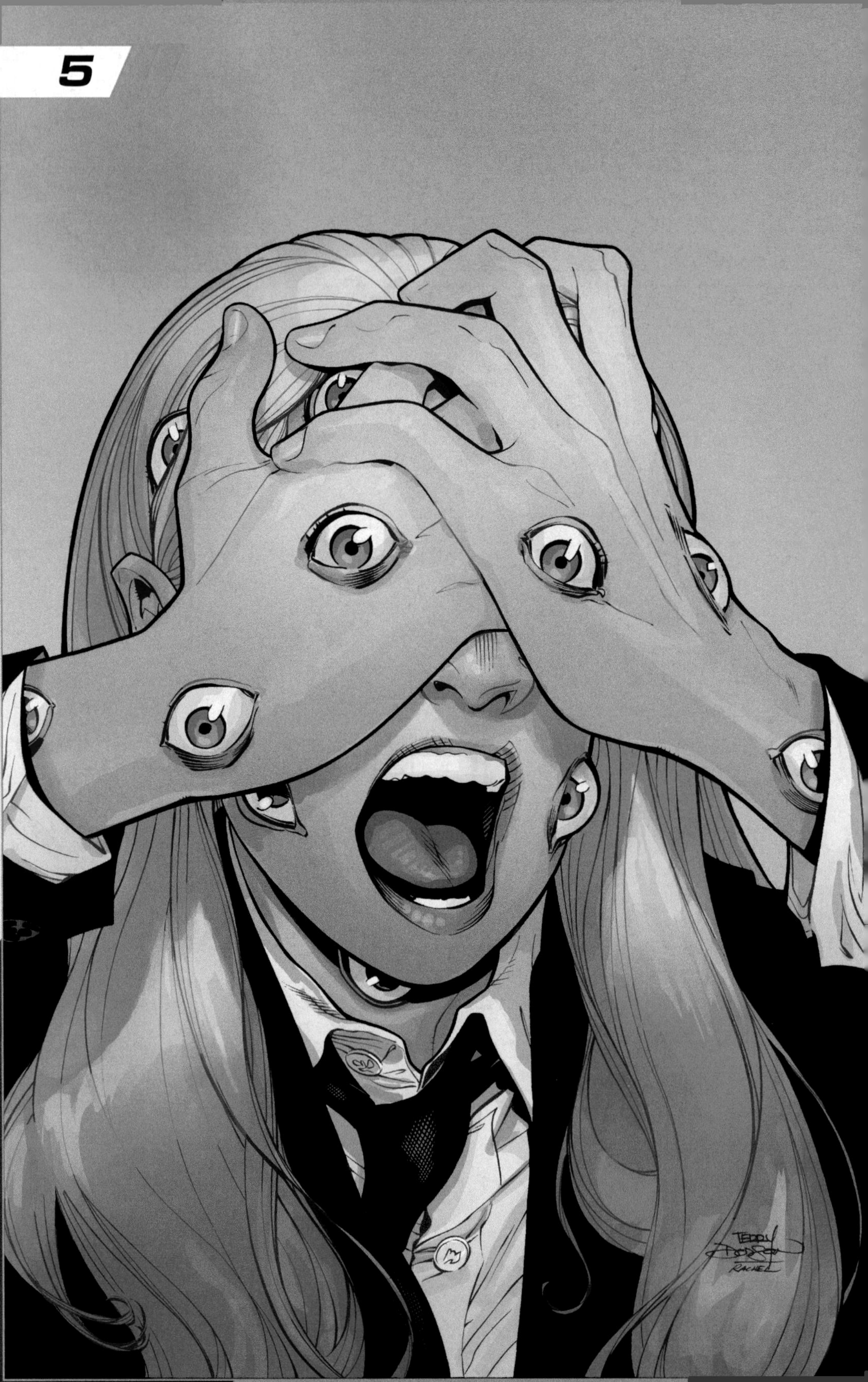

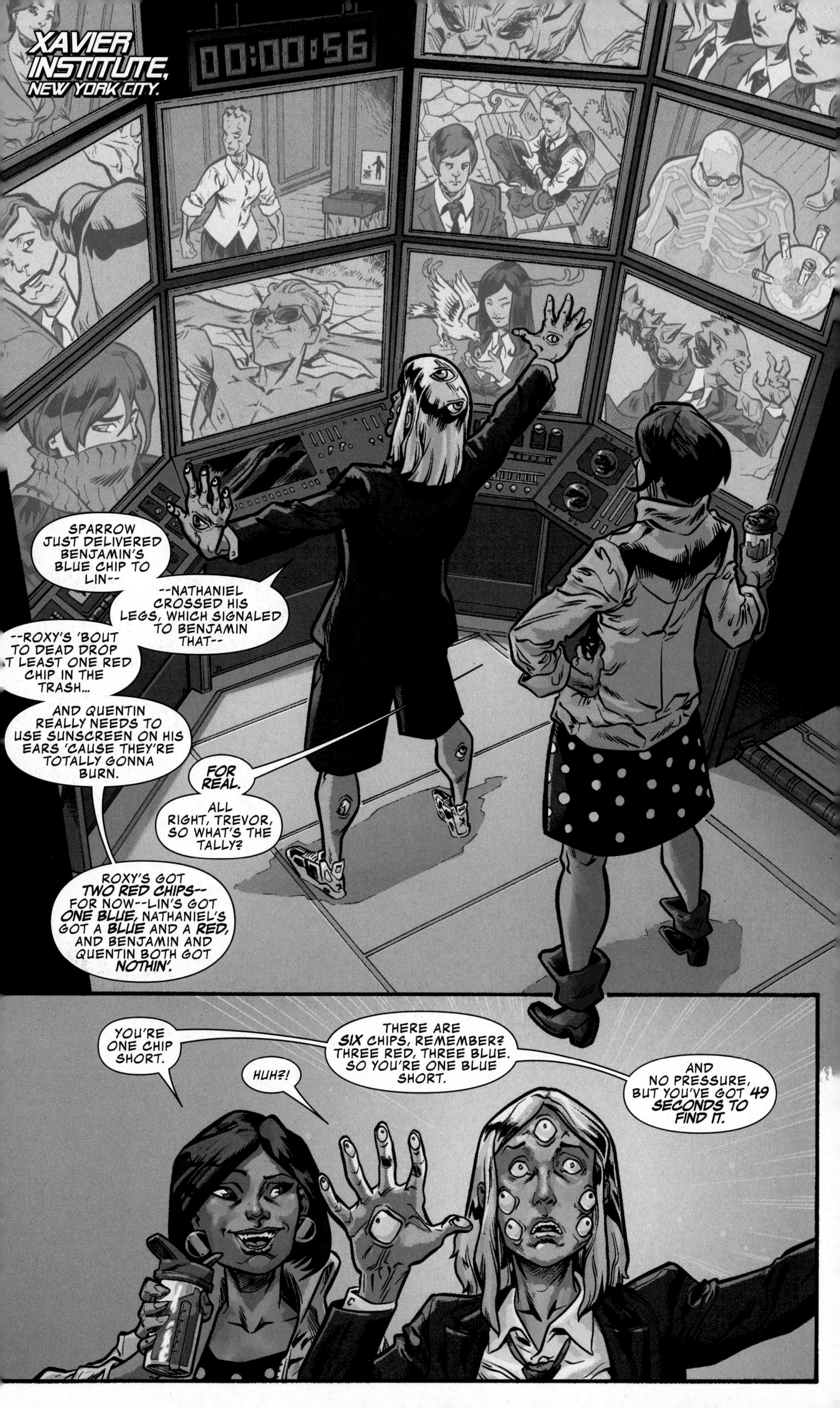

XAVIER INSTITUTE, NEW YORK CITY.
00:00:56
SPARROW JUST DELIVERED BENJAMIN'S BLUE CHIP TO LIN--
--NATHANIEL CROSSED HIS LEGS, WHICH SIGNALED TO BENJAMIN THAT--
--ROXY'S 'BOUT TO DEAD DROP AT LEAST ONE RED CHIP IN THE TRASH...
AND QUENTIN REALLY NEEDS TO USE SUNSCREEN ON HIS EARS 'CAUSE THEY'RE TOTALLY GONNA BURN.
FOR REAL.
ALL RIGHT, TREVOR, SO WHAT'S THE TALLY?
ROXY'S GOT TWO RED CHIPS-- FOR NOW--LIN'S GOT ONE BLUE, NATHANIEL'S GOT A BLUE AND A RED, AND BENJAMIN AND QUENTIN BOTH GOT NOTHIN'.
YOU'RE ONE CHIP SHORT.
HUH?!
THERE ARE SIX CHIPS, REMEMBER? THREE RED, THREE BLUE. SO YOU'RE ONE BLUE SHORT.
AND NO PRESSURE, BUT YOU'VE GOT 49 SECONDS TO FIND IT.

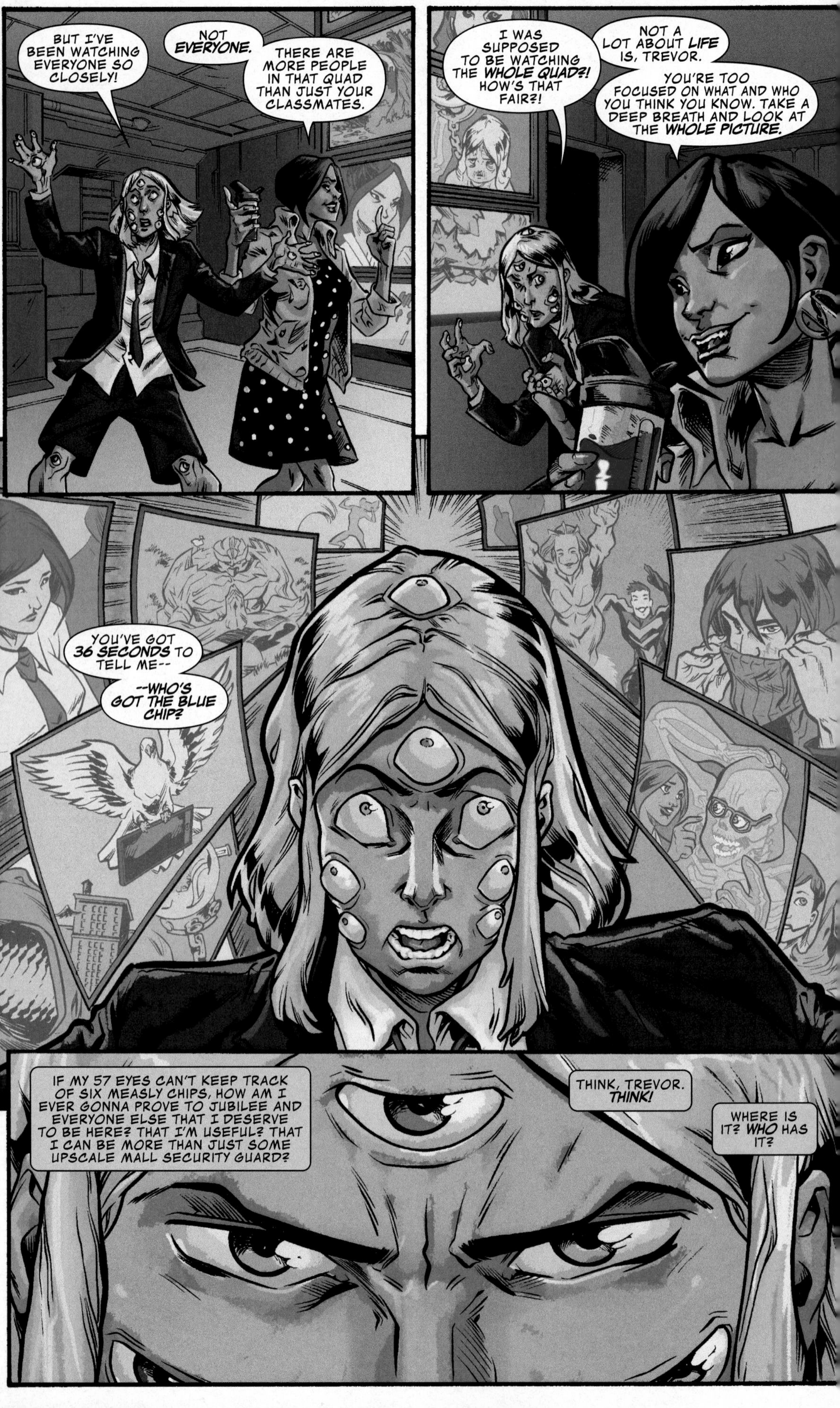

BUT I'VE BEEN WATCHING EVERYONE SO CLOSELY!
NOT EVERYONE.
THERE ARE MORE PEOPLE IN THAT QUAD THAN JUST YOUR CLASSMATES.
I WAS SUPPOSED TO BE WATCHING THE WHOLE QUAD?! HOW'S THAT FAIR?!
NOT A LOT ABOUT LIFE IS, TREVOR.
YOU'RE TOO FOCUSED ON WHAT AND WHO YOU THINK YOU KNOW. TAKE A DEEP BREATH AND LOOK AT THE WHOLE PICTURE.
YOU'VE GOT 36 SECONDS TO TELL ME--
--WHO'S GOT THE BLUE CHIP?
IF MY 57 EYES CAN'T KEEP TRACK OF SIX MEASLY CHIPS, HOW AM I EVER GONNA PROVE TO JUBILEE AND EVERYONE ELSE THAT I DESERVE TO BE HERE? THAT I'M USEFUL? THAT I CAN BE MORE THAN JUST SOME UPSCALE MALL SECURITY GUARD?
THINK, TREVOR. THINK!
WHERE IS IT? WHO HAS IT?

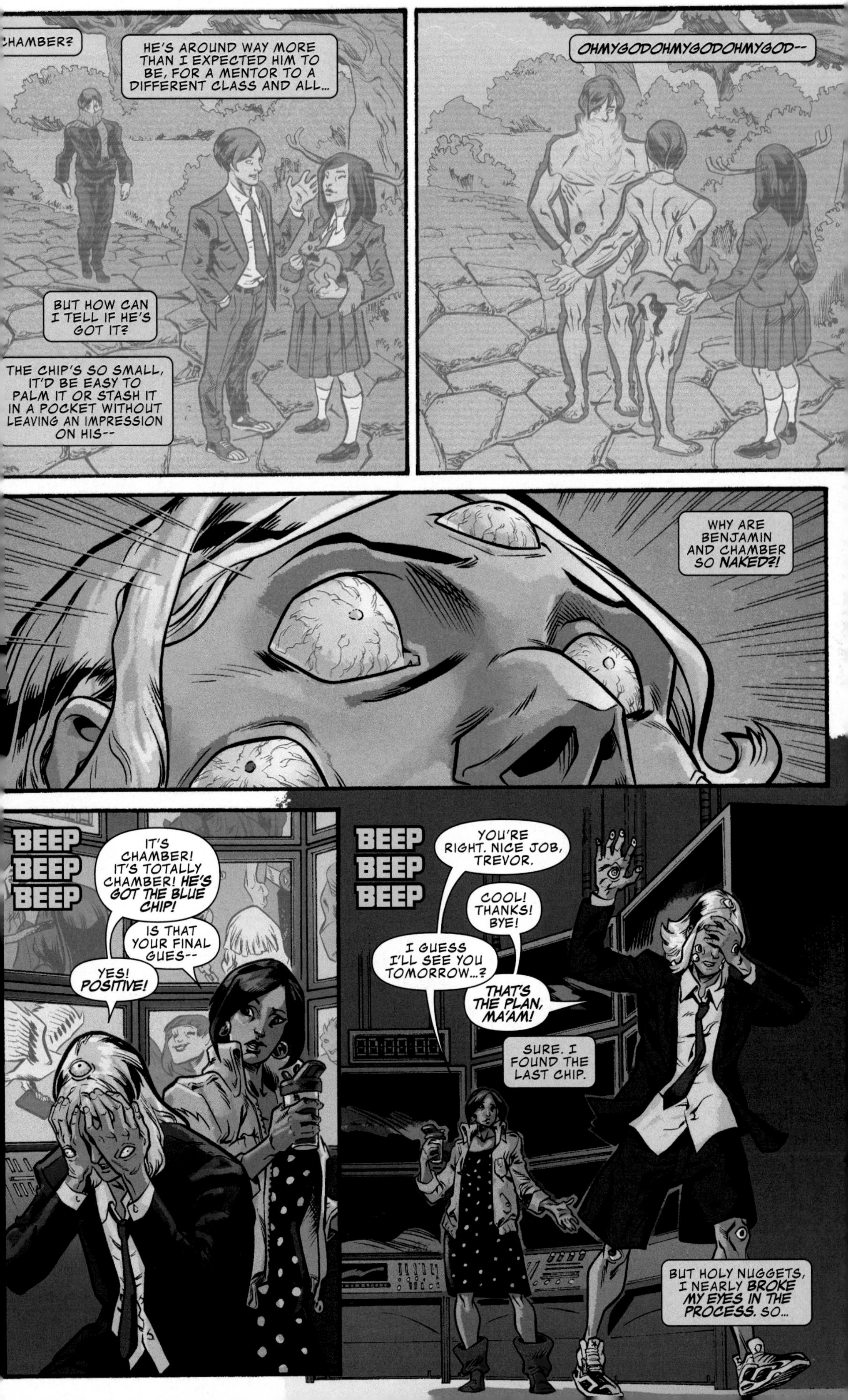

CHAMBER?
HE'S AROUND WAY MORE THAN I EXPECTED HIM TO BE, FOR A MENTOR TO A DIFFERENT CLASS AND ALL...
BUT HOW CAN I TELL IF HE'S GOT IT?
THE CHIP'S SO SMALL, IT'D BE EASY TO PALM IT OR STASH IT IN A POCKET WITHOUT LEAVING AN IMPRESSION ON HIS--
OHMYGODOHMYGODOHMYGOD--
WHY ARE BENJAMIN AND CHAMBER SO NAKED?!
BEEP BEEP BEEP
IT'S CHAMBER! IT'S TOTALLY CHAMBER! HE'S GOT THE BLUE CHIP!
IS THAT YOUR FINAL GUES--
YES! POSITIVE!
BEEP BEEP BEEP
YOU'RE RIGHT. NICE JOB, TREVOR.
COOL! THANKS! BYE!
I GUESS I'LL SEE YOU TOMORROW...?
THAT'S THE PLAN, MA'AM!
SURE. I FOUND THE LAST CHIP.
BUT HOLY NUGGETS, I NEARLY BROKE MY EYES IN THE PROCESS. SO...

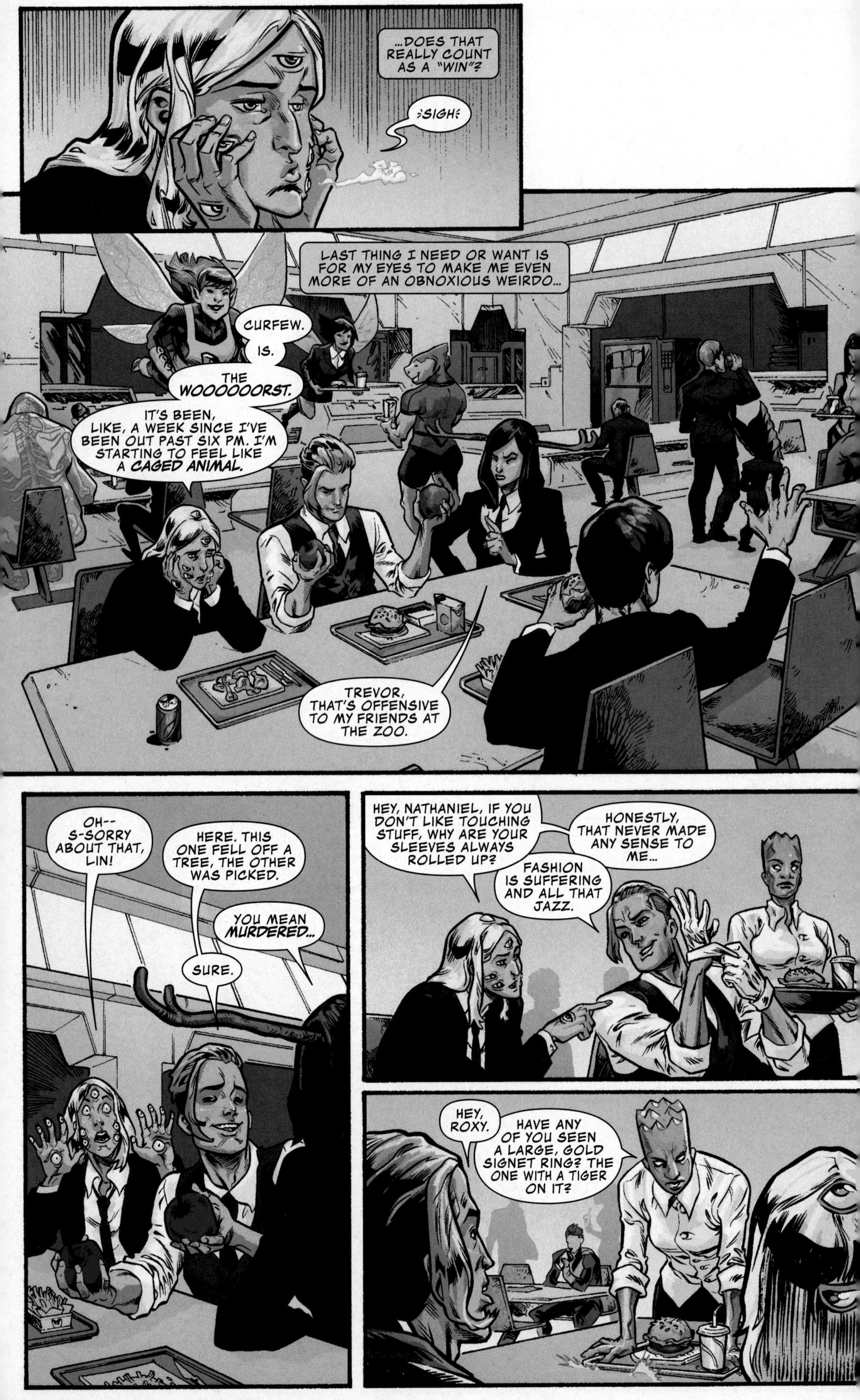

...DOES THAT REALLY COUNT AS A "WIN"?
SIGH
LAST THING I NEED OR WANT IS FOR MY EYES TO MAKE ME EVEN MORE OF AN OBNOXIOUS WEIRDO...
CURFEW.
IS.
THE WOOOOOORST.
IT'S BEEN, LIKE, A WEEK SINCE I'VE BEEN OUT PAST SIX PM. I'M STARTING TO FEEL LIKE A CAGED ANIMAL.
TREVOR, THAT'S OFFENSIVE TO MY FRIENDS AT THE ZOO.
OH-- S-SORRY ABOUT THAT, LIN!
HERE. THIS ONE FELL OFF A TREE, THE OTHER WAS PICKED.
YOU MEAN MURDERED...
SURE.
HEY, NATHANIEL, IF YOU DON'T LIKE TOUCHING STUFF, WHY ARE YOUR SLEEVES ALWAYS ROLLED UP?
HONESTLY, THAT NEVER MADE ANY SENSE TO ME...
FASHION IS SUFFERING AND ALL THAT JAZZ.
HEY, ROXY.
HAVE ANY OF YOU SEEN A LARGE, GOLD SIGNET RING? THE ONE WITH A TIGER ON IT?

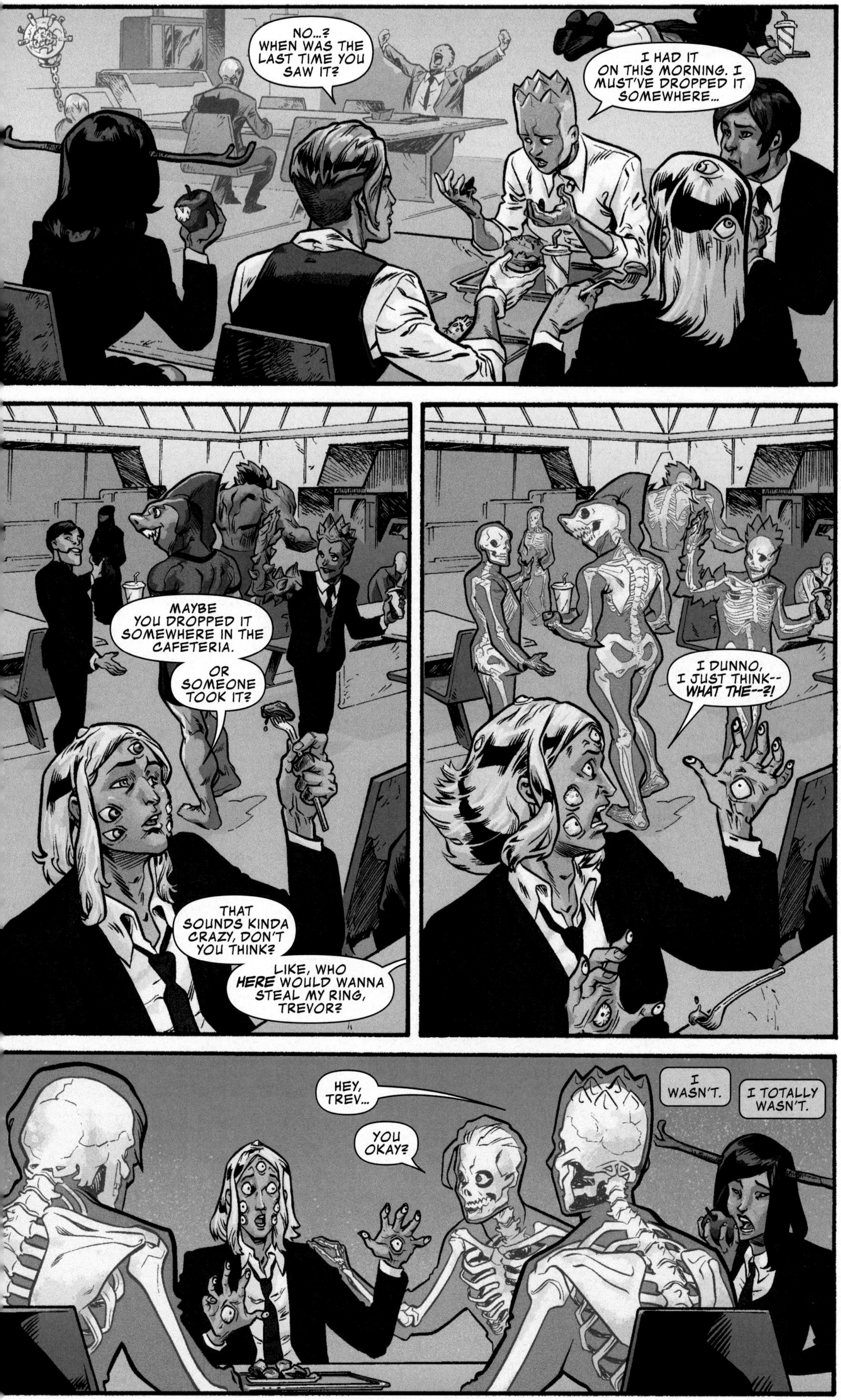
NO...? WHEN WAS THE LAST TIME YOU SAW IT?
I HAD IT ON THIS MORNING. I MUST'VE DROPPED IT SOMEWHERE...
MAYBE YOU DROPPED IT SOMEWHERE IN THE CAFETERIA.
OR SOMEONE TOOK IT?
THAT SOUNDS KINDA CRAZY, DON'T YOU THINK?
LIKE, WHO HERE WOULD WANNA STEAL MY RING, TREVOR?
I DUNNO, I JUST THINK-- WHAT THE--?!
HEY, TREV...
YOU OKAY?
I WASN'T.
I TOTALLY WASN'T.

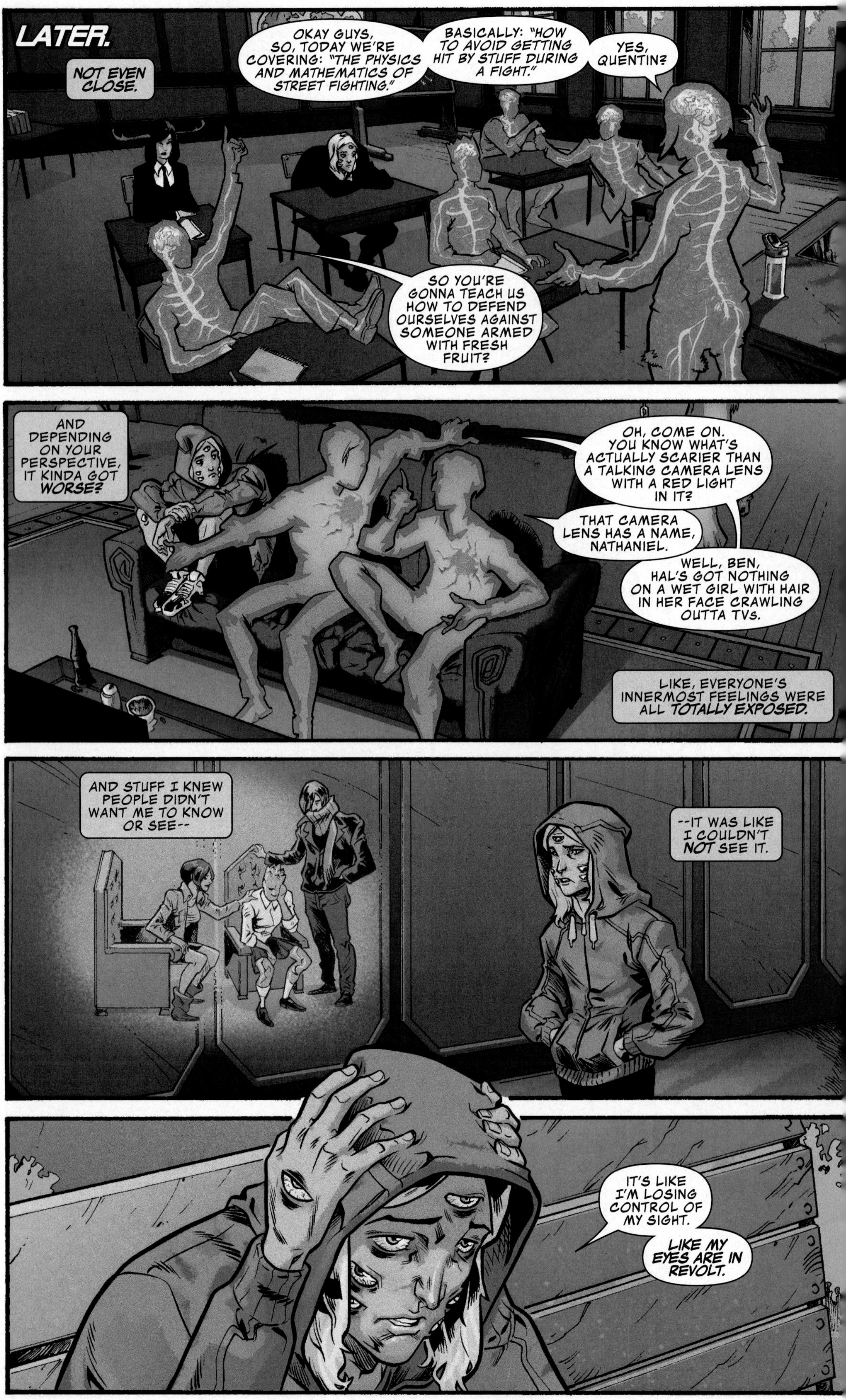
LATER.
NOT EVEN CLOSE.
OKAY GUYS, SO, TODAY WE'RE COVERING: "THE PHYSICS AND MATHEMATICS OF STREET FIGHTING."
BASICALLY: "HOW TO AVOID GETTING HIT BY STUFF DURING A FIGHT."
YES, QUENTIN?
SO YOU'RE GONNA TEACH US HOW TO DEFEND OURSELVES AGAINST SOMEONE ARMED WITH FRESH FRUIT?
AND DEPENDING ON YOUR PERSPECTIVE, IT KINDA GOT WORSE?
OH, COME ON. YOU KNOW WHAT'S ACTUALLY SCARIER THAN A TALKING CAMERA LENS WITH A RED LIGHT IN IT?
THAT CAMERA LENS HAS A NAME, NATHANIEL.
WELL, BEN, HAL'S GOT NOTHING ON A WET GIRL WITH HAIR IN HER FACE CRAWLING OUTTA TVS.
LIKE, EVERYONE'S INNERMOST FEELINGS WERE ALL TOTALLY EXPOSED.
AND STUFF I KNEW PEOPLE DIDN'T WANT ME TO KNOW OR SEE--
--IT WAS LIKE I COULDN'T NOT SEE IT.
IT'S LIKE I'M LOSING CONTROL OF MY SIGHT.
LIKE MY EYES ARE IN REVOLT.

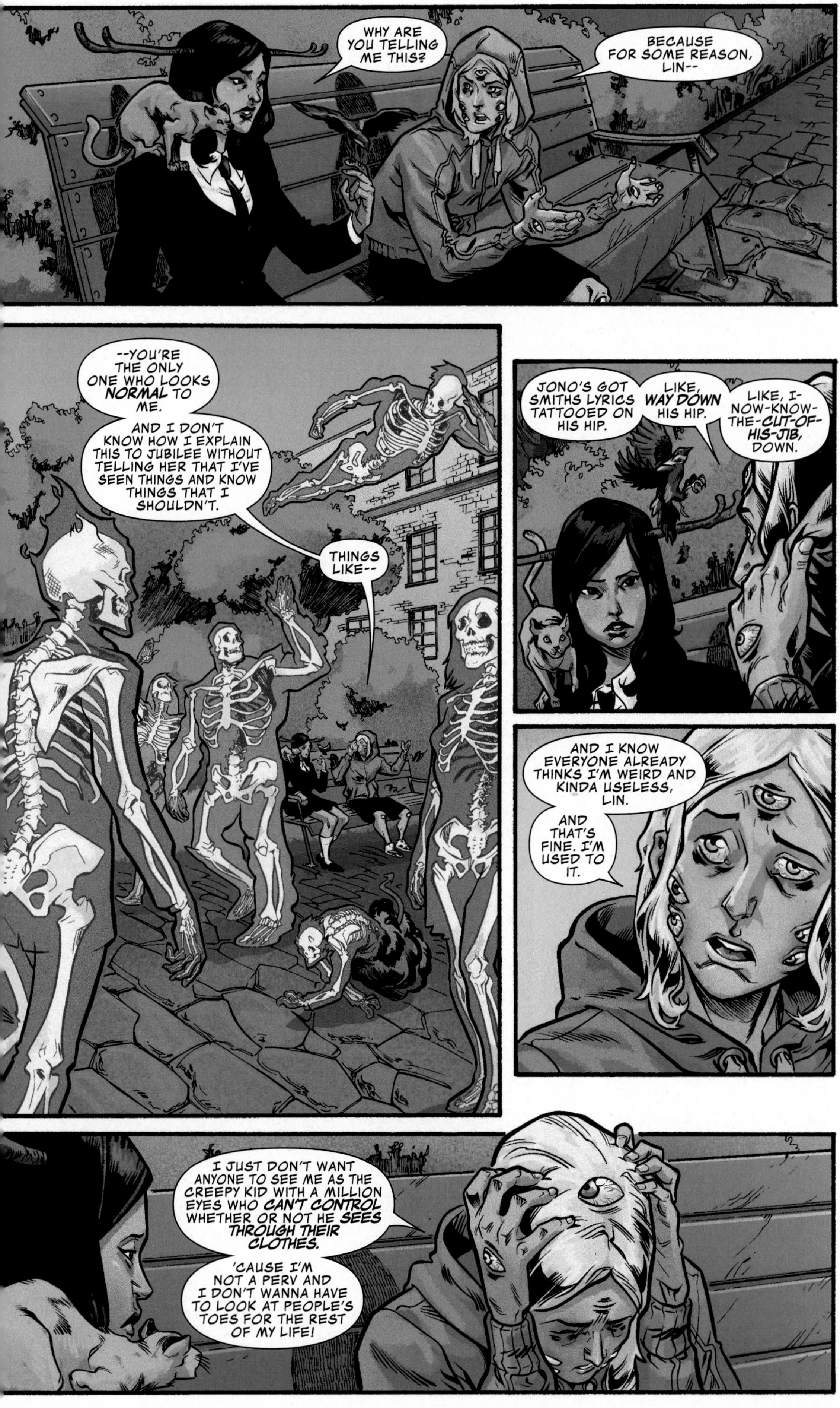
WHY ARE YOU TELLING ME THIS?
BECAUSE FOR SOME REASON, LIN--
--YOU'RE THE ONLY ONE WHO LOOKS NORMAL TO ME.
AND I DON'T KNOW HOW I EXPLAIN THIS TO JUBILEE WITHOUT TELLING HER THAT I'VE SEEN THINGS AND KNOW THINGS THAT I SHOULDN'T.
THINGS LIKE--
JONO'S GOT SMITHS LYRICS TATTOOED ON HIS HIP.
LIKE, WAY DOWN HIS HIP.
LIKE, I-NOW-KNOW-THE-CUT-OF-HIS-JIB, DOWN.
AND I KNOW EVERYONE ALREADY THINKS I'M WEIRD AND KINDA USELESS, LIN.
AND THAT'S FINE. I'M USED TO IT.
I JUST DON'T WANT ANYONE TO SEE ME AS THE CREEPY KID WITH A MILLION EYES WHO CAN'T CONTROL WHETHER OR NOT HE SEES THROUGH THEIR CLOTHES.
'CAUSE I'M NOT A PERV AND I DON'T WANNA HAVE TO LOOK AT PEOPLE'S TOES FOR THE REST OF MY LIFE!

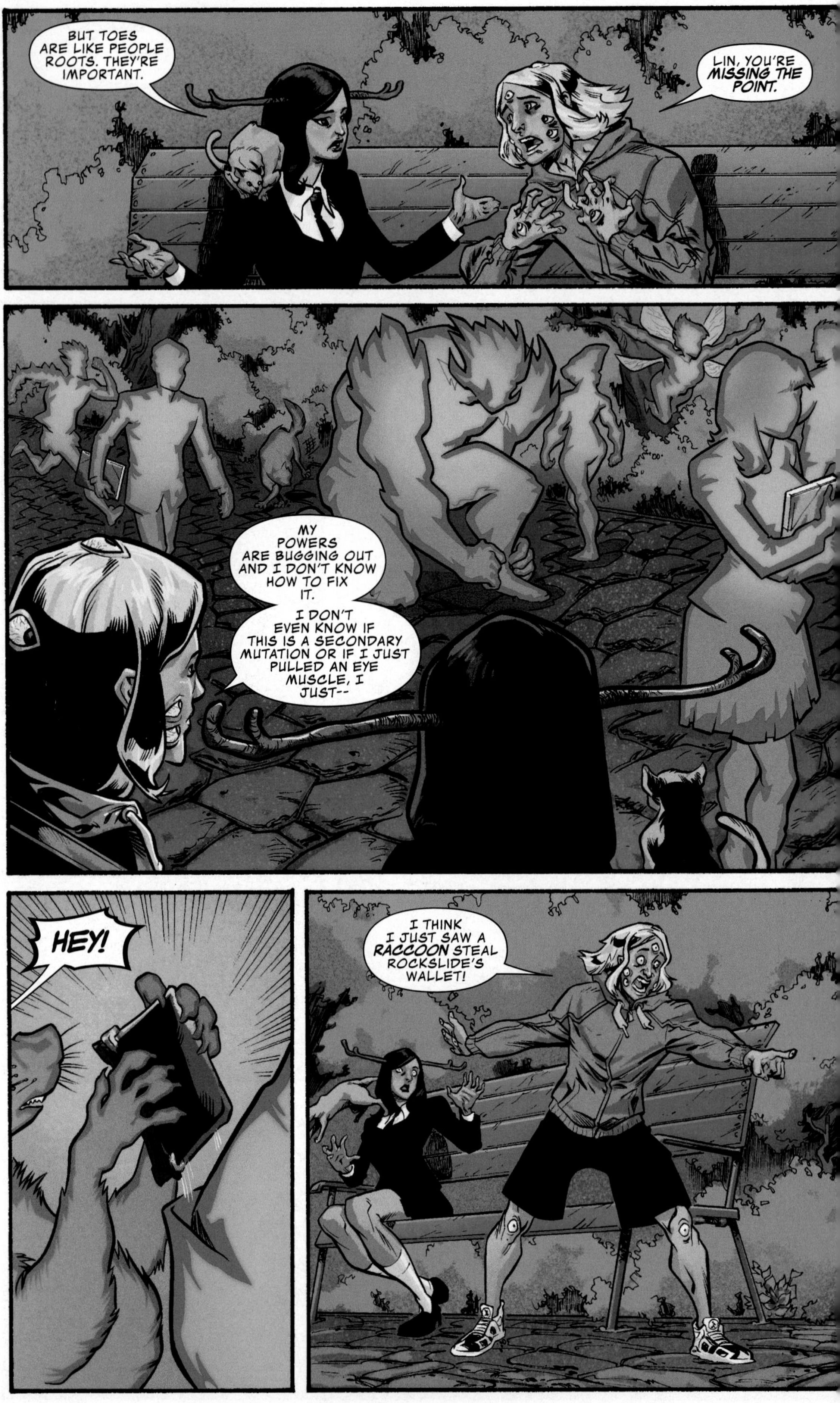

BUT TOES ARE LIKE PEOPLE ROOTS. THEY'RE IMPORTANT.
LIN, YOU'RE MISSING THE POINT.
MY POWERS ARE BUGGING OUT AND I DON'T KNOW HOW TO FIX IT.
I DON'T EVEN KNOW IF THIS IS A SECONDARY MUTATION OR IF I JUST PULLED AN EYE MUSCLE, I JUST--
HEY!
I THINK I JUST SAW A RACCOON STEAL ROCKSLIDE'S WALLET!

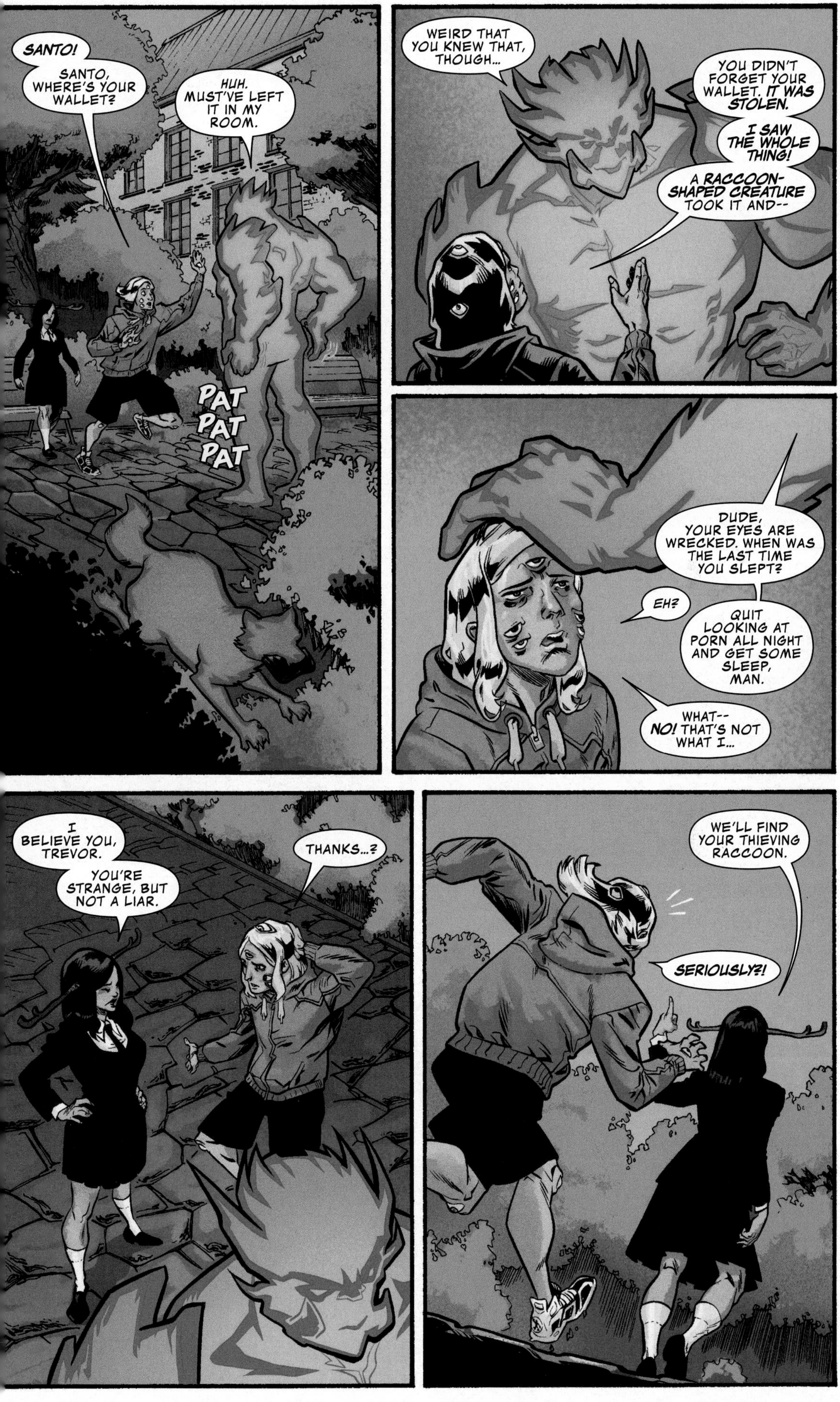
SANTO!
SANTO, WHERE'S YOUR WALLET?
HUH. MUST'VE LEFT IT IN MY ROOM.
PAT PAT PAT
WEIRD THAT YOU KNEW THAT, THOUGH...
YOU DIDN'T FORGET YOUR WALLET. IT WAS STOLEN.
I SAW THE WHOLE THING!
A RACCOON-SHAPED CREATURE TOOK IT AND--
DUDE, YOUR EYES ARE WRECKED. WHEN WAS THE LAST TIME YOU SLEPT?
EH?
QUIT LOOKING AT PORN ALL NIGHT AND GET SOME SLEEP, MAN.
WHAT-- NO! THAT'S NOT WHAT I...
I BELIEVE YOU, TREVOR.
YOU'RE STRANGE, BUT NOT A LIAR.
THANKS...?
WE'LL FIND YOUR THIEVING RACCOON.
SERIOUSLY?!

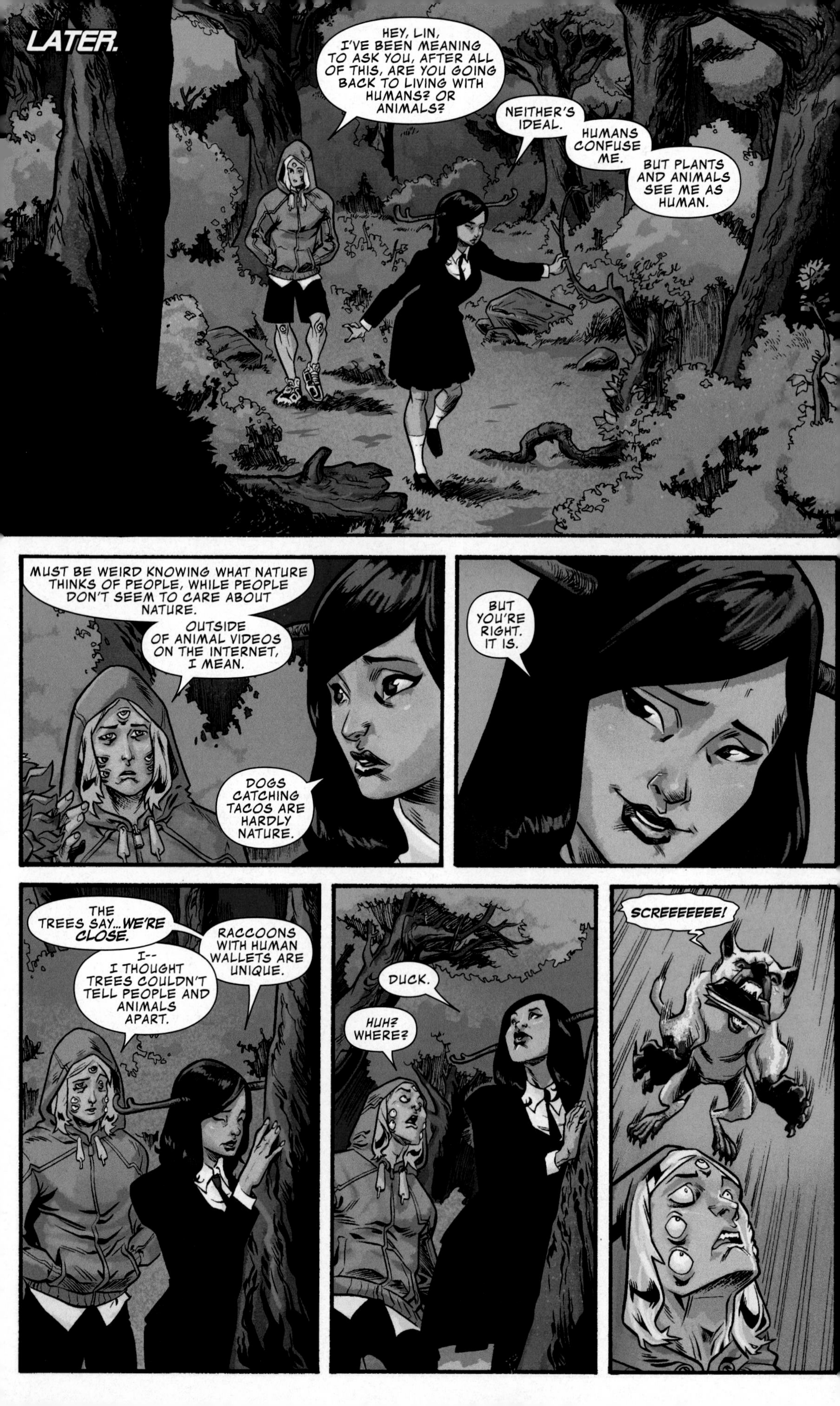
LATER.
HEY, LIN, I'VE BEEN MEANING TO ASK YOU, AFTER ALL OF THIS, ARE YOU GOING BACK TO LIVING WITH HUMANS? OR ANIMALS?
NEITHER'S IDEAL.
HUMANS CONFUSE ME.
BUT PLANTS AND ANIMALS SEE ME AS HUMAN.
MUST BE WEIRD KNOWING WHAT NATURE THINKS OF PEOPLE, WHILE PEOPLE DON'T SEEM TO CARE ABOUT NATURE.
OUTSIDE OF ANIMAL VIDEOS ON THE INTERNET, I MEAN.
DOGS CATCHING TACOS ARE HARDLY NATURE.
BUT YOU'RE RIGHT. IT IS.
THE TREES SAY...WE'RE CLOSE.
I-- I THOUGHT TREES COULDN'T TELL PEOPLE AND ANIMALS APART.
RACCOONS WITH HUMAN WALLETS ARE UNIQUE.
DUCK.
HUH? WHERE?
SCREEEEEEE!

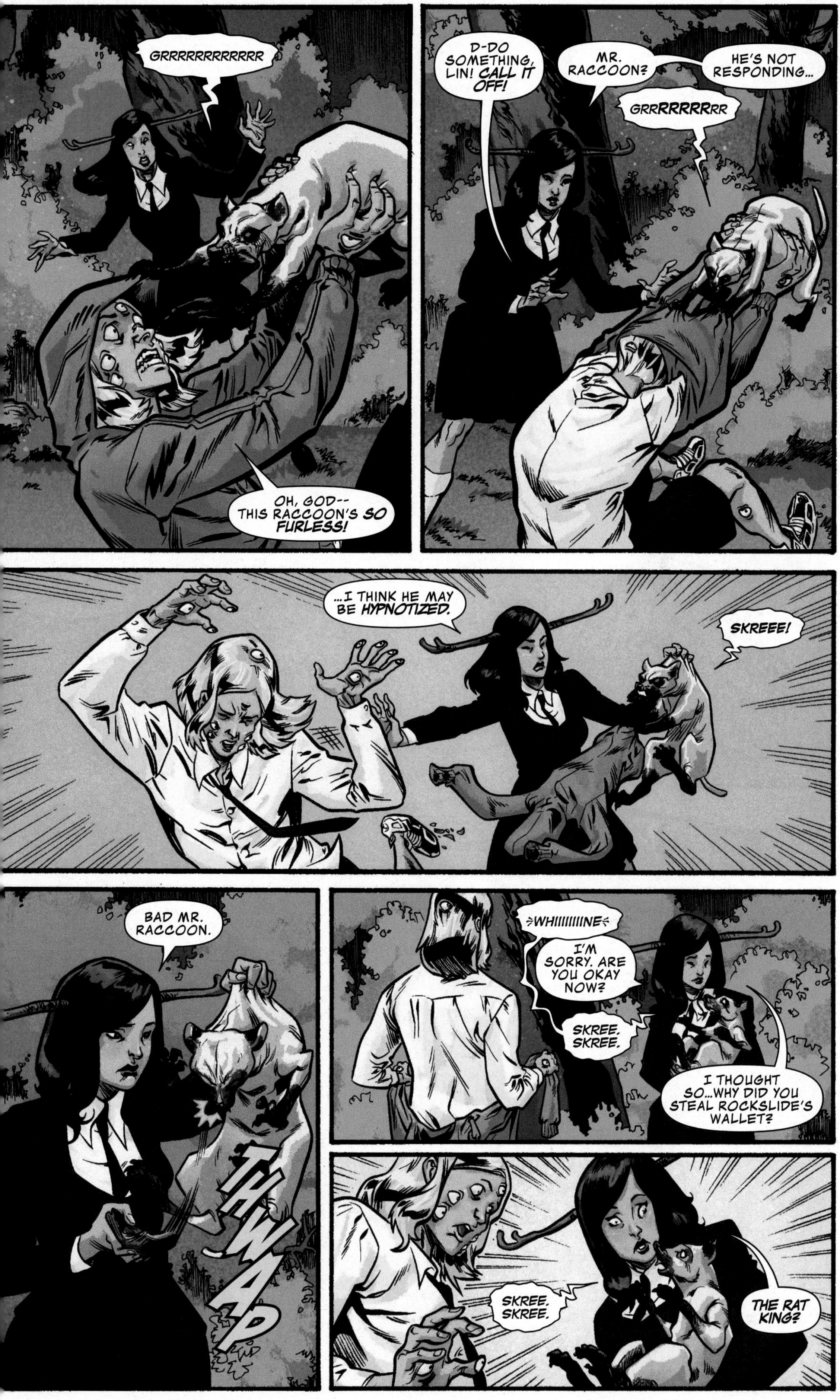
GRRRRRRRRRRR
OH, GOD-- THIS RACCOON'S SO FURLESS!
D-DO SOMETHING, LIN! CALL IT OFF!
MR. RACCOON?
HE'S NOT RESPONDING...
GRRRRRRRR
...I THINK HE MAY BE HYPNOTIZED.
SKREEE!
BAD MR. RACCOON.
THWAP
WHIIIIIIINE
I'M SORRY. ARE YOU OKAY NOW?
SKREE. SKREE.
I THOUGHT SO...WHY DID YOU STEAL ROCKSLIDE'S WALLET?
SKREE. SKREE.
THE RAT KING?

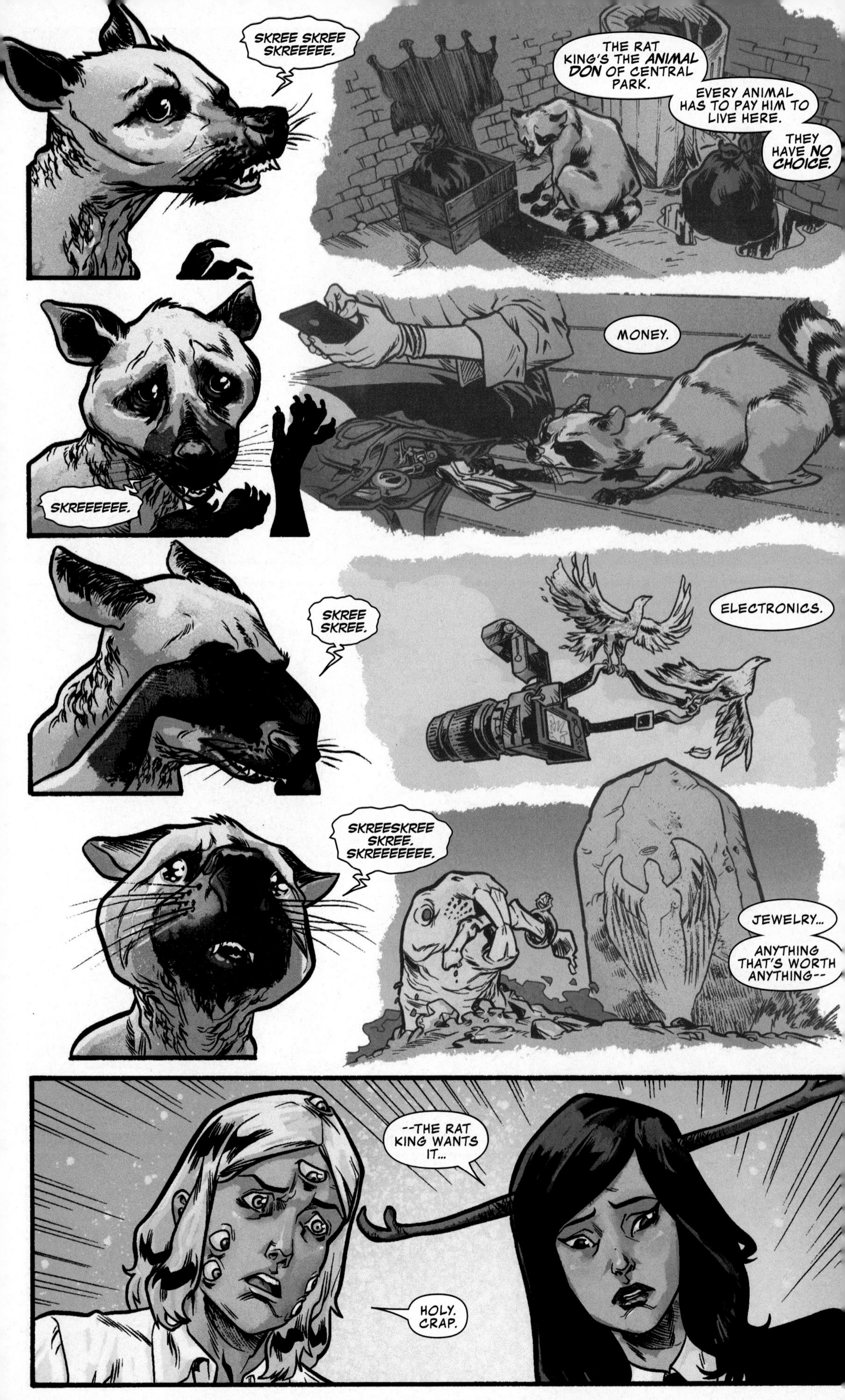
SKREE SKREE SKREEEEEE.
THE RAT KING'S THE ANIMAL DON OF CENTRAL PARK.
EVERY ANIMAL HAS TO PAY HIM TO LIVE HERE.
THEY HAVE NO CHOICE.
MONEY.
SKREEEEEEE.
SKREE SKREE.
ELECTRONICS.
SKREESKREE SKREE. SKREEEEEEEE.
JEWELRY...
ANYTHING THAT'S WORTH ANYTHING--
--THE RAT KING WANTS IT...
HOLY. CRAP.

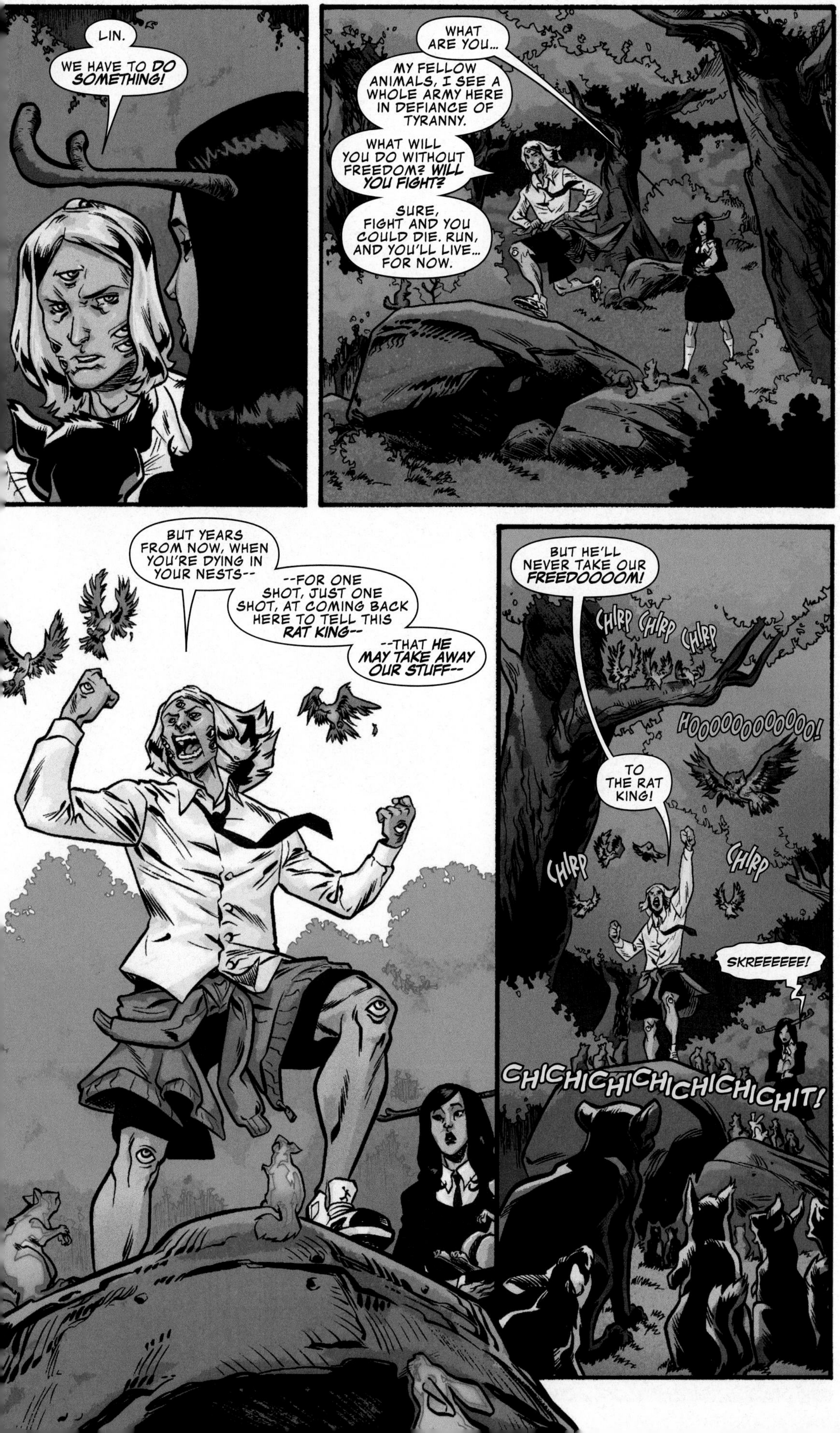
LIN.
WE HAVE TO *DO SOMETHING!*
WHAT ARE YOU...
MY FELLOW ANIMALS, I SEE A WHOLE ARMY HERE IN DEFIANCE OF TYRANNY.
WHAT WILL YOU DO WITHOUT FREEDOM? *WILL YOU FIGHT?*
SURE, FIGHT AND YOU COULD DIE. RUN, AND YOU'LL LIVE... FOR NOW.
BUT YEARS FROM NOW, WHEN YOU'RE DYING IN YOUR NESTS--
--FOR ONE SHOT, JUST ONE SHOT, AT COMING BACK HERE TO TELL THIS *RAT KING--*
--THAT *HE MAY TAKE AWAY OUR STUFF--*
BUT HE'LL NEVER TAKE OUR *FREEDOOOOM!*
CHIRP CHIRP CHIRP
HOOOOOOOOOOOO!
TO THE RAT KING!
CHIRP
CHIRP
SKREEEEEE!
CHICHICHICHICHICHICHIT!

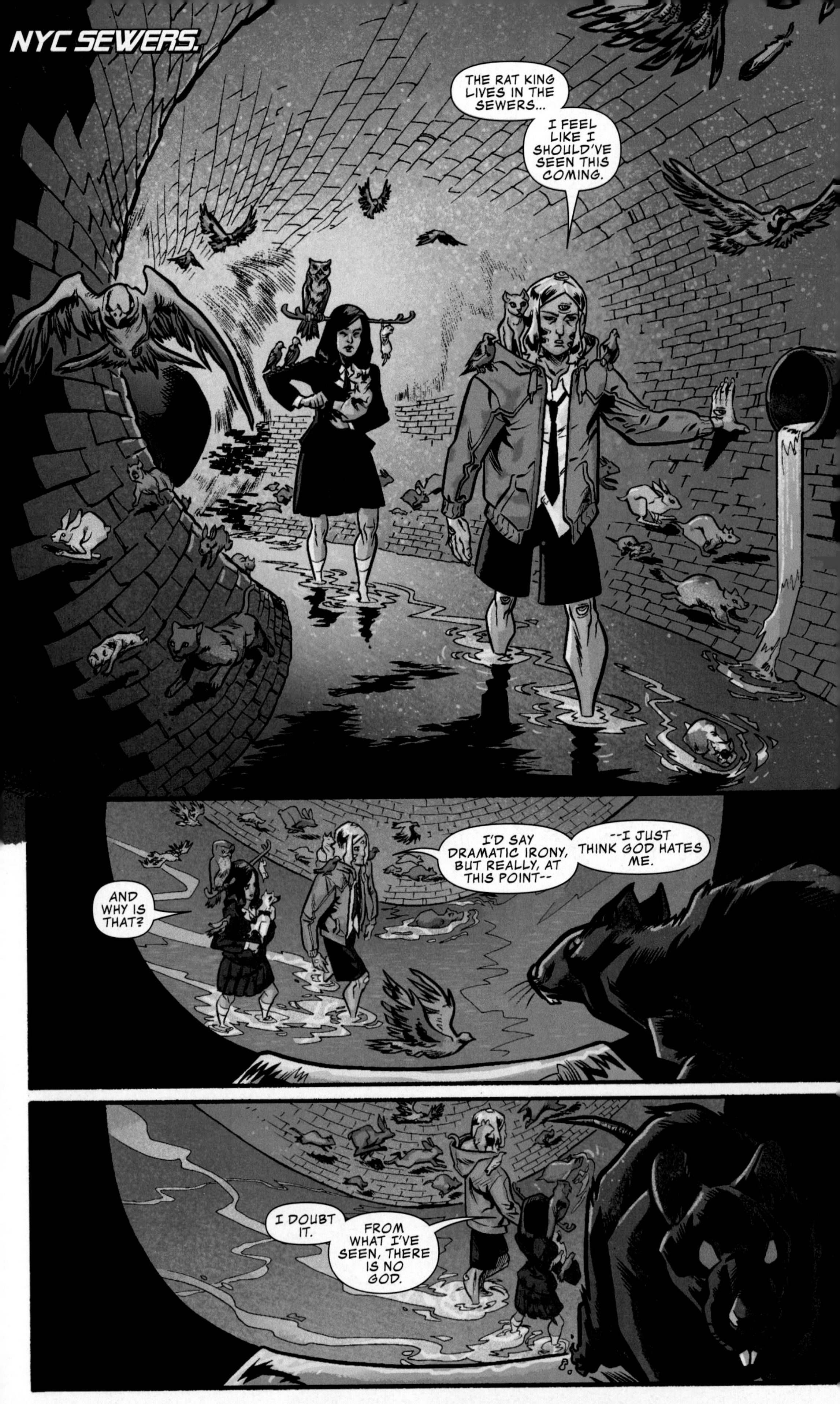
NYC SEWERS.
THE RAT KING LIVES IN THE SEWERS...
I FEEL LIKE I SHOULD'VE SEEN THIS COMING.
I'D SAY DRAMATIC IRONY, BUT REALLY, AT THIS POINT--
--I JUST THINK GOD HATES ME.
AND WHY IS THAT?
I DOUBT IT.
FROM WHAT I'VE SEEN, THERE IS NO GOD.

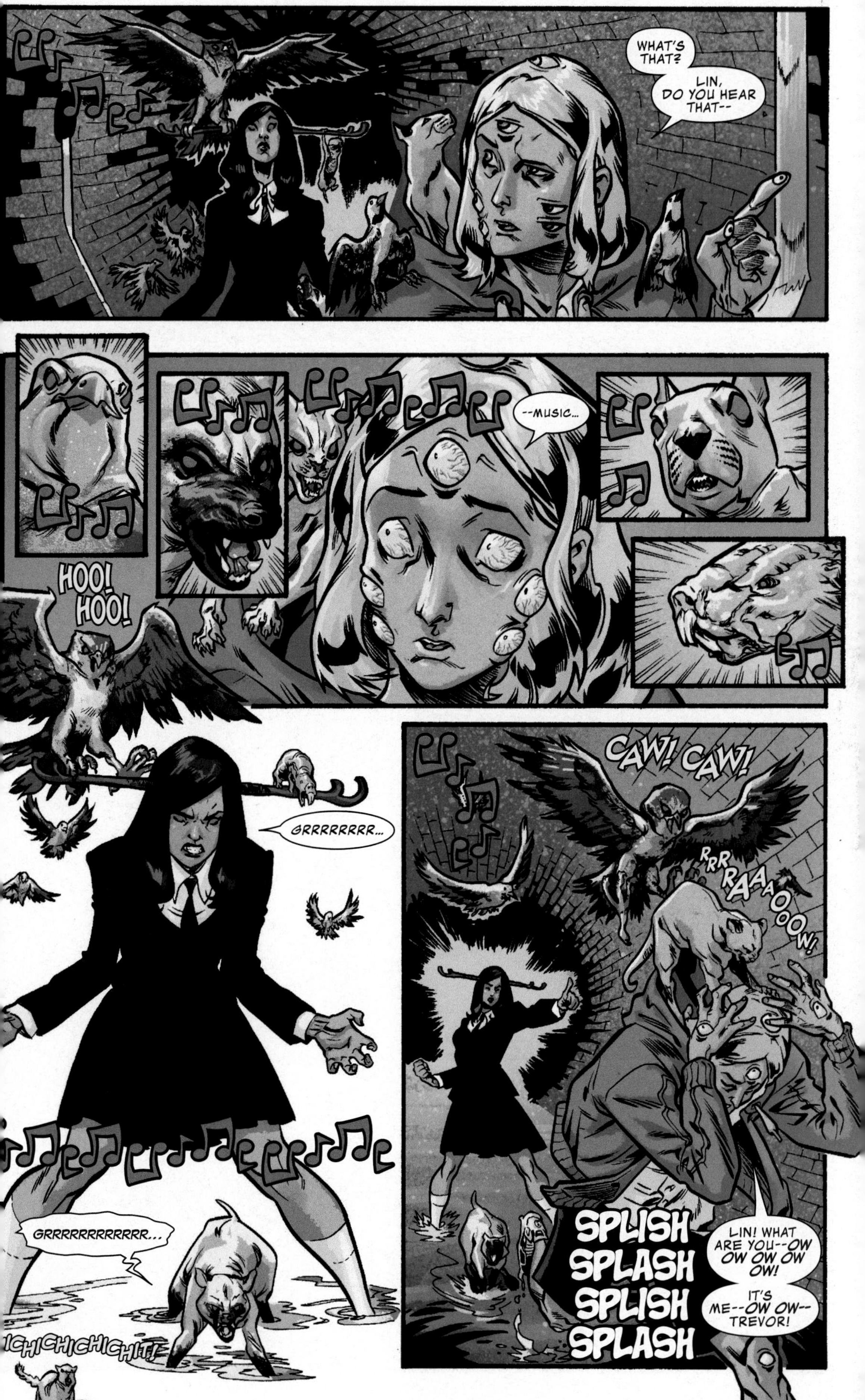

WHAT'S THAT?
LIN, DO YOU HEAR THAT--
--MUSIC...
HOO! HOO!
GRRRRRRRR...
GRRRRRRRRRRRR...
ICHICHICHICHIT!
CAW! CAW!
RRRRAAAOOOW!
SPLISH SPLASH SPLISH SPLASH
LIN! WHAT ARE YOU--OW OW OW OW OW!
IT'S ME--OW OW--TREVOR!

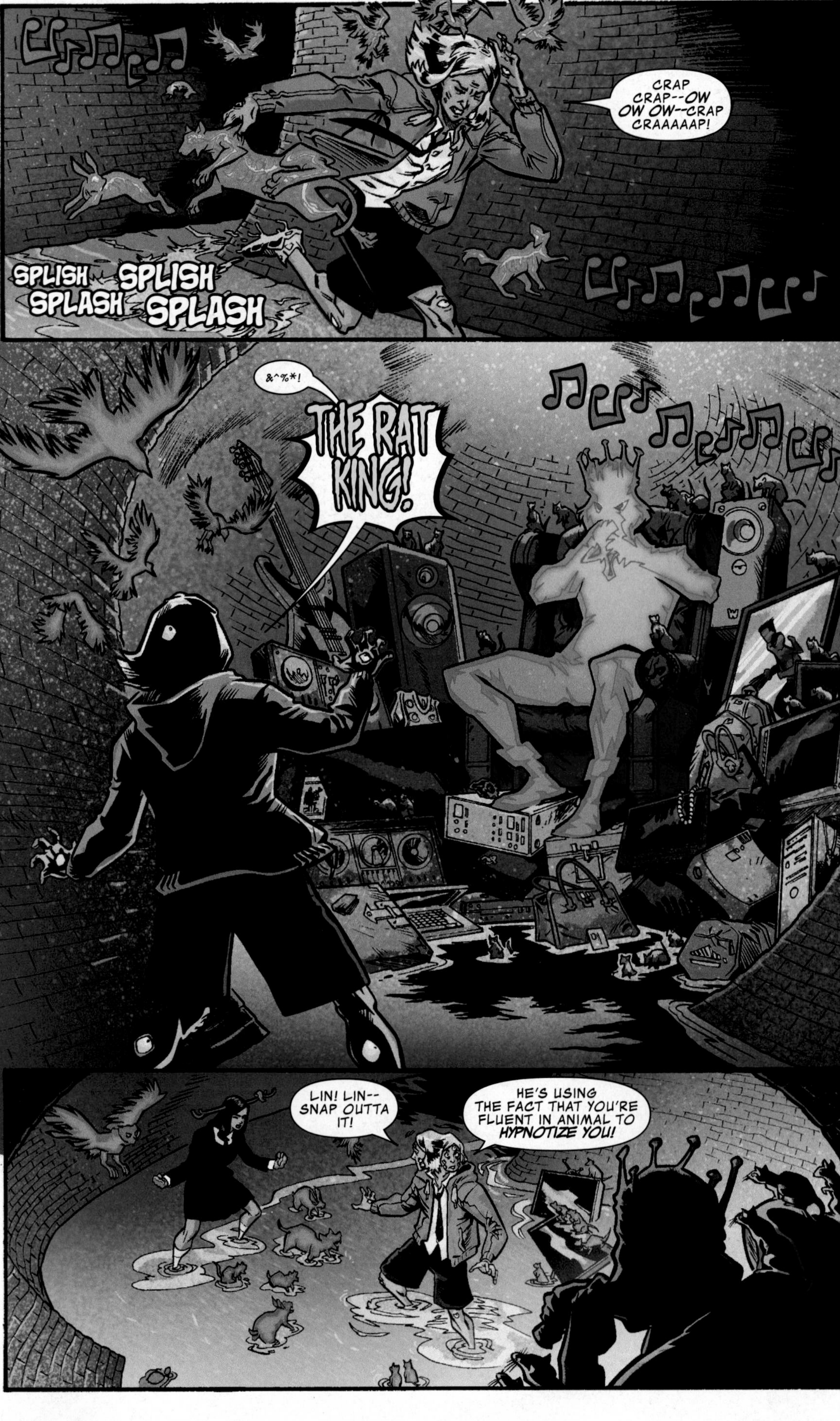
CRAP CRAP--OW OW OW--CRAP CRAAAAAP!
SPLISH SPLASH SPLISH SPLASH
&^%*!
THE RAT KING!
LIN! LIN-- SNAP OUTTA IT!
HE'S USING THE FACT THAT YOU'RE FLUENT IN ANIMAL TO HYPNOTIZE YOU!

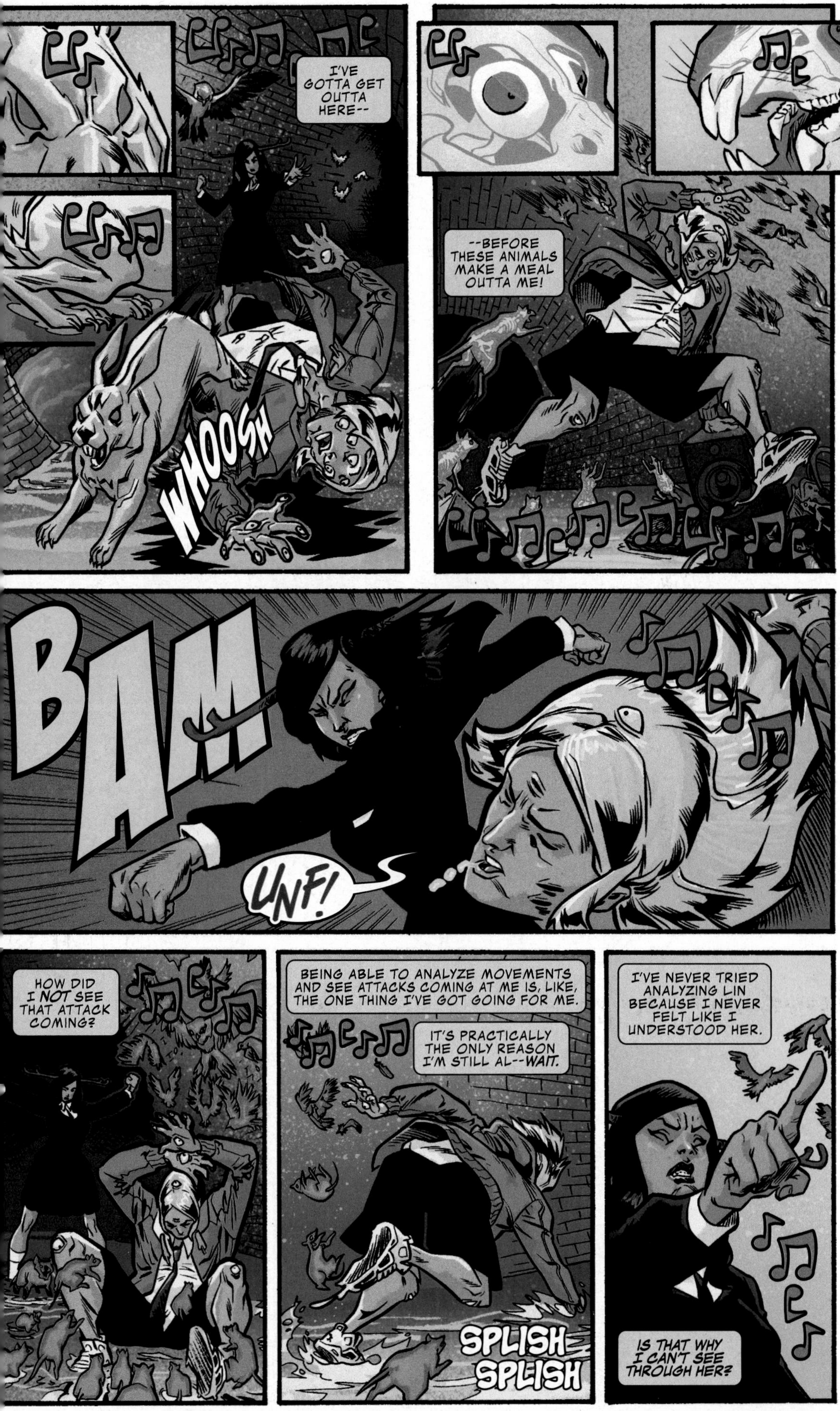
I'VE GOTTA GET OUTTA HERE--
WHOOSH
--BEFORE THESE ANIMALS MAKE A MEAL OUTTA ME!
BAM
UNF!
HOW DID I NOT SEE THAT ATTACK COMING?
BEING ABLE TO ANALYZE MOVEMENTS AND SEE ATTACKS COMING AT ME IS, LIKE, THE ONE THING I'VE GOT GOING FOR ME.
IT'S PRACTICALLY THE ONLY REASON I'M STILL AL--WAIT.
SPLISH SPLISH
I'VE NEVER TRIED ANALYZING LIN BECAUSE I NEVER FELT LIKE I UNDERSTOOD HER.
IS THAT WHY I CAN'T SEE THROUGH HER?

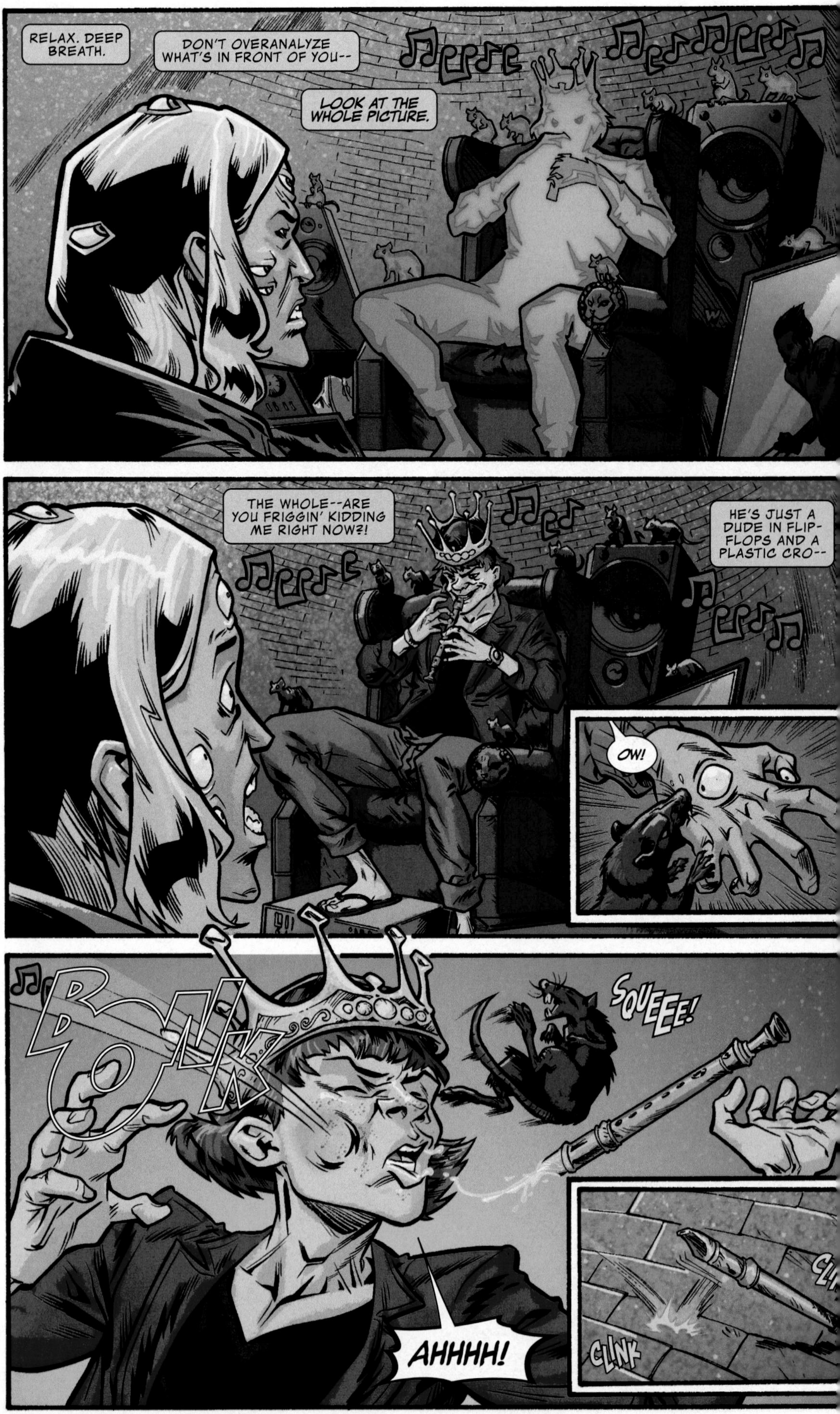
RELAX. DEEP BREATH.
DON'T OVERANALYZE WHAT'S IN FRONT OF YOU--
LOOK AT THE WHOLE PICTURE.
THE WHOLE--ARE YOU FRIGGIN' KIDDING ME RIGHT NOW?!
HE'S JUST A DUDE IN FLIP-FLOPS AND A PLASTIC CRO--
OW!
BONK
SQUEEEE!
AHHHH!
CLINK

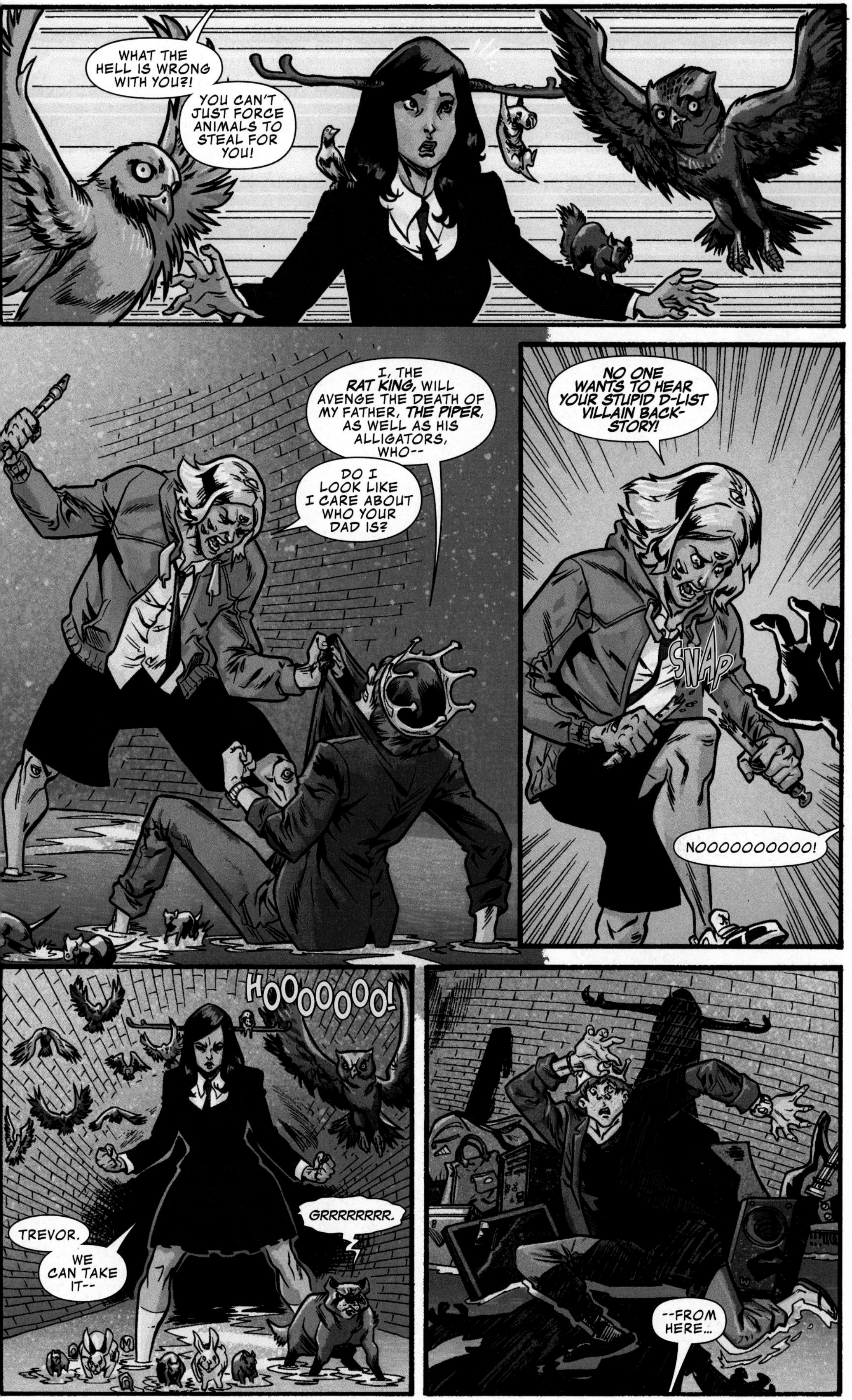
WHAT THE HELL IS WRONG WITH YOU?!
YOU CAN'T JUST FORCE ANIMALS TO STEAL FOR YOU!
I, THE RAT KING, WILL AVENGE THE DEATH OF MY FATHER, THE PIPER, AS WELL AS HIS ALLIGATORS, WHO--
DO I LOOK LIKE I CARE ABOUT WHO YOUR DAD IS?
NO ONE WANTS TO HEAR YOUR STUPID D-LIST VILLAIN BACK-STORY!
SNAP
NOOOOOOOOOO!
HOOOOOOO!
GRRRRRRRR.
TREVOR.
WE CAN TAKE IT--
--FROM HERE...

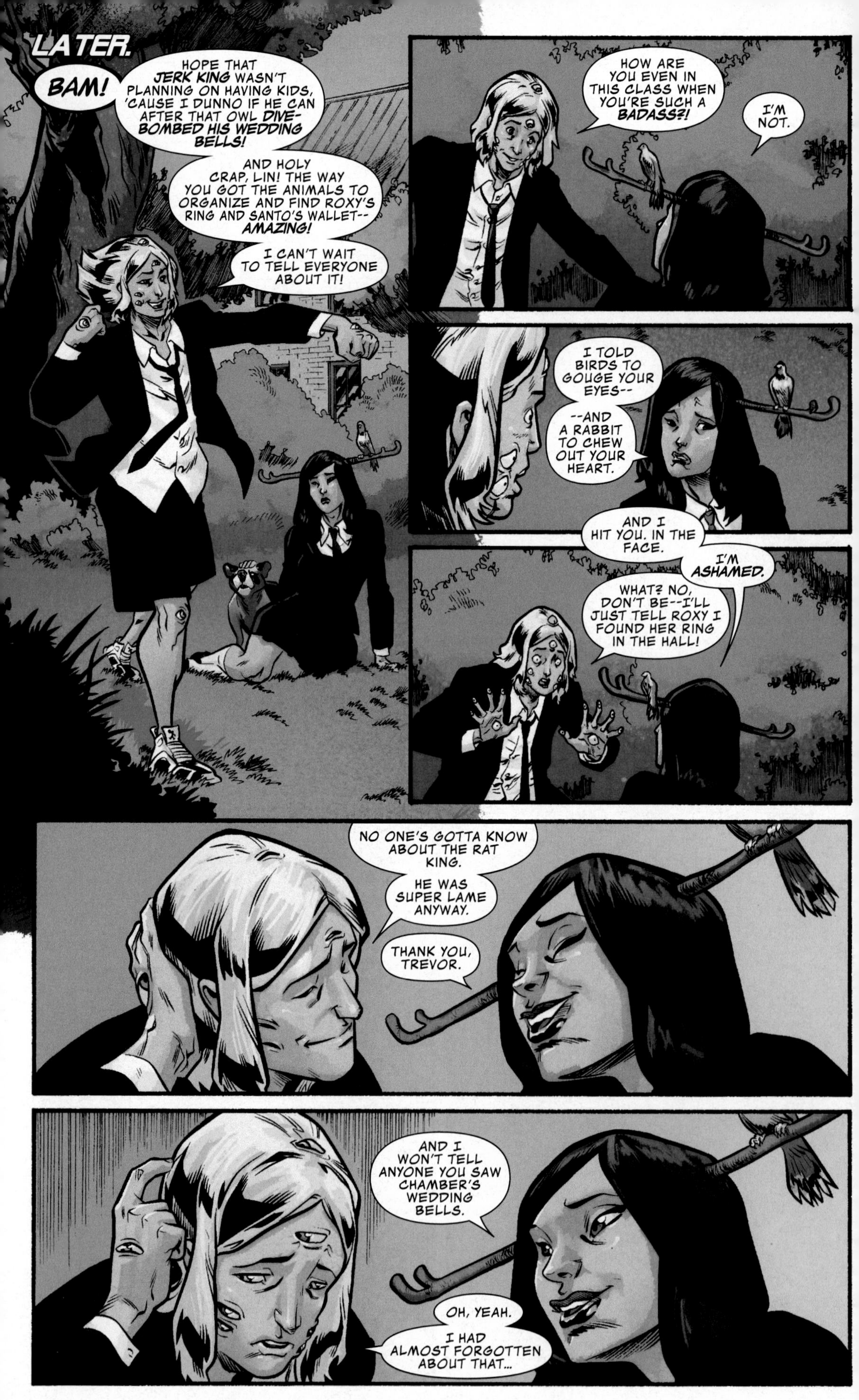
LATER.
BAM!
HOPE THAT JERK KING WASN'T PLANNING ON HAVING KIDS, 'CAUSE I DUNNO IF HE CAN AFTER THAT OWL DIVE-BOMBED HIS WEDDING BELLS!
AND HOLY CRAP, LIN! THE WAY YOU GOT THE ANIMALS TO ORGANIZE AND FIND ROXY'S RING AND SANTO'S WALLET--AMAZING!
I CAN'T WAIT TO TELL EVERYONE ABOUT IT!
HOW ARE YOU EVEN IN THIS CLASS WHEN YOU'RE SUCH A BADASS?!
I'M NOT.
I TOLD BIRDS TO GOUGE YOUR EYES--
--AND A RABBIT TO CHEW OUT YOUR HEART.
AND I HIT YOU. IN THE FACE.
I'M ASHAMED.
WHAT? NO, DON'T BE--I'LL JUST TELL ROXY I FOUND HER RING IN THE HALL!
NO ONE'S GOTTA KNOW ABOUT THE RAT KING.
HE WAS SUPER LAME ANYWAY.
THANK YOU, TREVOR.
AND I WON'T TELL ANYONE YOU SAW CHAMBER'S WEDDING BELLS.
OH, YEAH.
I HAD ALMOST FORGOTTEN ABOUT THAT...

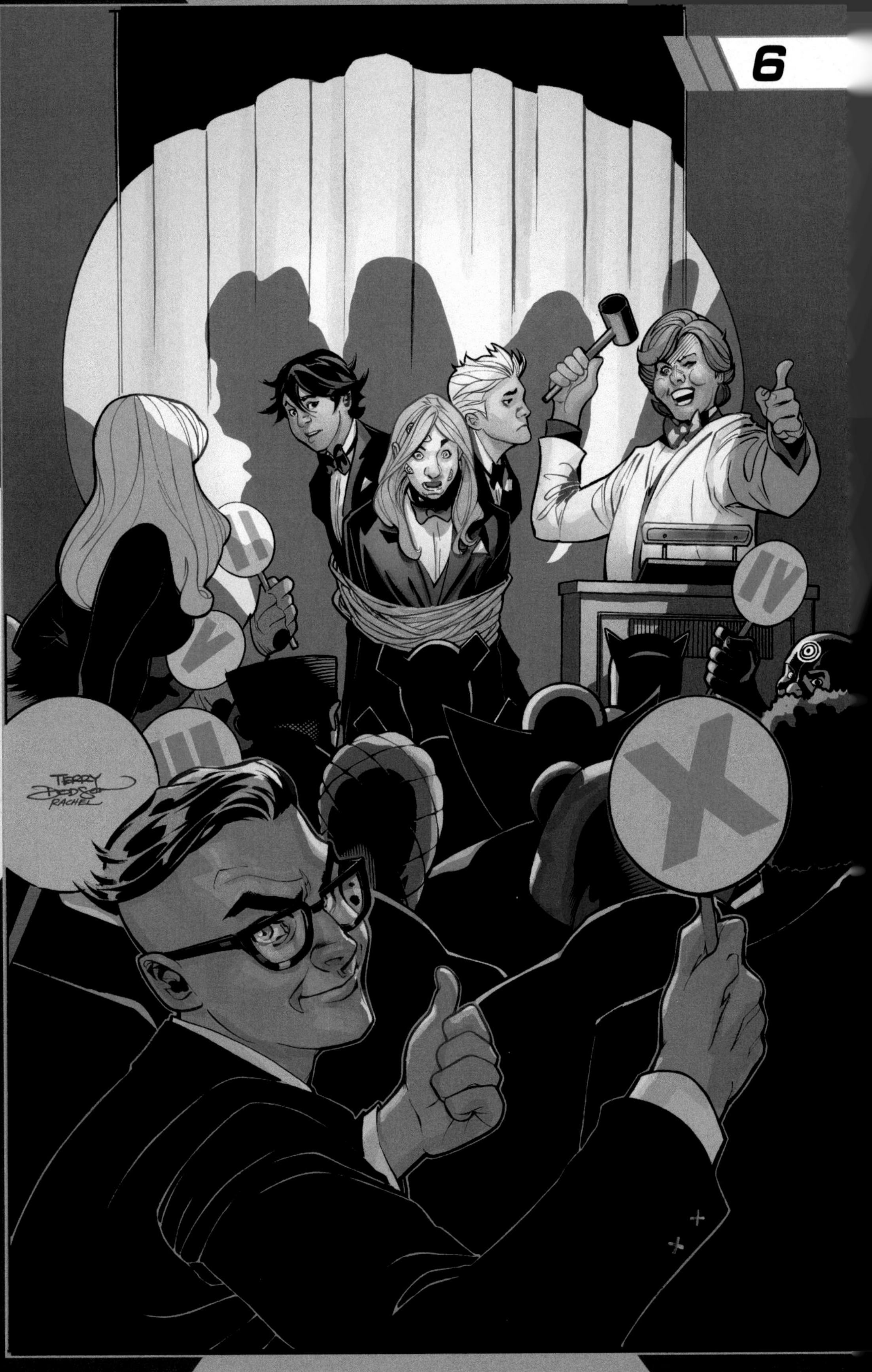
6
TERRY DODSON
RACHEL

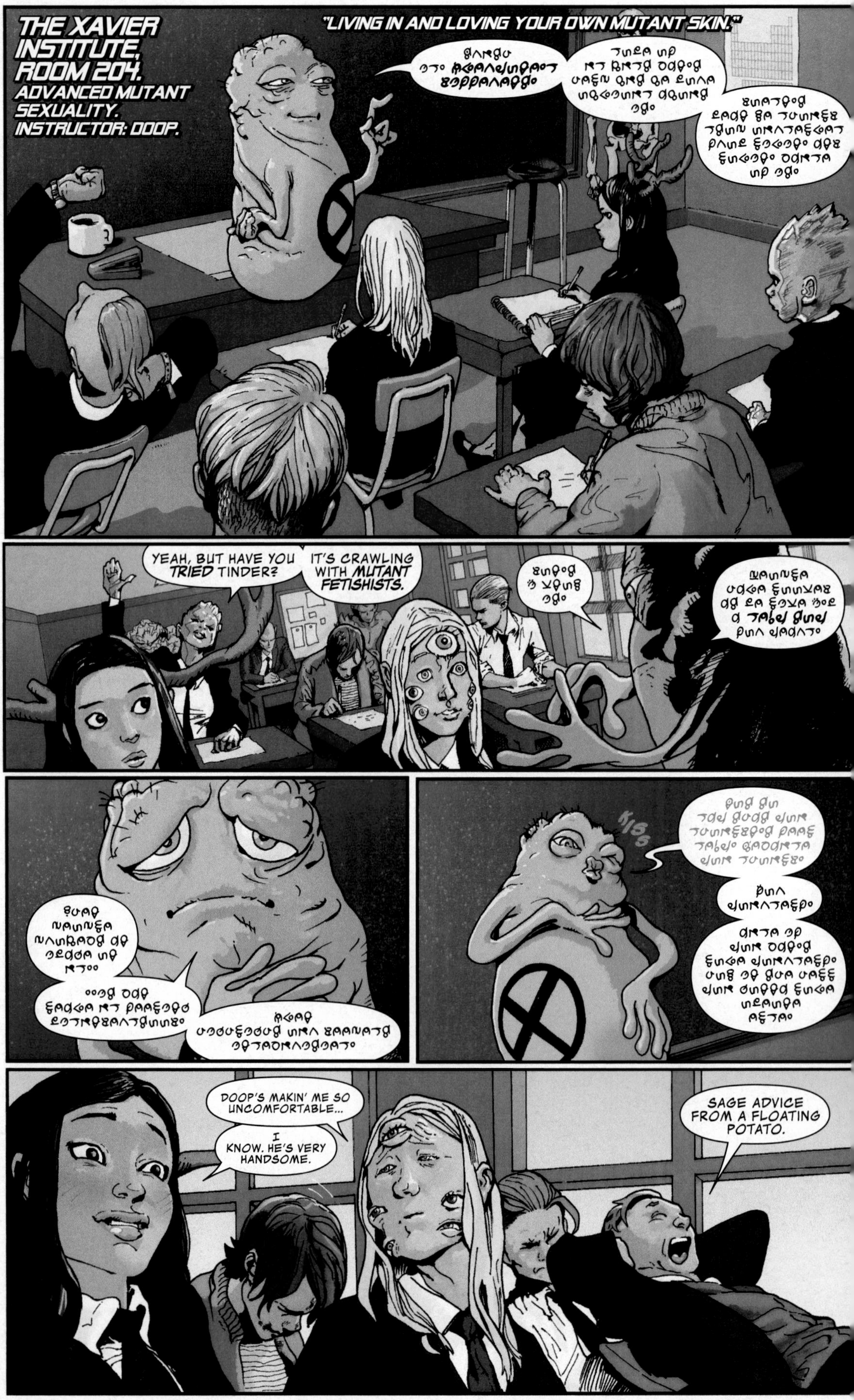
THE XAVIER INSTITUTE, ROOM 204.
ADVANCED MUTANT SEXUALITY.
INSTRUCTOR: DOOP.
"LIVING IN AND LOVING YOUR OWN MUTANT SKIN."
YEAH, BUT HAVE YOU TRIED TINDER?
IT'S CRAWLING WITH MUTANT FETISHISTS.
KISS
DOOP'S MAKIN' ME SO UNCOMFORTABLE...
I KNOW. HE'S VERY HANDSOME.
SAGE ADVICE FROM A FLOATING POTATO.

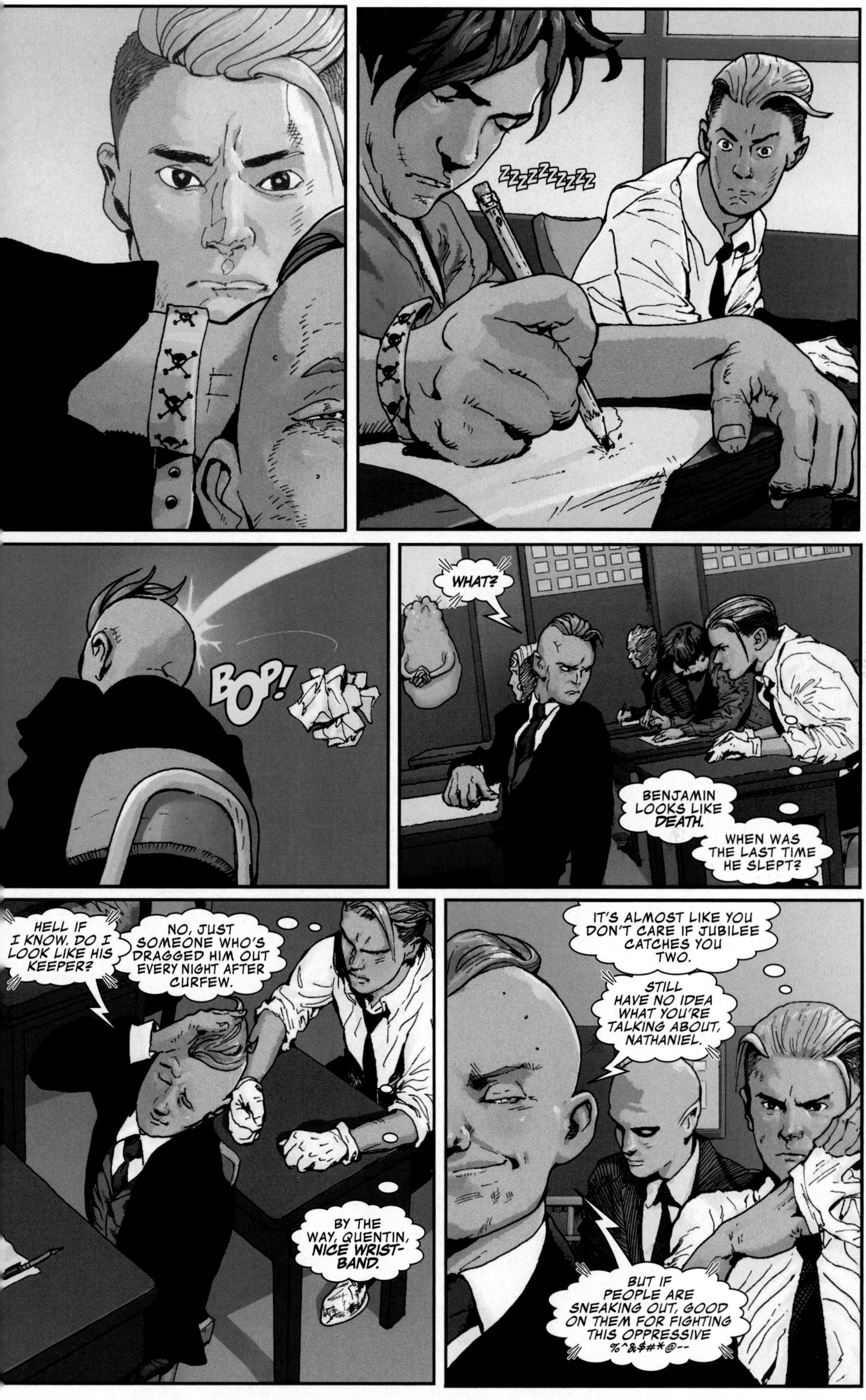
ZZZZZZZZZ
BOP!
WHAT?
BENJAMIN LOOKS LIKE DEATH.
WHEN WAS THE LAST TIME HE SLEPT?
HELL IF I KNOW. DO I LOOK LIKE HIS KEEPER?
NO, JUST SOMEONE WHO'S DRAGGED HIM OUT EVERY NIGHT AFTER CURFEW.
BY THE WAY, QUENTIN, NICE WRIST-BAND.
IT'S ALMOST LIKE YOU DON'T CARE IF JUBILEE CATCHES YOU TWO.
STILL HAVE NO IDEA WHAT YOU'RE TALKING ABOUT, NATHANIEL.
BUT IF PEOPLE ARE SNEAKING OUT, GOOD ON THEM FOR FIGHTING THIS OPPRESSIVE %^&$#*@--

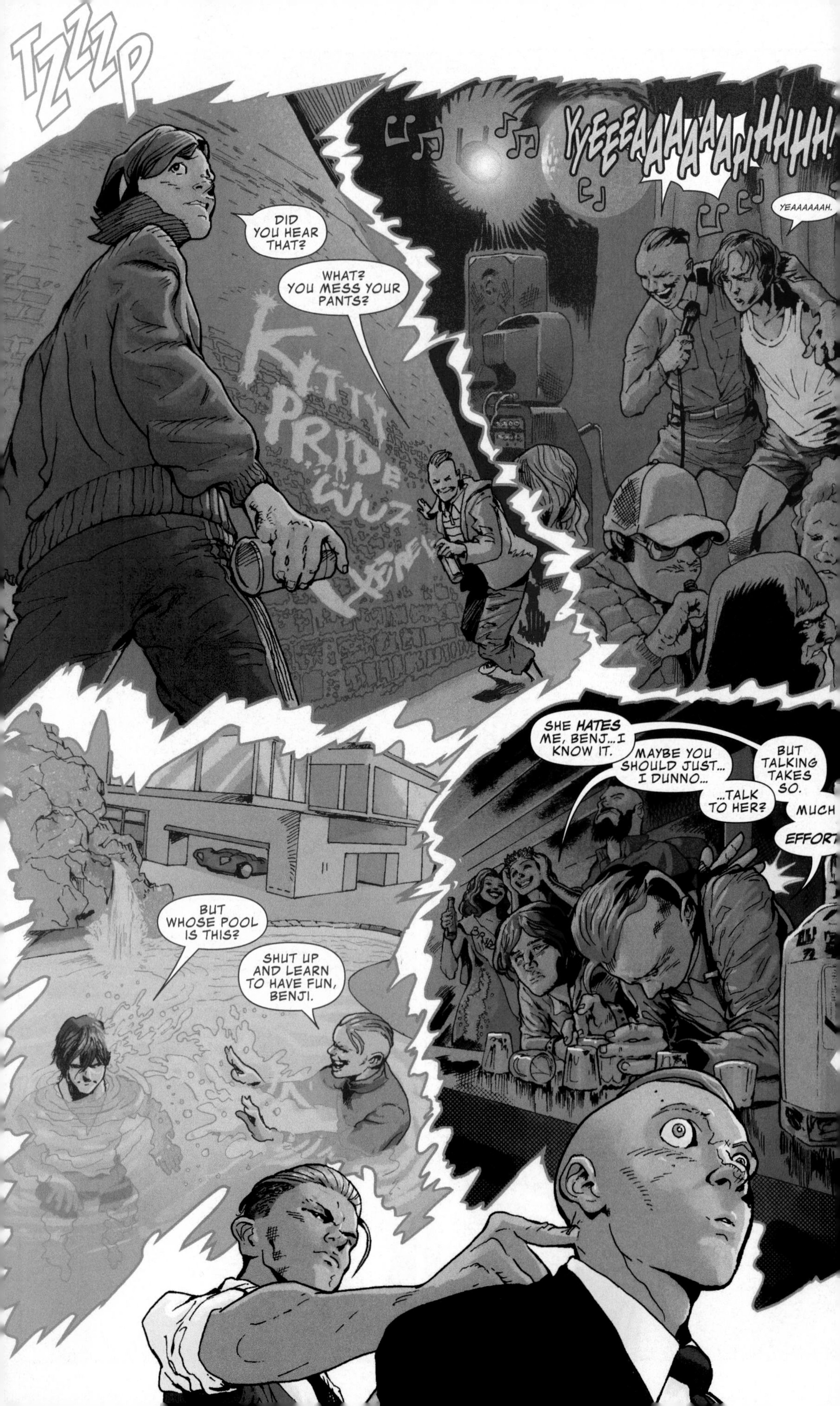
TZZZP
DID YOU HEAR THAT?
WHAT? YOU MESS YOUR PANTS?
KITTY PRIDE WUZ HERE!
YYEEEAAAAAAHHHH!
YEAAAAAAH.
BUT WHOSE POOL IS THIS?
SHUT UP AND LEARN TO HAVE FUN, BENJI.
SHE HATES ME, BENJ... I KNOW IT.
MAYBE YOU SHOULD JUST... I DUNNO...
...TALK TO HER?
BUT TALKING TAKES SO.
MUCH
EFFORT

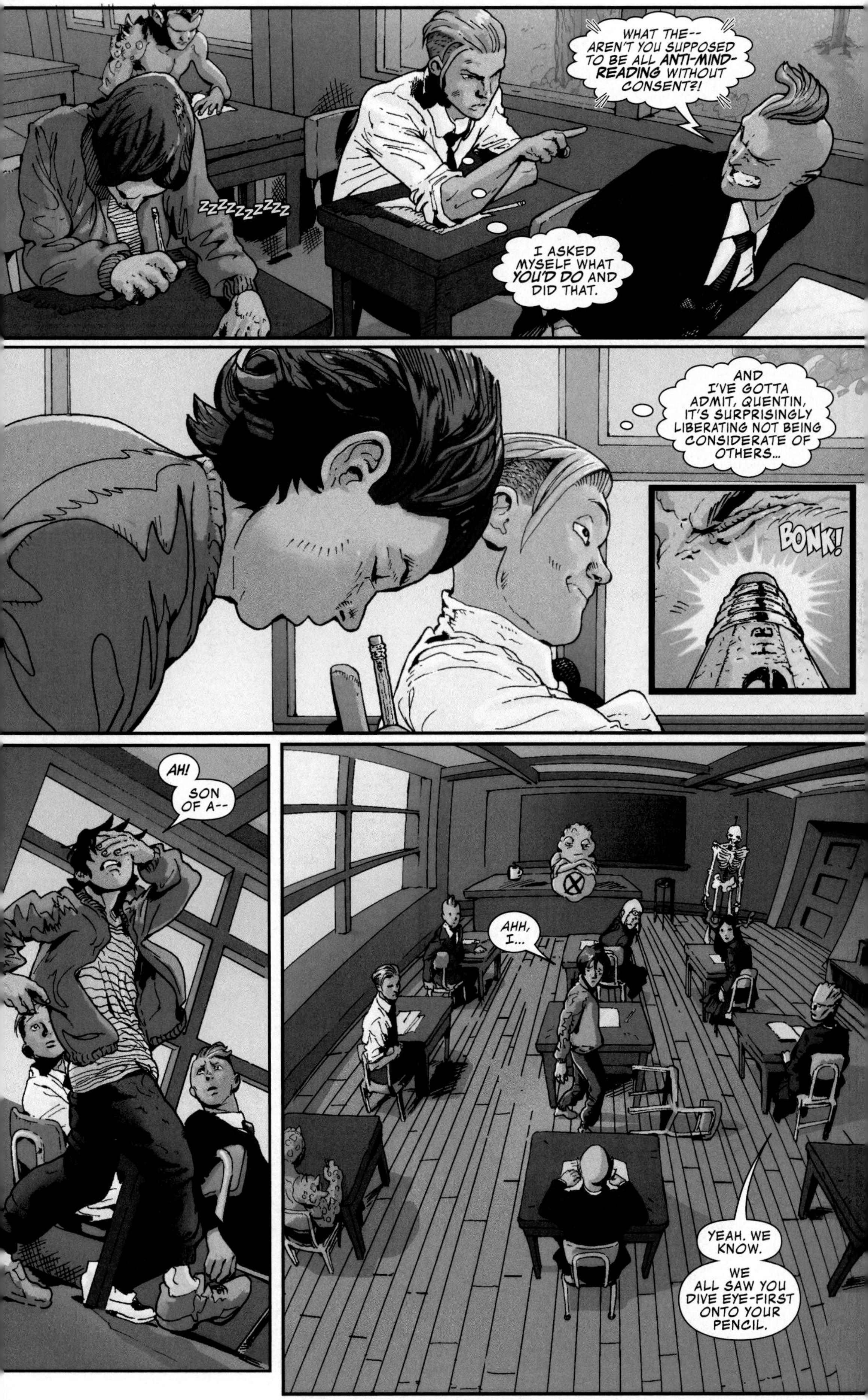

WHAT THE-- AREN'T YOU SUPPOSED TO BE ALL ANTI-MIND-READING WITHOUT CONSENT?!
ZZZZZZZZZZ
I ASKED MYSELF WHAT YOU'D DO AND DID THAT.
AND I'VE GOTTA ADMIT, QUENTIN, IT'S SURPRISINGLY LIBERATING NOT BEING CONSIDERATE OF OTHERS...
BONK!
AH!
SON OF A--
AHH, I...
YEAH. WE KNOW.
WE ALL SAW YOU DIVE EYE-FIRST ONTO YOUR PENCIL.

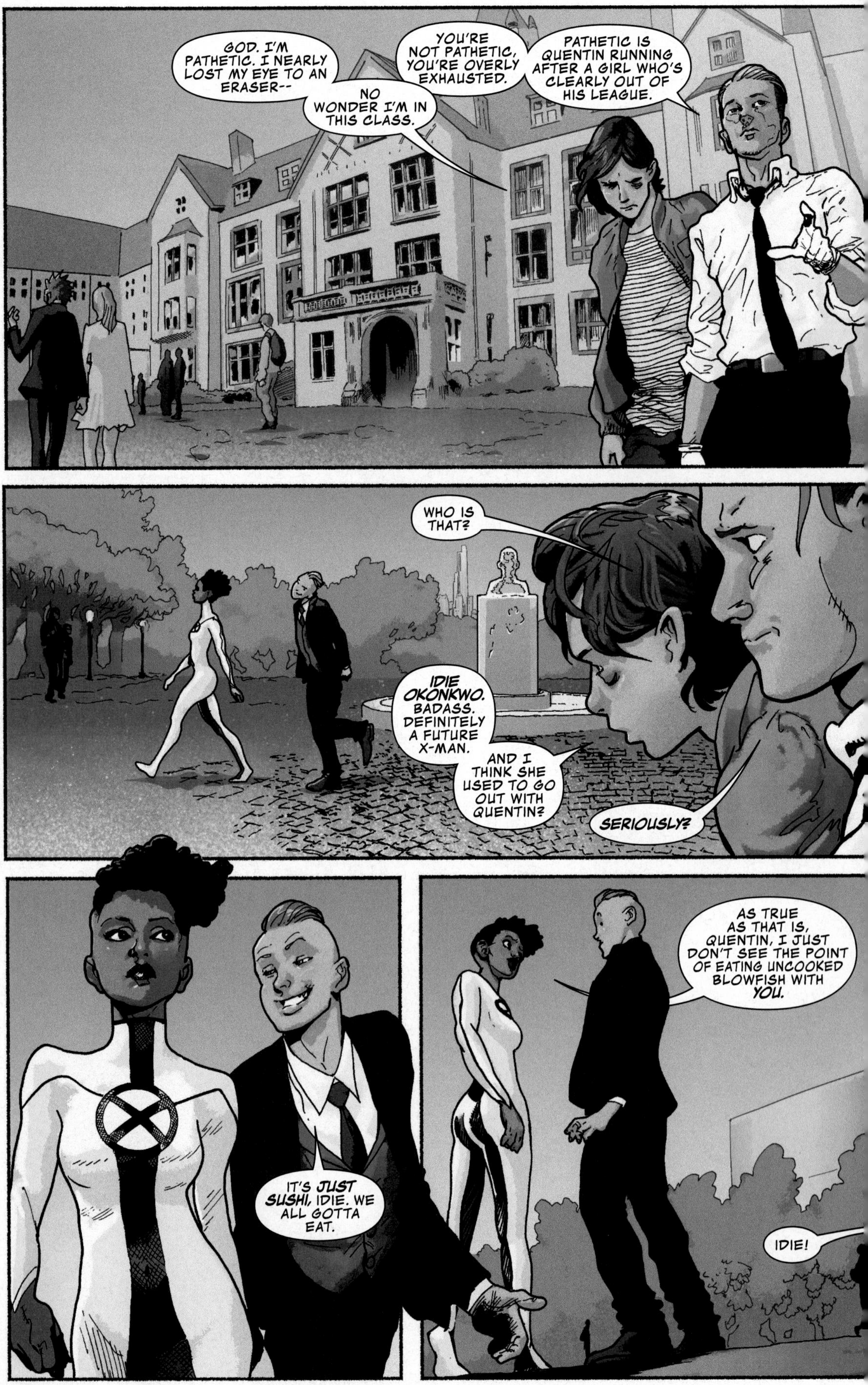
GOD. I'M PATHETIC. I NEARLY LOST MY EYE TO AN ERASER--
NO WONDER I'M IN THIS CLASS.
YOU'RE NOT PATHETIC, YOU'RE OVERLY EXHAUSTED.
PATHETIC IS QUENTIN RUNNING AFTER A GIRL WHO'S CLEARLY OUT OF HIS LEAGUE.
WHO IS THAT?
IDIE OKONKWO. BADASS. DEFINITELY A FUTURE X-MAN.
AND I THINK SHE USED TO GO OUT WITH QUENTIN?
SERIOUSLY?
IT'S JUST SUSHI, IDIE. WE ALL GOTTA EAT.
AS TRUE AS THAT IS, QUENTIN, I JUST DON'T SEE THE POINT OF EATING UNCOOKED BLOWFISH WITH YOU.
IDIE!

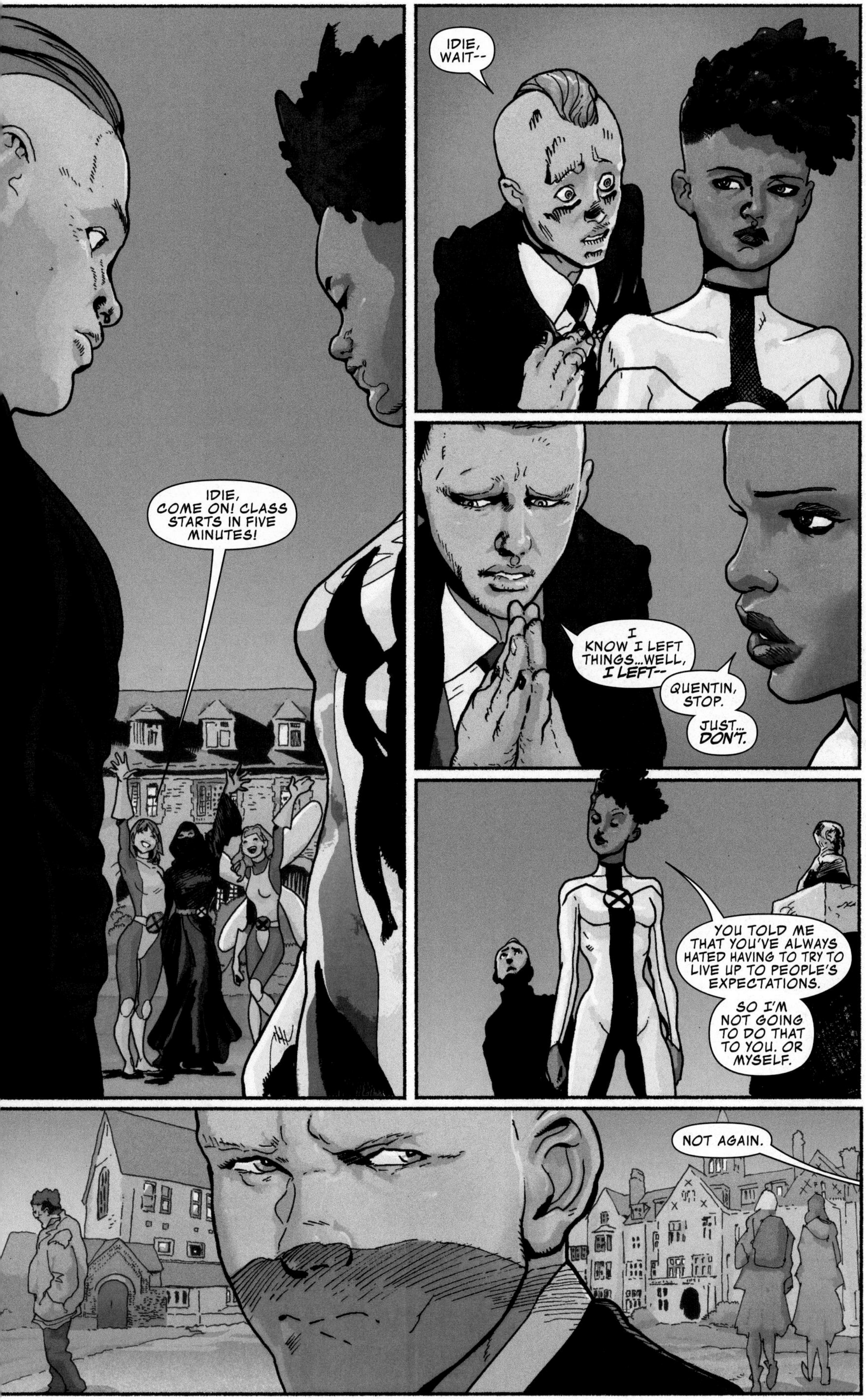
IDIE, COME ON! CLASS STARTS IN FIVE MINUTES!
IDIE, WAIT--
I KNOW I LEFT THINGS...WELL, *I LEFT*--
QUENTIN, STOP.
JUST... *DON'T.*
YOU TOLD ME THAT YOU'VE ALWAYS HATED HAVING TO TRY TO LIVE UP TO PEOPLE'S EXPECTATIONS.
SO I'M NOT GOING TO DO THAT TO YOU. OR MYSELF.
NOT AGAIN.

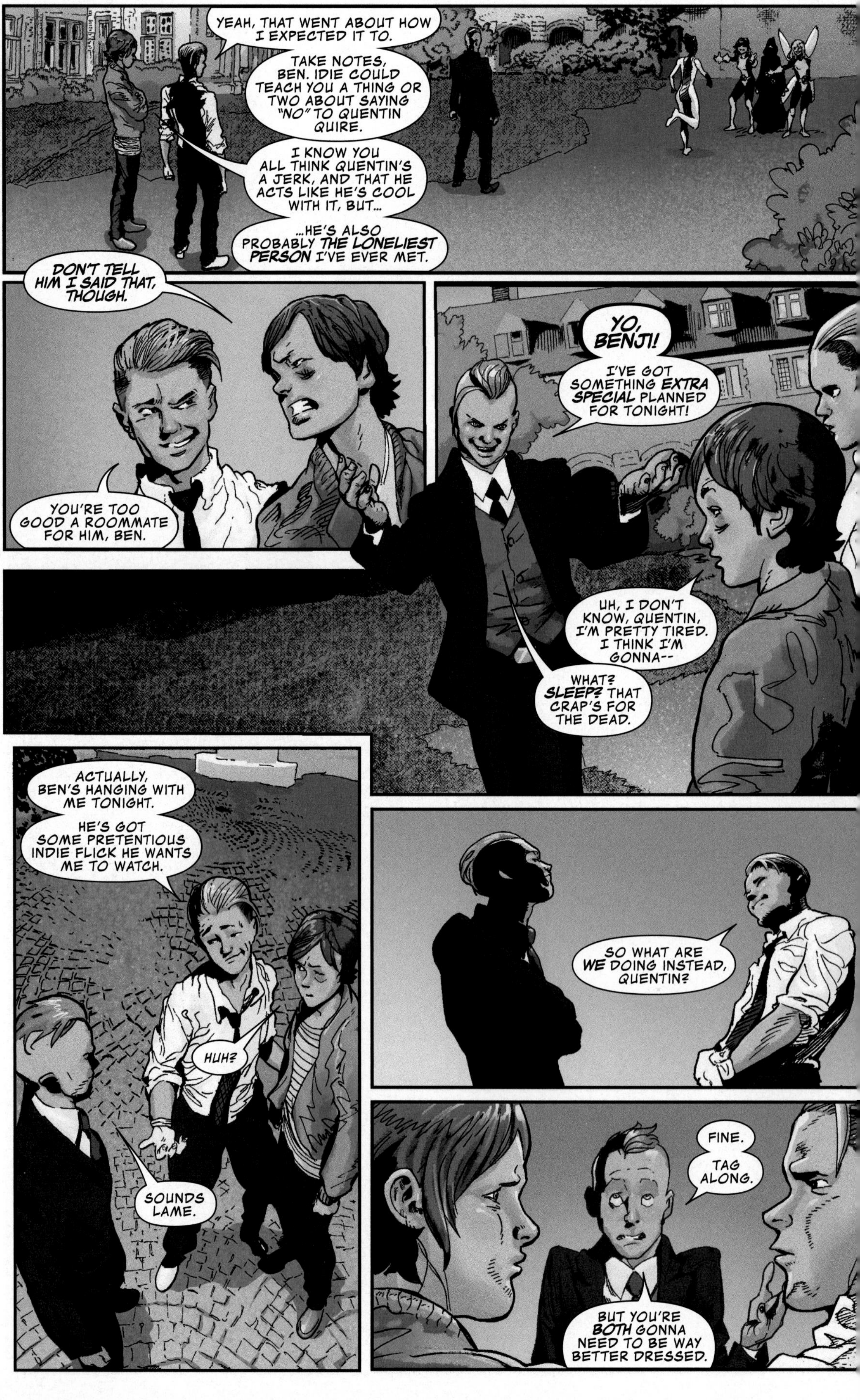
YEAH, THAT WENT ABOUT HOW I EXPECTED IT TO.
TAKE NOTES, BEN. IDIE COULD TEACH YOU A THING OR TWO ABOUT SAYING "NO" TO QUENTIN QUIRE.
I KNOW YOU ALL THINK QUENTIN'S A JERK, AND THAT HE ACTS LIKE HE'S COOL WITH IT, BUT...
...HE'S ALSO PROBABLY THE LONELIEST PERSON I'VE EVER MET.
DON'T TELL HIM I SAID THAT, THOUGH.
YOU'RE TOO GOOD A ROOMMATE FOR HIM, BEN.
YO, BENJI!
I'VE GOT SOMETHING EXTRA SPECIAL PLANNED FOR TONIGHT!
UH, I DON'T KNOW, QUENTIN, I'M PRETTY TIRED. I THINK I'M GONNA--
WHAT? SLEEP? THAT CRAP'S FOR THE DEAD.
ACTUALLY, BEN'S HANGING WITH ME TONIGHT.
HE'S GOT SOME PRETENTIOUS INDIE FLICK HE WANTS ME TO WATCH.
HUH?
SOUNDS LAME.
SO WHAT ARE WE DOING INSTEAD, QUENTIN?
FINE.
TAG ALONG.
BUT YOU'RE BOTH GONNA NEED TO BE WAY BETTER DRESSED.

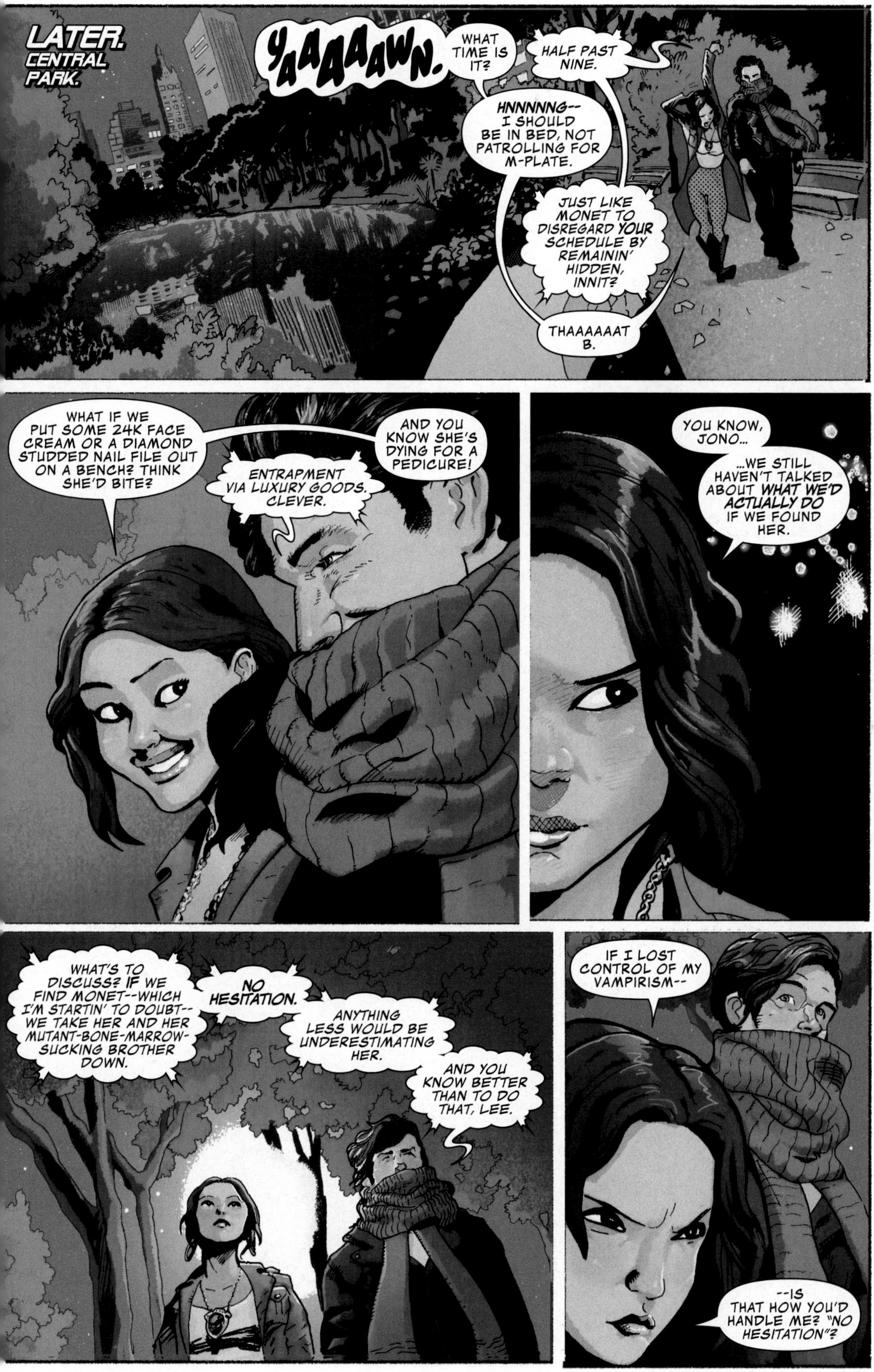
LATER. CENTRAL PARK.
YAAAAAWN.
WHAT TIME IS IT?
HALF PAST NINE.
HNNNNNG-- I SHOULD BE IN BED, NOT PATROLLING FOR M-PLATE.
JUST LIKE MONET TO DISREGARD YOUR SCHEDULE BY REMAININ' HIDDEN, INNIT?
THAAAAAAT B.
WHAT IF WE PUT SOME 24K FACE CREAM OR A DIAMOND STUDDED NAIL FILE OUT ON A BENCH? THINK SHE'D BITE?
ENTRAPMENT VIA LUXURY GOODS. CLEVER.
AND YOU KNOW SHE'S DYING FOR A PEDICURE!
YOU KNOW, JONO...
...WE STILL HAVEN'T TALKED ABOUT WHAT WE'D ACTUALLY DO IF WE FOUND HER.
WHAT'S TO DISCUSS? IF WE FIND MONET--WHICH I'M STARTIN' TO DOUBT--WE TAKE HER AND HER MUTANT-BONE-MARROW-SUCKING BROTHER DOWN.
NO HESITATION.
ANYTHING LESS WOULD BE UNDERESTIMATING HER.
AND YOU KNOW BETTER THAN TO DO THAT, LEE.
IF I LOST CONTROL OF MY VAMPIRISM--
--IS THAT HOW YOU'D HANDLE ME? "NO HESITATION"?

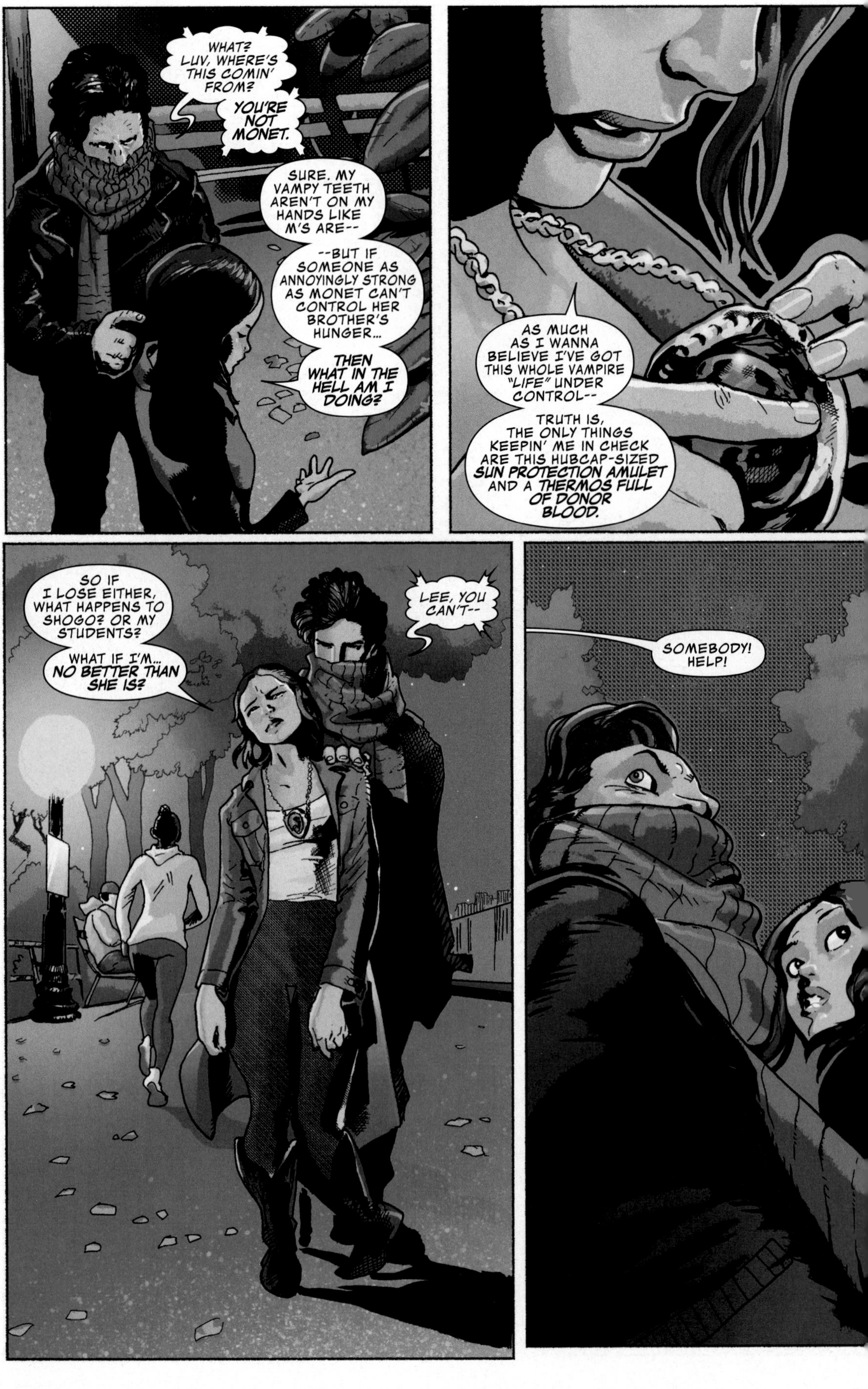
WHAT? LUV, WHERE'S THIS COMIN' FROM?
YOU'RE NOT MONET.
SURE. MY VAMPY TEETH AREN'T ON MY HANDS LIKE M'S ARE--
--BUT IF SOMEONE AS ANNOYINGLY STRONG AS MONET CAN'T CONTROL HER BROTHER'S HUNGER...
THEN WHAT IN THE HELL AM I DOING?
AS MUCH AS I WANNA BELIEVE I'VE GOT THIS WHOLE VAMPIRE "LIFE" UNDER CONTROL--
TRUTH IS, THE ONLY THINGS KEEPIN' ME IN CHECK ARE THIS HUBCAP-SIZED SUN PROTECTION AMULET AND A THERMOS FULL OF DONOR BLOOD.
SO IF I LOSE EITHER, WHAT HAPPENS TO SHOGO? OR MY STUDENTS?
WHAT IF I'M... NO BETTER THAN SHE IS?
LEE, YOU CAN'T--
SOMEBODY! HELP!

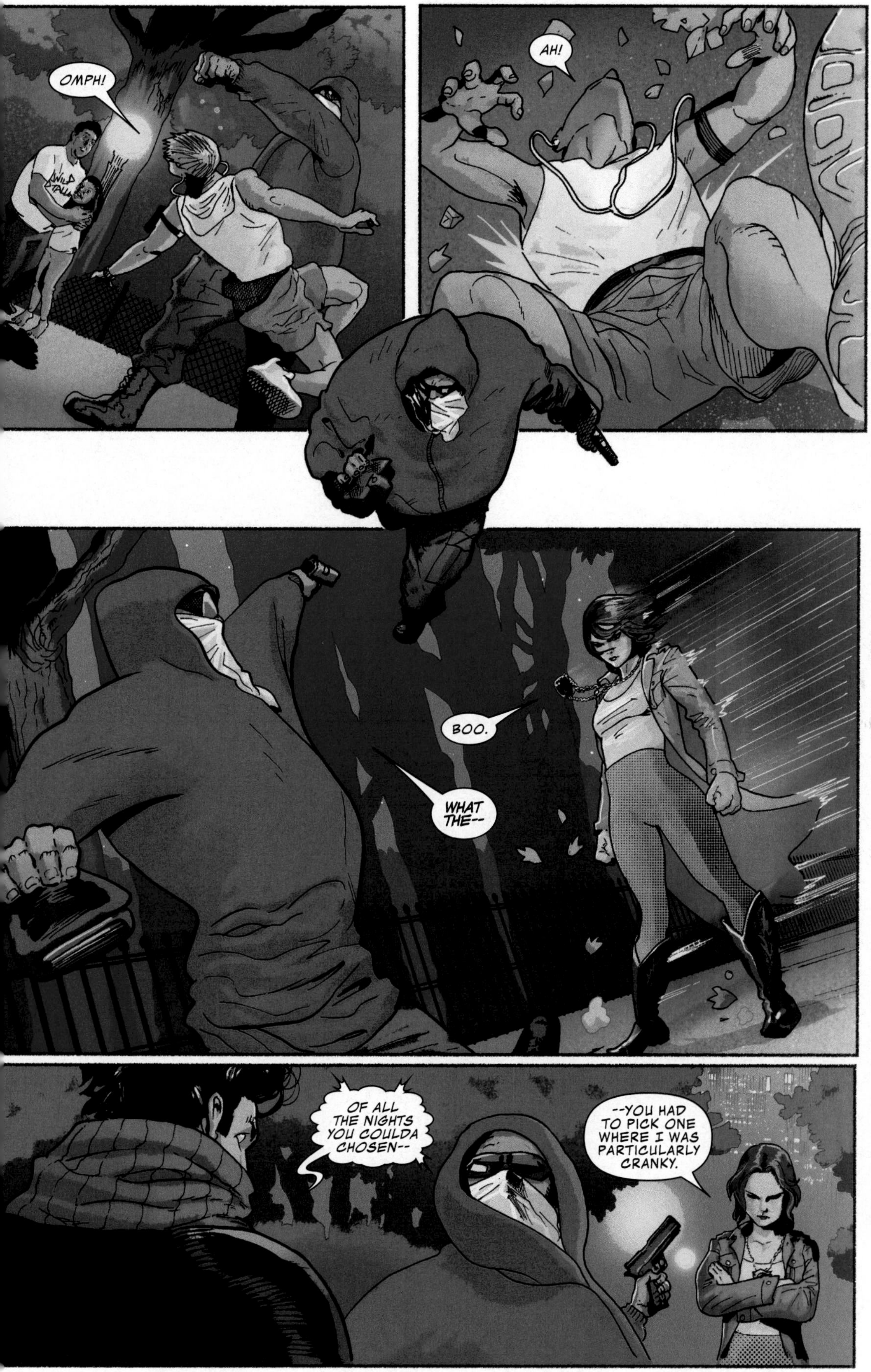
OMPH!
AH!
BOO.
WHAT THE--
OF ALL THE NIGHTS YOU COULDA CHOSEN--
--YOU HAD TO PICK ONE WHERE I WAS PARTICULARLY CRANKY.

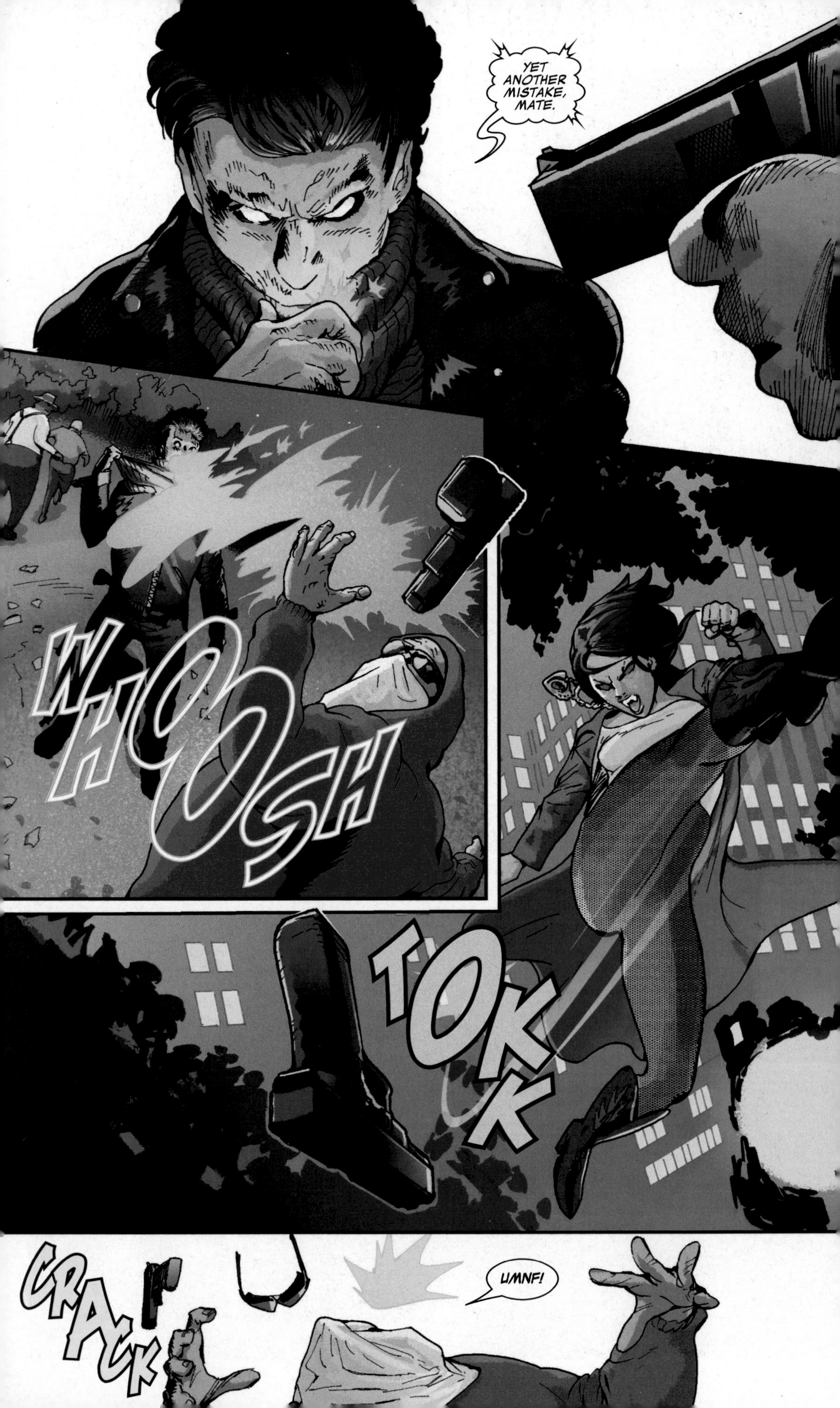
YET ANOTHER MISTAKE, MATE.
WHOOSH
TOK
CRACK
UMNF!

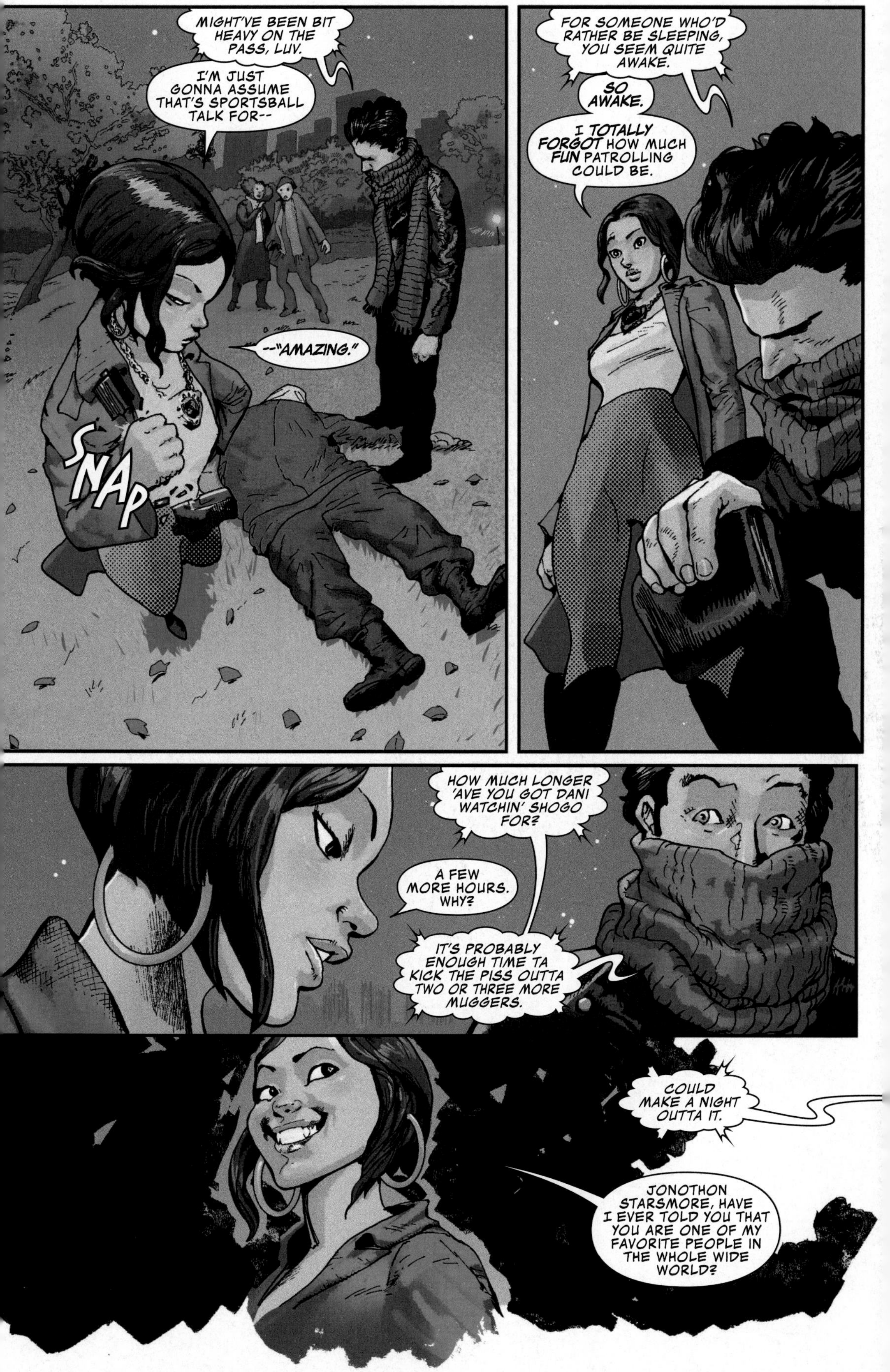

MIGHT'VE BEEN BIT HEAVY ON THE PASS, LUV.
I'M JUST GONNA ASSUME THAT'S SPORTSBALL TALK FOR--
--"AMAZING."
SNAP
FOR SOMEONE WHO'D RATHER BE SLEEPING, YOU SEEM QUITE AWAKE.
SO AWAKE.
I TOTALLY FORGOT HOW MUCH FUN PATROLLING COULD BE.
HOW MUCH LONGER 'AVE YOU GOT DANI WATCHIN' SHOGO FOR?
A FEW MORE HOURS. WHY?
IT'S PROBABLY ENOUGH TIME TA KICK THE PISS OUTTA TWO OR THREE MORE MUGGERS.
COULD MAKE A NIGHT OUTTA IT.
JONOTHON STARSMORE, HAVE I EVER TOLD YOU THAT YOU ARE ONE OF MY FAVORITE PEOPLE IN THE WHOLE WIDE WORLD?

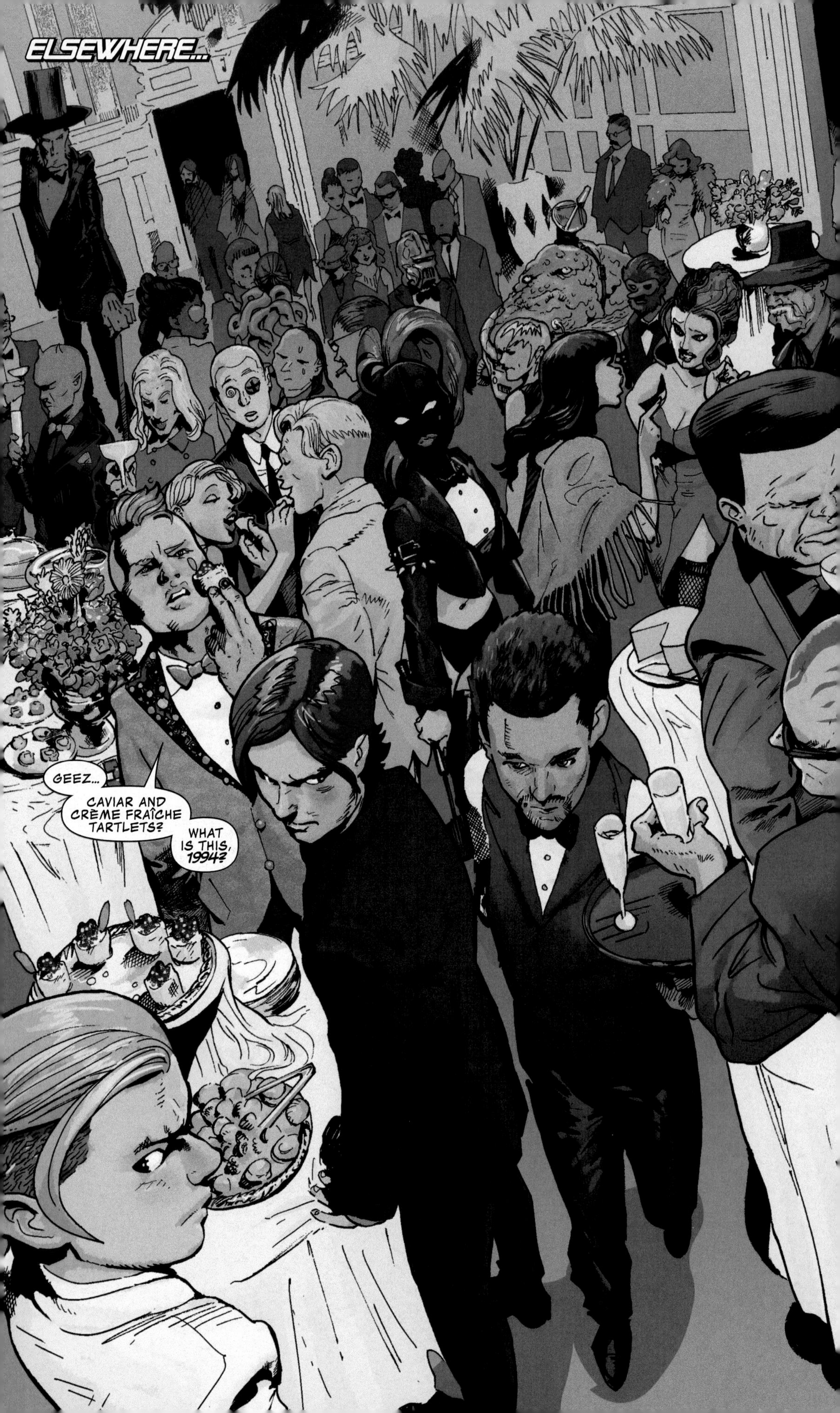
ELSEWHERE...
GEEZ...
CAVIAR AND CRÈME FRAÎCHE TARTLETS?
WHAT IS THIS, 1994?

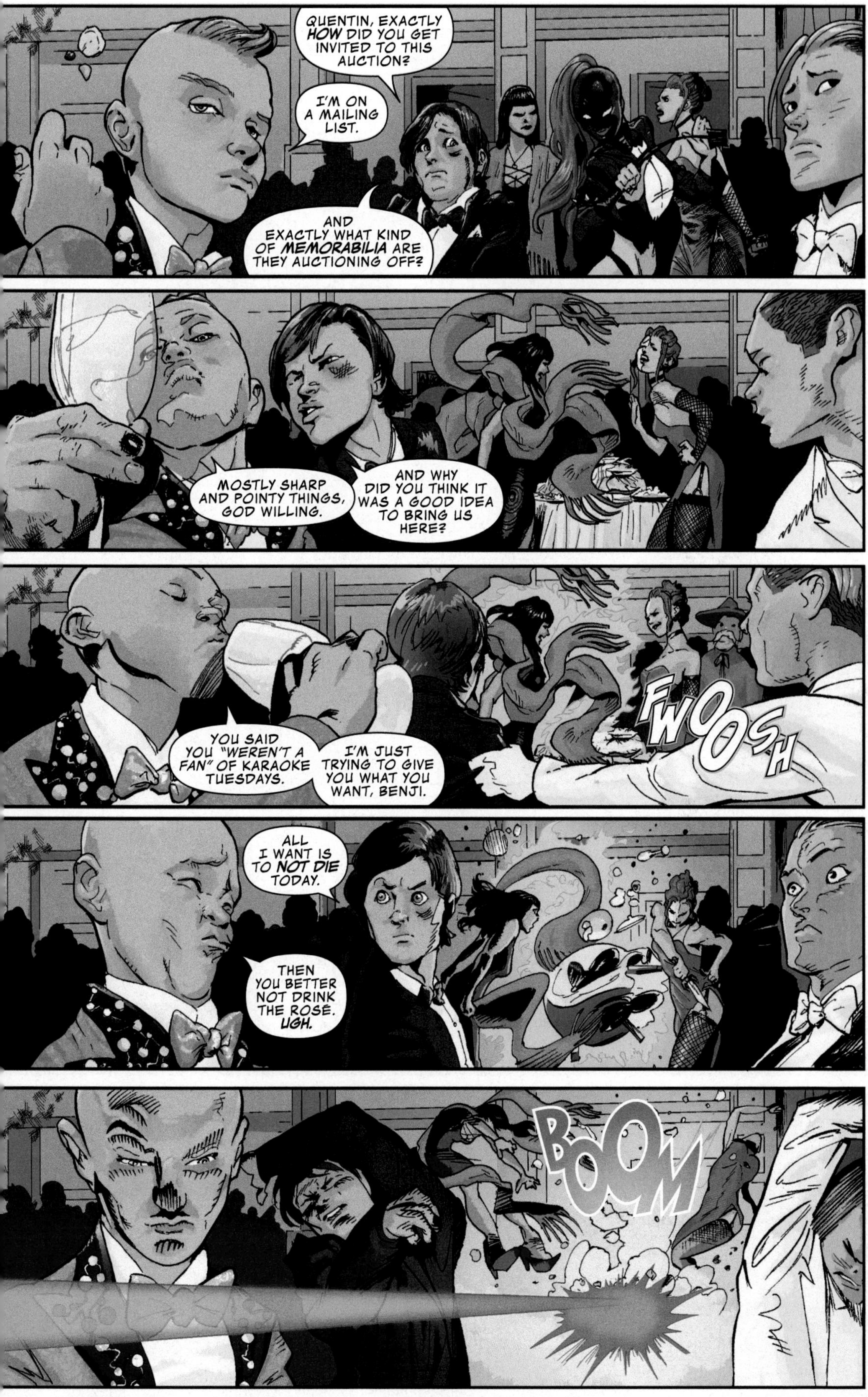
QUENTIN, EXACTLY HOW DID YOU GET INVITED TO THIS AUCTION?
I'M ON A MAILING LIST.
AND EXACTLY WHAT KIND OF MEMORABILIA ARE THEY AUCTIONING OFF?
MOSTLY SHARP AND POINTY THINGS, GOD WILLING.
AND WHY DID YOU THINK IT WAS A GOOD IDEA TO BRING US HERE?
YOU SAID YOU "WEREN'T A FAN" OF KARAOKE TUESDAYS.
I'M JUST TRYING TO GIVE YOU WHAT YOU WANT, BENJI.
FWOOSH
ALL I WANT IS TO NOT DIE TODAY.
THEN YOU BETTER NOT DRINK THE ROSE. UGH.
BOOM

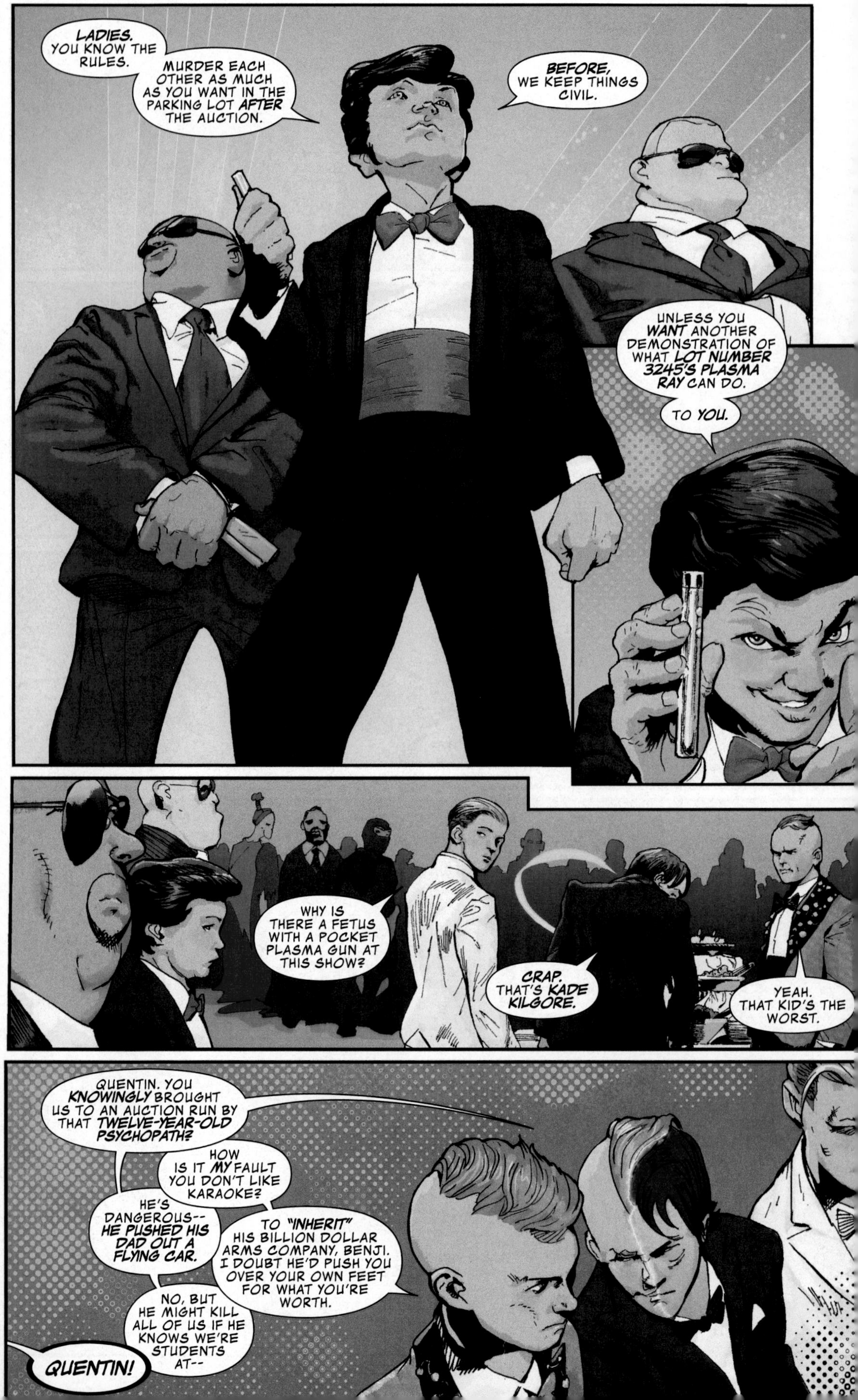

LADIES. YOU KNOW THE RULES.
MURDER EACH OTHER AS MUCH AS YOU WANT IN THE PARKING LOT AFTER THE AUCTION.
BEFORE, WE KEEP THINGS CIVIL.
UNLESS YOU WANT ANOTHER DEMONSTRATION OF WHAT LOT NUMBER 3245'S PLASMA RAY CAN DO.
TO YOU.
WHY IS THERE A FETUS WITH A POCKET PLASMA GUN AT THIS SHOW?
CRAP. THAT'S KADE KILGORE.
YEAH. THAT KID'S THE WORST.
QUENTIN. YOU KNOWINGLY BROUGHT US TO AN AUCTION RUN BY THAT TWELVE-YEAR-OLD PSYCHOPATH?
HOW IS IT MY FAULT YOU DON'T LIKE KARAOKE?
HE'S DANGEROUS-- HE PUSHED HIS DAD OUT A FLYING CAR.
TO "INHERIT" HIS BILLION DOLLAR ARMS COMPANY, BENJI. I DOUBT HE'D PUSH YOU OVER YOUR OWN FEET FOR WHAT YOU'RE WORTH.
NO, BUT HE MIGHT KILL ALL OF US IF HE KNOWS WE'RE STUDENTS AT--
QUENTIN!

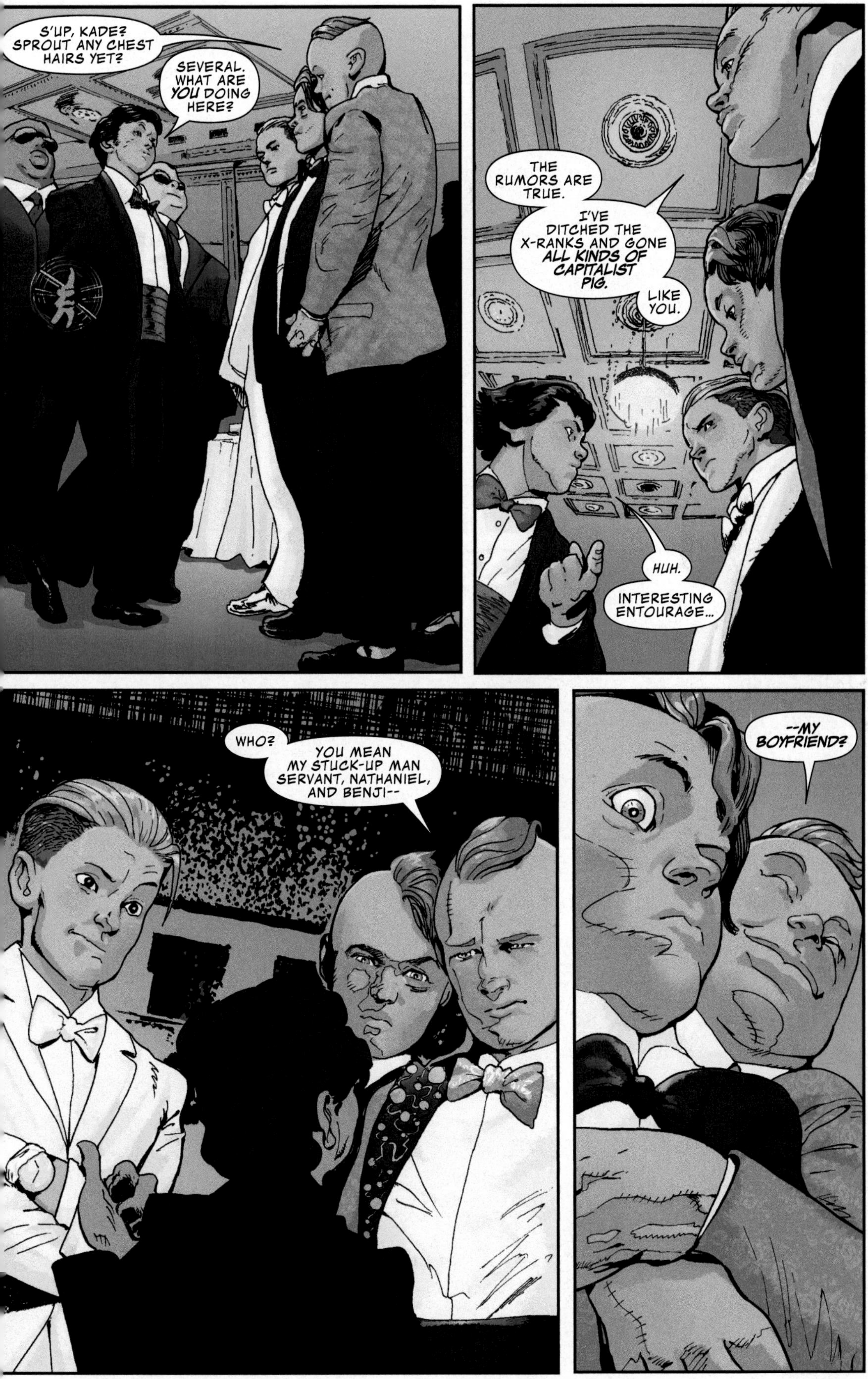
S'UP, KADE? SPROUT ANY CHEST HAIRS YET?
SEVERAL. WHAT ARE *YOU* DOING HERE?
THE RUMORS ARE TRUE.
I'VE DITCHED THE X-RANKS AND GONE ***ALL KINDS OF CAPITALIST PIG.***
LIKE YOU.
HUH.
INTERESTING ENTOURAGE...
WHO?
YOU MEAN MY STUCK-UP MAN SERVANT, NATHANIEL, AND BENJI--
--MY BOYFRIEND?

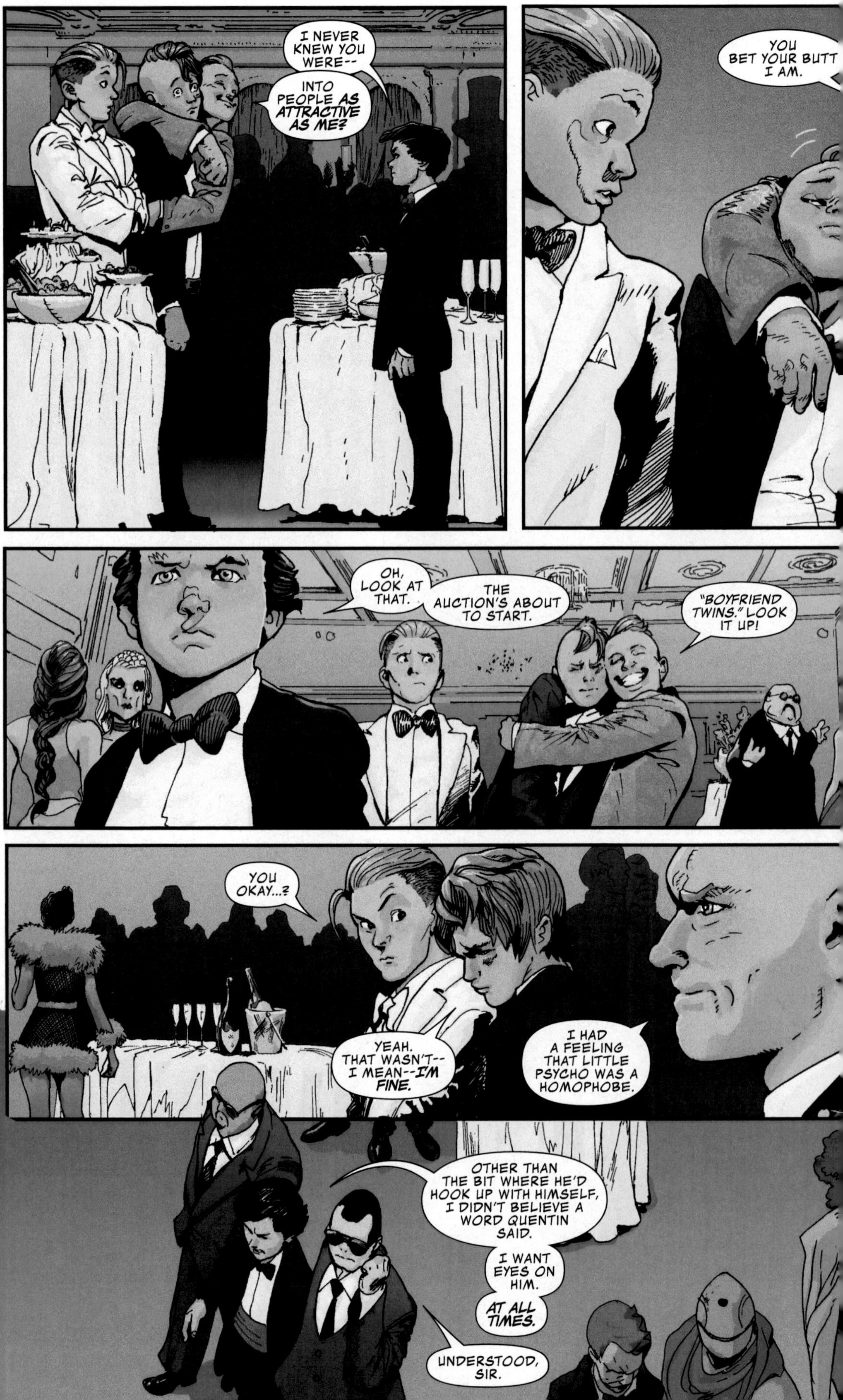
I NEVER KNEW YOU WERE--
INTO PEOPLE AS ATTRACTIVE AS ME?
YOU BET YOUR BUTT I AM.
OH, LOOK AT THAT.
THE AUCTION'S ABOUT TO START.
"BOYFRIEND TWINS." LOOK IT UP!
YOU OKAY...?
YEAH. THAT WASN'T-- I MEAN--I'M FINE.
I HAD A FEELING THAT LITTLE PSYCHO WAS A HOMOPHOBE.
OTHER THAN THE BIT WHERE HE'D HOOK UP WITH HIMSELF, I DIDN'T BELIEVE A WORD QUENTIN SAID.
I WANT EYES ON HIM.
AT ALL TIMES.
UNDERSTOOD, SIR.

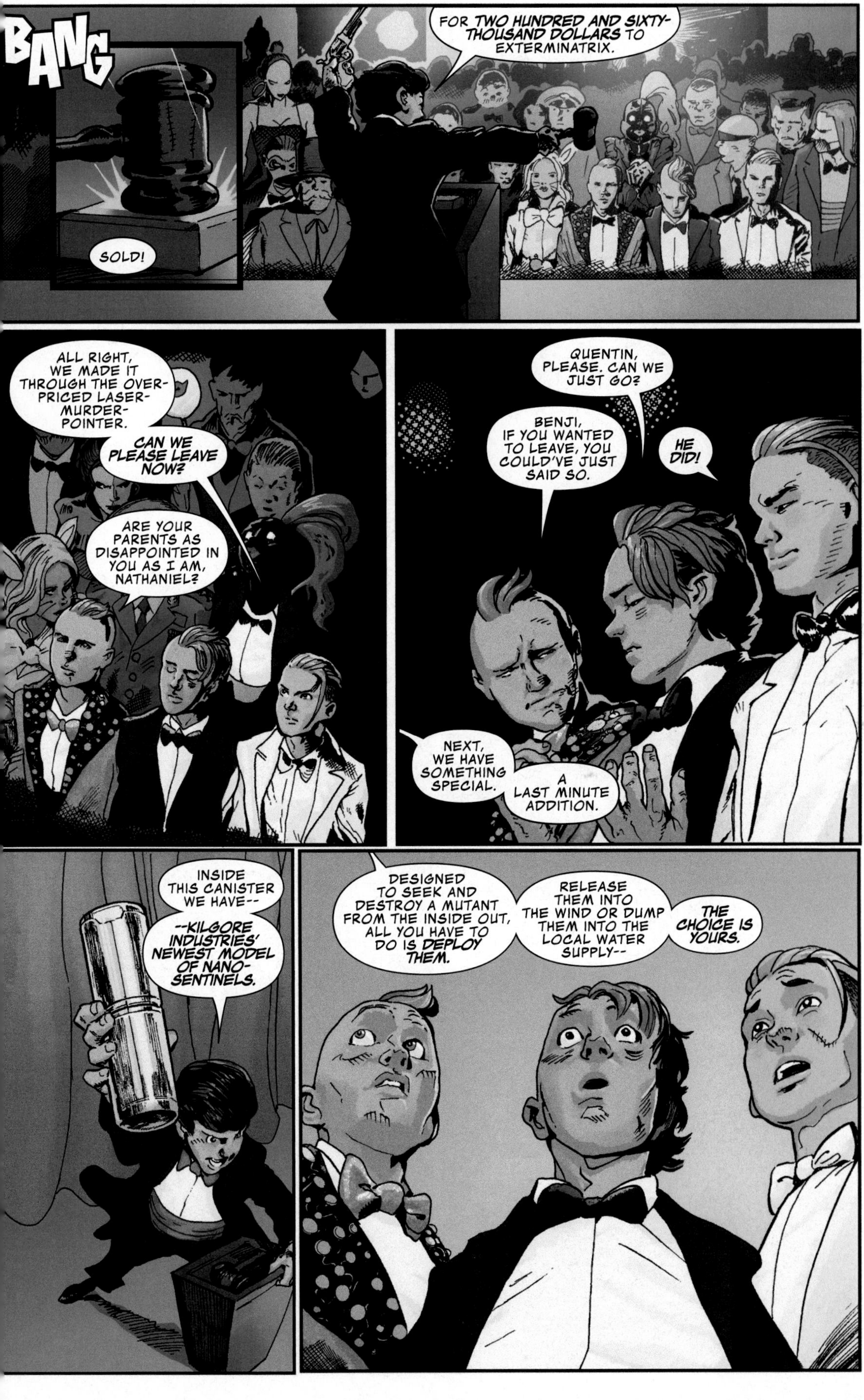
BANG
SOLD!
FOR TWO HUNDRED AND SIXTY-THOUSAND DOLLARS TO EXTERMINATRIX.
ALL RIGHT, WE MADE IT THROUGH THE OVER-PRICED LASER-MURDER-POINTER.
CAN WE PLEASE LEAVE NOW?
ARE YOUR PARENTS AS DISAPPOINTED IN YOU AS I AM, NATHANIEL?
QUENTIN, PLEASE. CAN WE JUST GO?
BENJI, IF YOU WANTED TO LEAVE, YOU COULD'VE JUST SAID SO.
HE DID!
NEXT, WE HAVE SOMETHING SPECIAL.
A LAST MINUTE ADDITION.
INSIDE THIS CANISTER WE HAVE--
--KILGORE INDUSTRIES' NEWEST MODEL OF NANO-SENTINELS.
DESIGNED TO SEEK AND DESTROY A MUTANT FROM THE INSIDE OUT, ALL YOU HAVE TO DO IS DEPLOY THEM.
RELEASE THEM INTO THE WIND OR DUMP THEM INTO THE LOCAL WATER SUPPLY--
THE CHOICE IS YOURS.

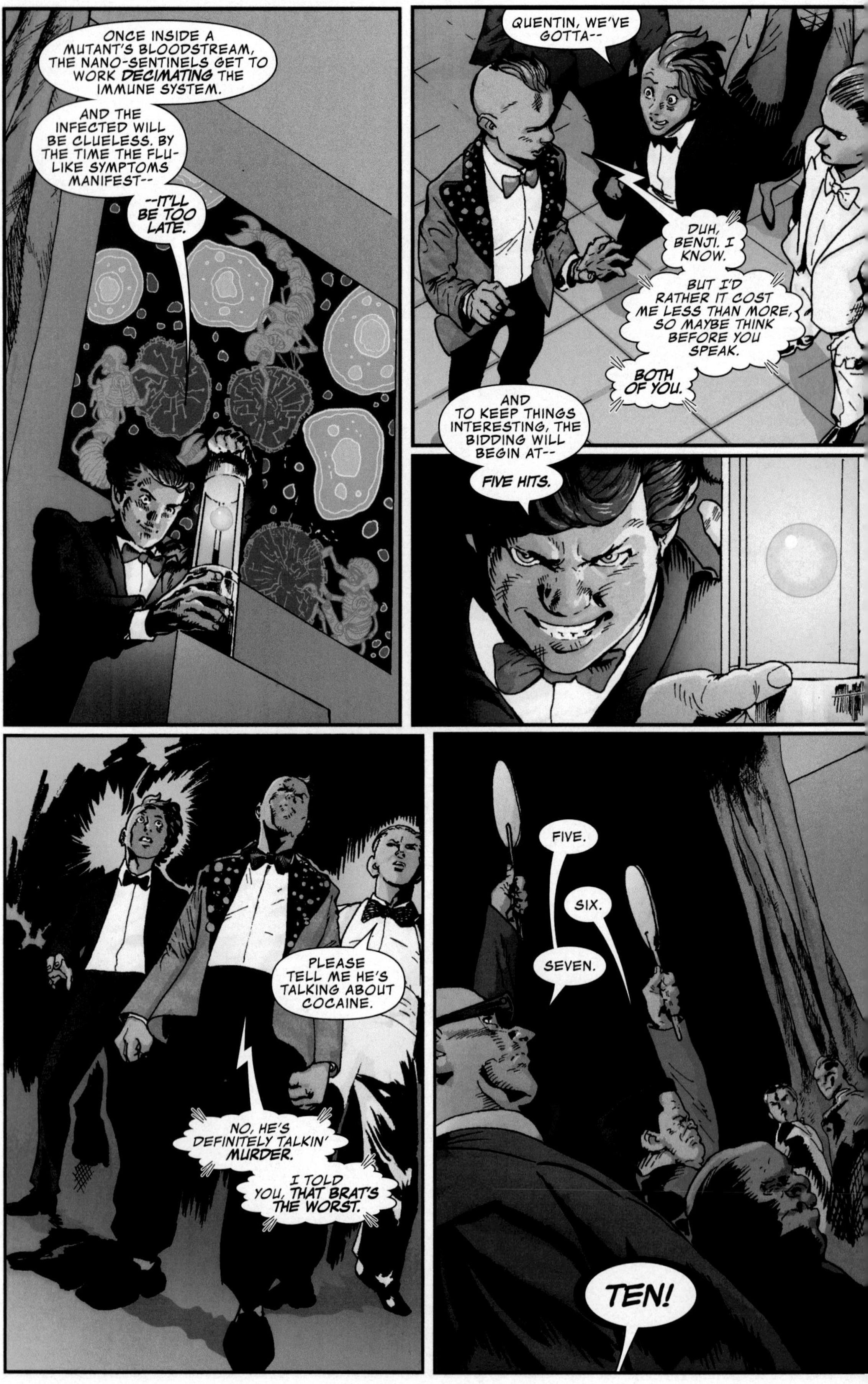

ONCE INSIDE A MUTANT'S BLOODSTREAM, THE NANO-SENTINELS GET TO WORK DECIMATING THE IMMUNE SYSTEM.
AND THE INFECTED WILL BE CLUELESS. BY THE TIME THE FLU-LIKE SYMPTOMS MANIFEST--
--IT'LL BE TOO LATE.
QUENTIN, WE'VE GOTTA--
DUH, BENJI. I KNOW.
BUT I'D RATHER IT COST ME LESS THAN MORE, SO MAYBE THINK BEFORE YOU SPEAK.
BOTH OF YOU.
AND TO KEEP THINGS INTERESTING, THE BIDDING WILL BEGIN AT--
FIVE HITS.
PLEASE TELL ME HE'S TALKING ABOUT COCAINE.
NO, HE'S DEFINITELY TALKIN' MURDER.
I TOLD YOU, THAT BRAT'S THE WORST.
FIVE.
SIX.
SEVEN.
TEN!

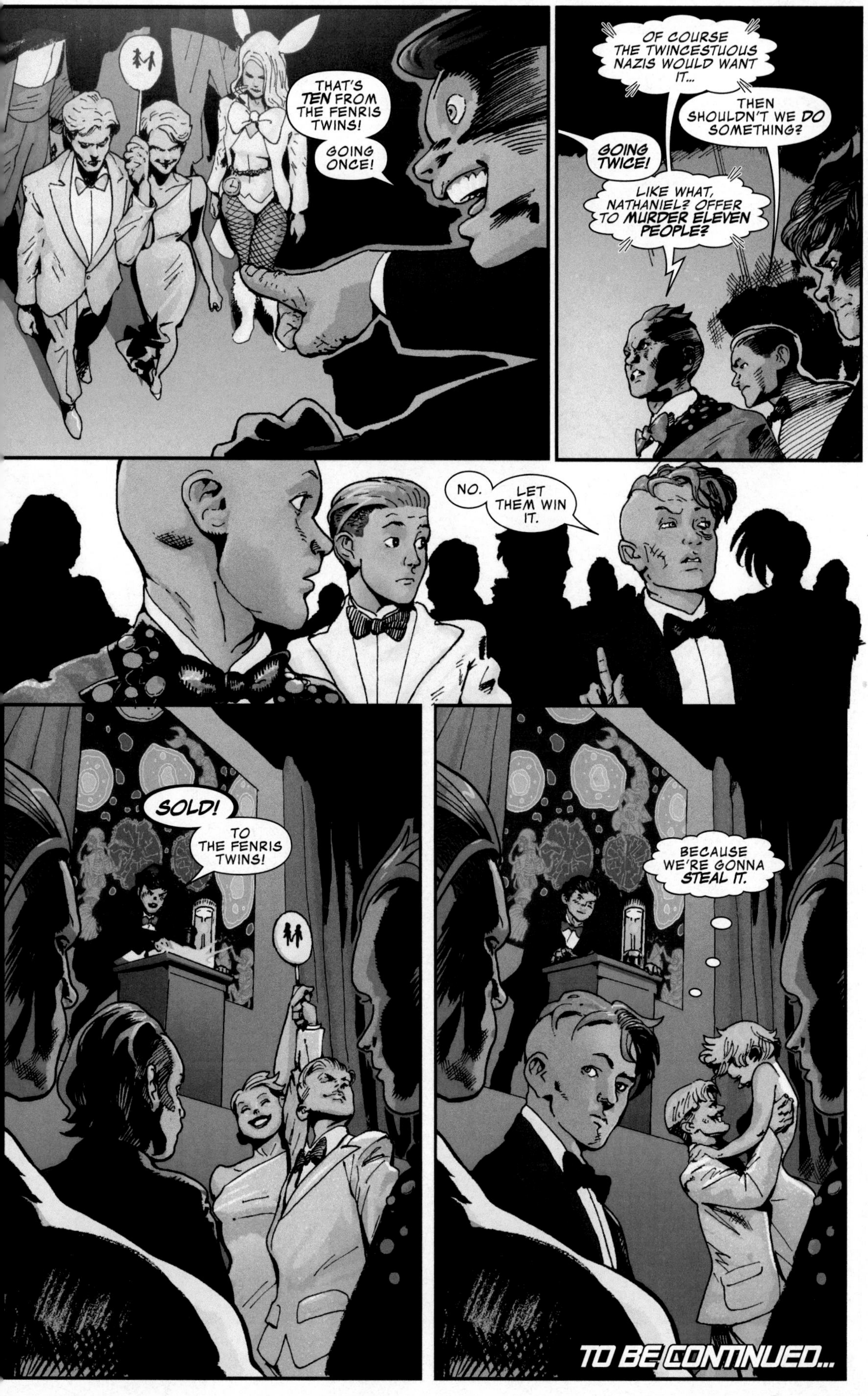
THAT'S TEN FROM THE FENRIS TWINS!
GOING ONCE!
OF COURSE THE TWINCESTUOUS NAZIS WOULD WANT IT...
THEN SHOULDN'T WE DO SOMETHING?
GOING TWICE!
LIKE WHAT, NATHANIEL? OFFER TO MURDER ELEVEN PEOPLE?
NO.
LET THEM WIN IT.
SOLD!
TO THE FENRIS TWINS!
BECAUSE WE'RE GONNA STEAL IT.
TO BE CONTINUED...

#1 REMASTERED VARIANT
BY **BRYAN HITCH, CAM SMITH & PAUL MOUNTS**

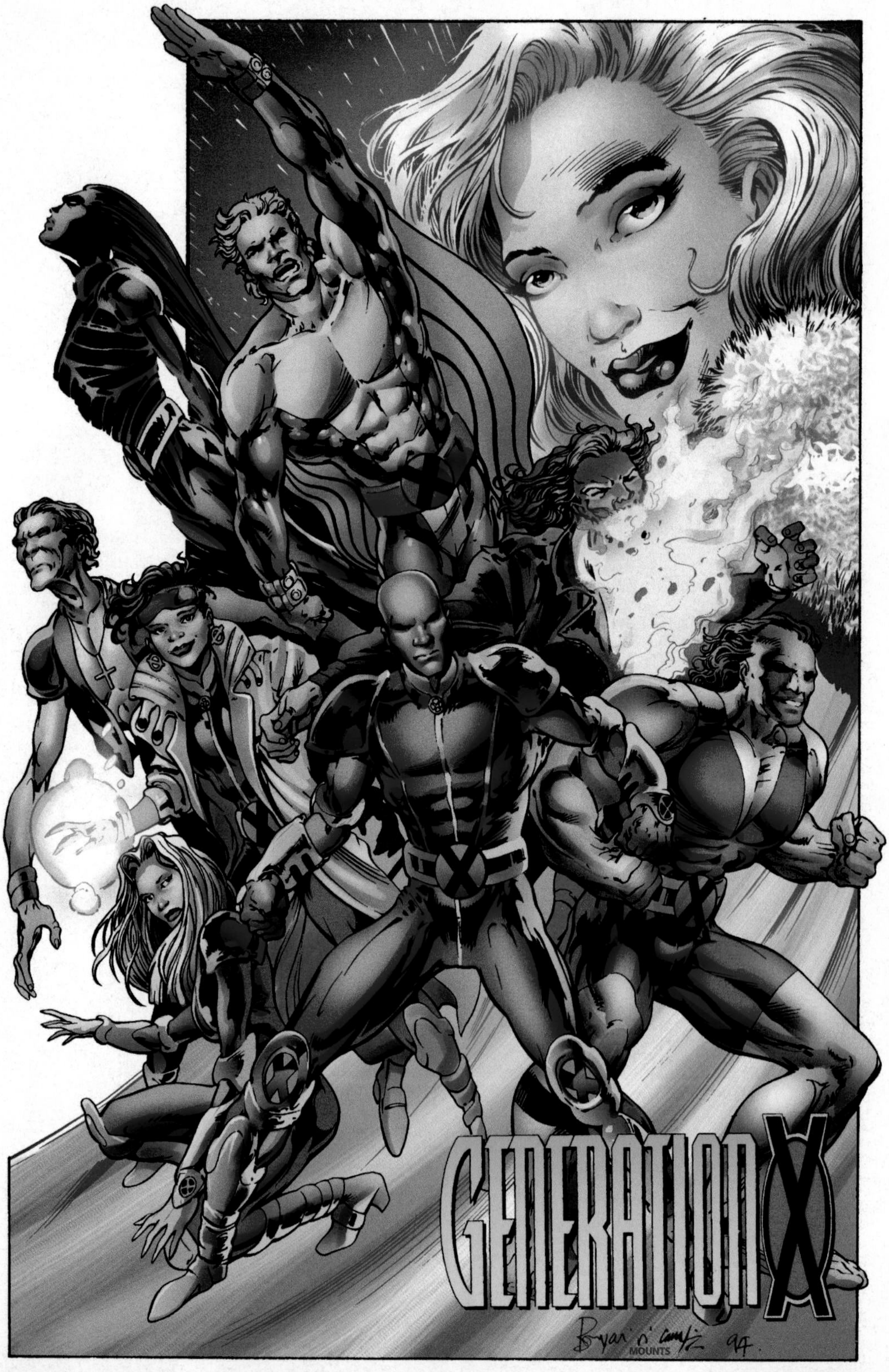
GENERATION X
MOUNTS
94

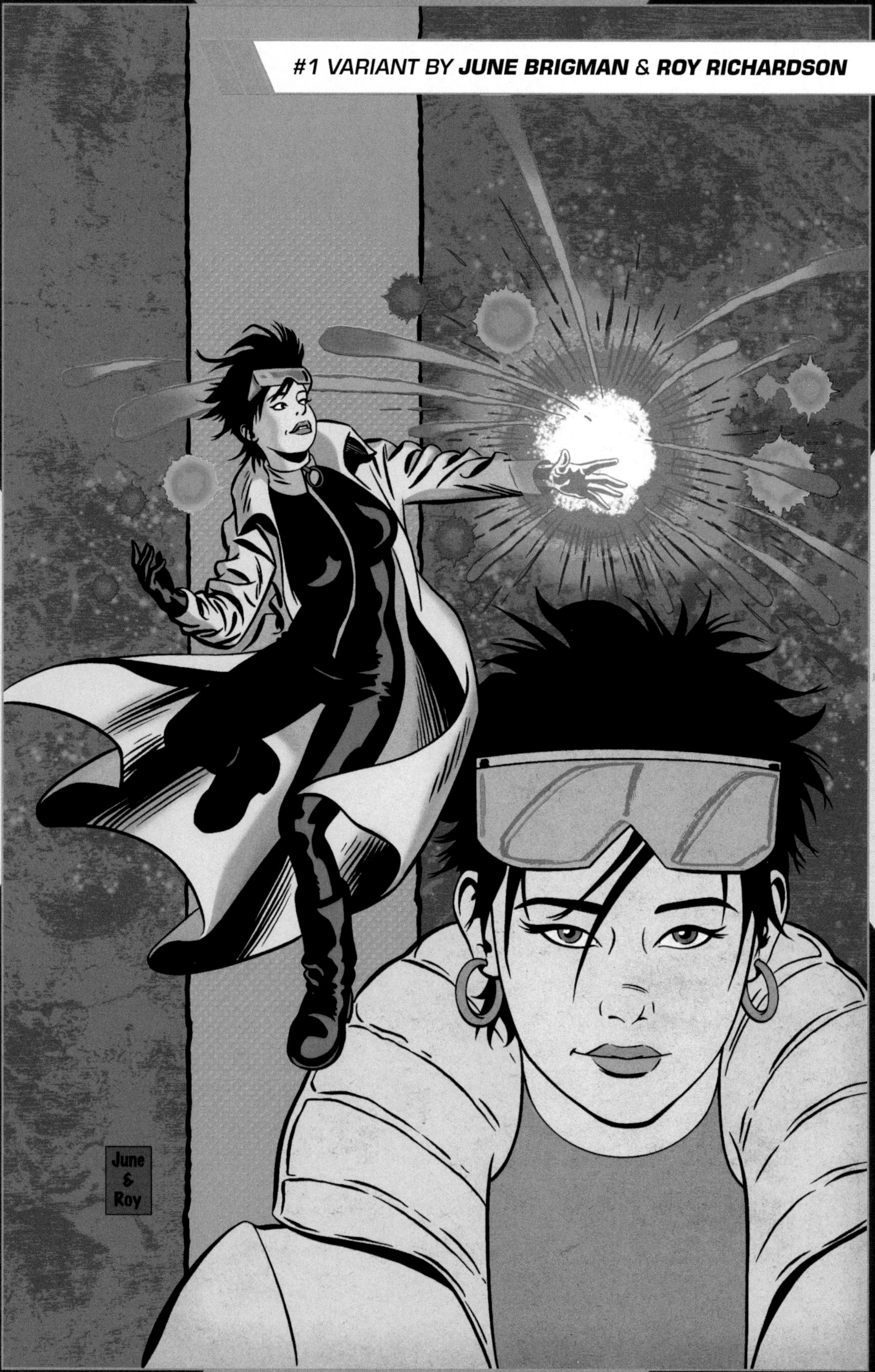
June & Roy

#1 VARIANT BY **JUNE BRIGMAN** & **ROY RICHARDSON**

#1 VARIANT BY **RAHZZAH**

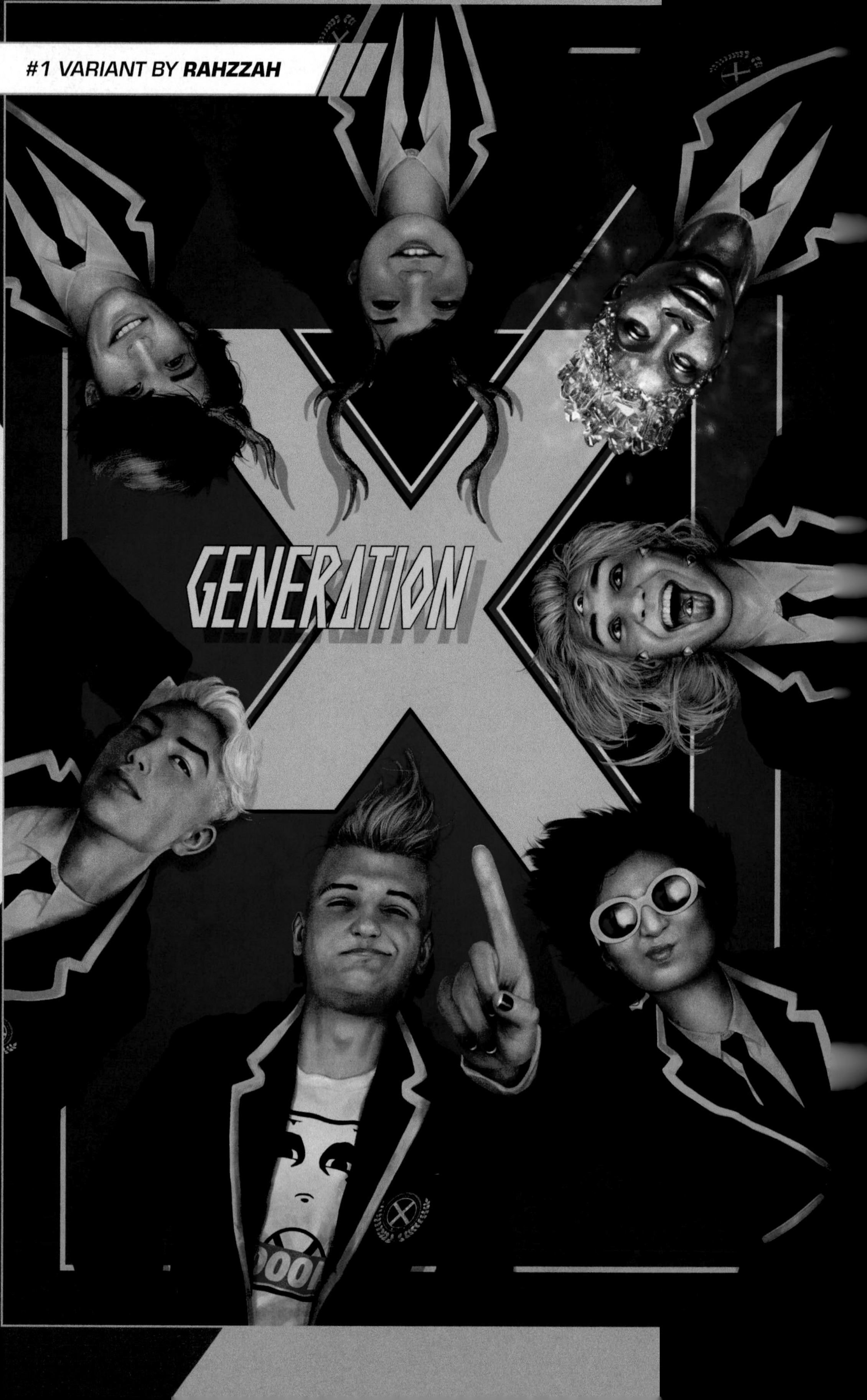
GENERATION

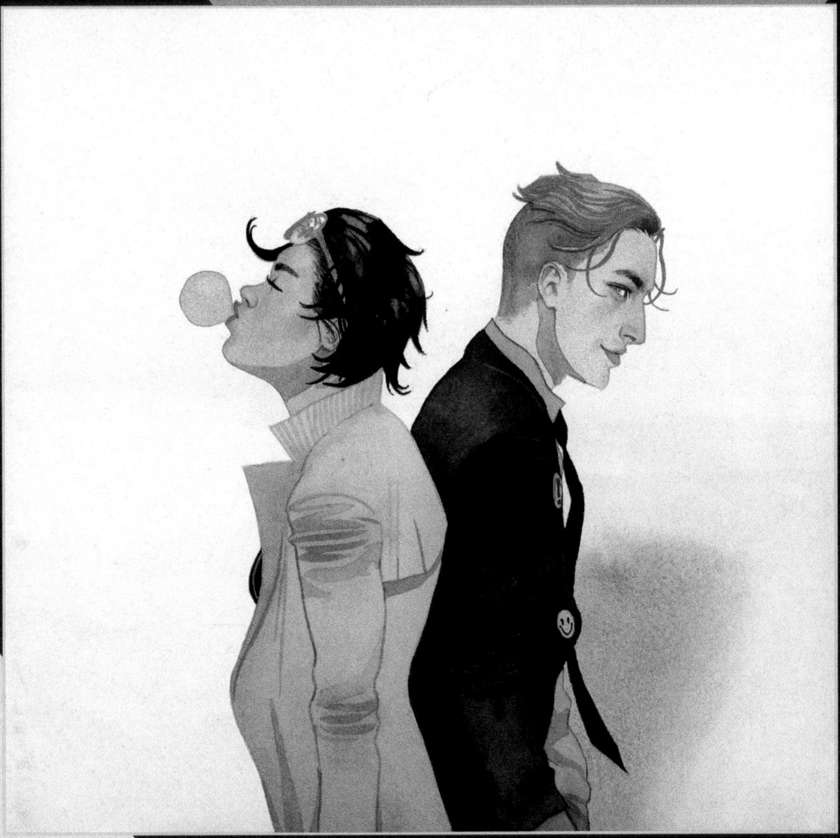

#1 HIP-HOP VARIANT
BY **KEVIN WADA**

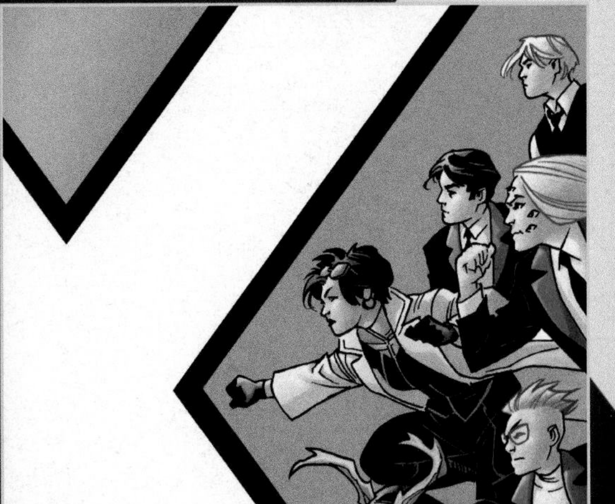

#1 CORNER BOX VARIANT
BY **LEONARD KIRK**
& **MICHAEL GARLAND**

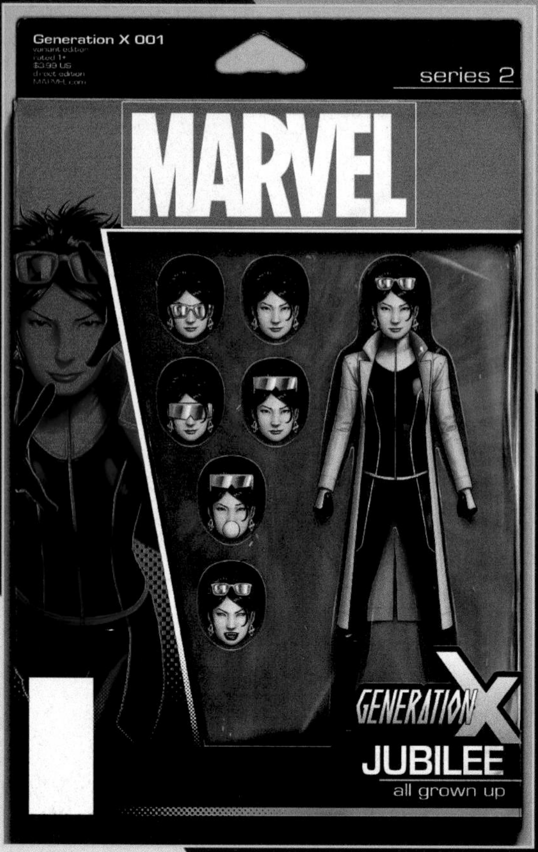
Generation X 001
series 2
MARVEL
GENERATION X
JUBILEE
all grown up

#1 ACTION FIGURE VARIANT
*BY **JOHN TYLER CHRISTOPHER***

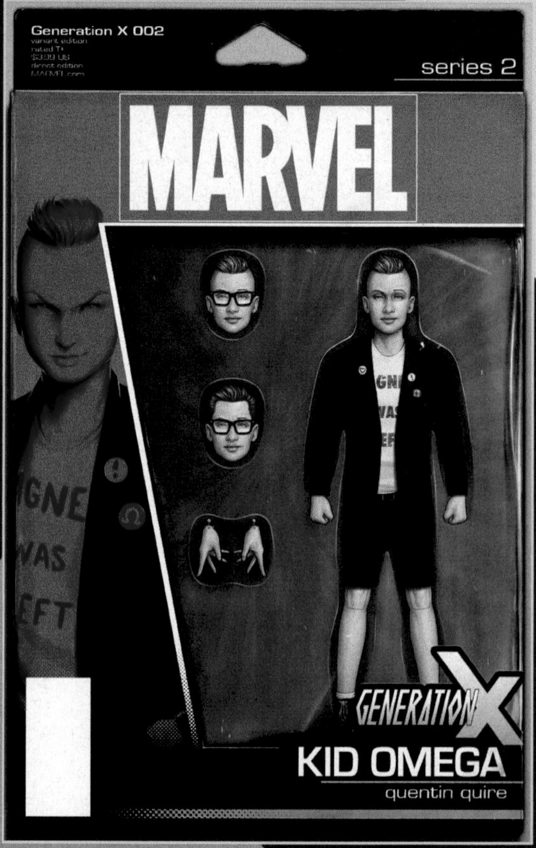
Generation X 002
series 2
MARVEL
GENERATION X
KID OMEGA
quentin quire

#4 ACTION FIGURE VARIANT
*BY **JOHN TYLER CHRISTOPHER***

#2 VARIANT BY **DAVID LOPEZ**

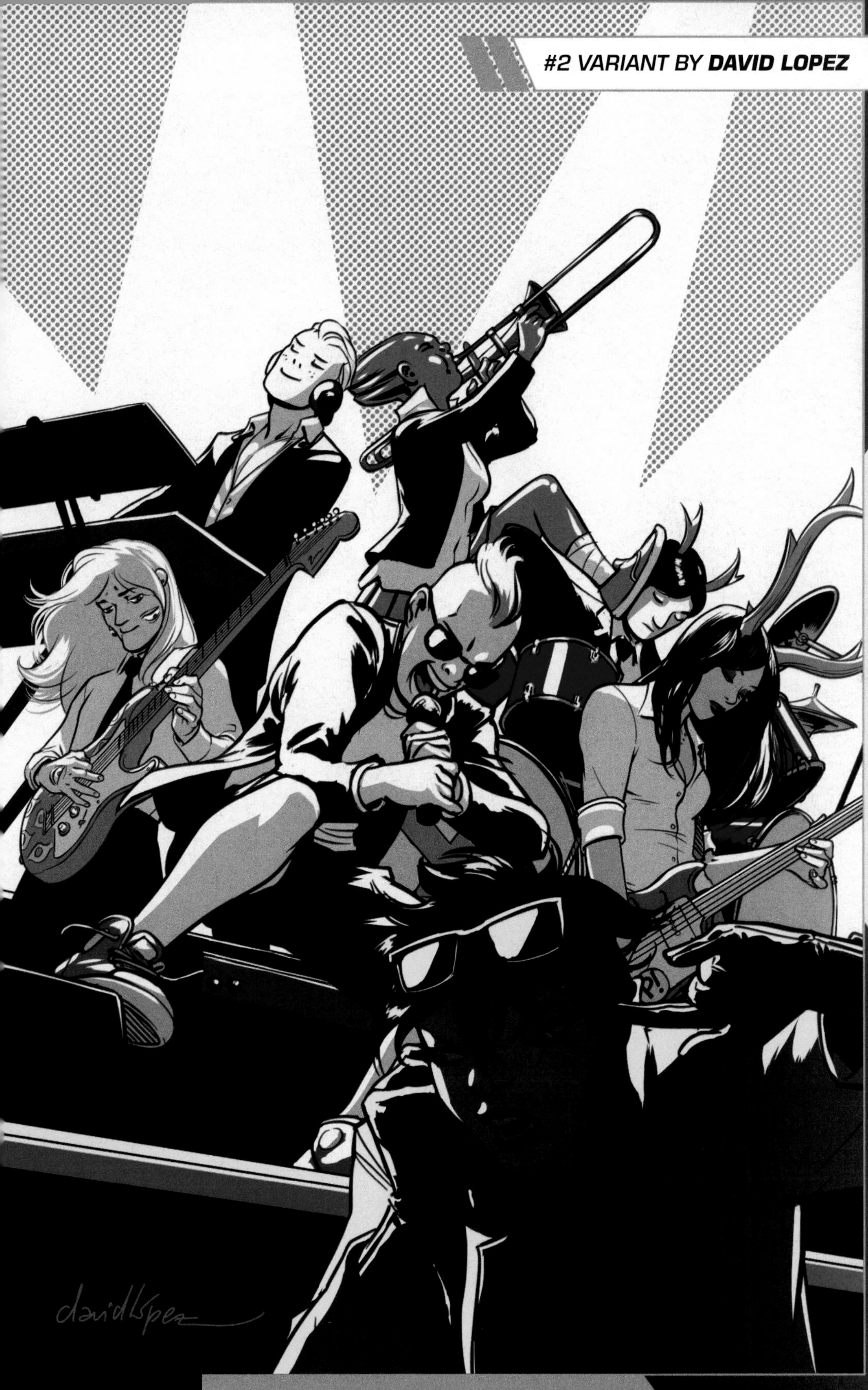

#4 VARIANT BY **JIM LEE** & **ISRAEL SILVA** WITH **MICHAEL KELLEHER**

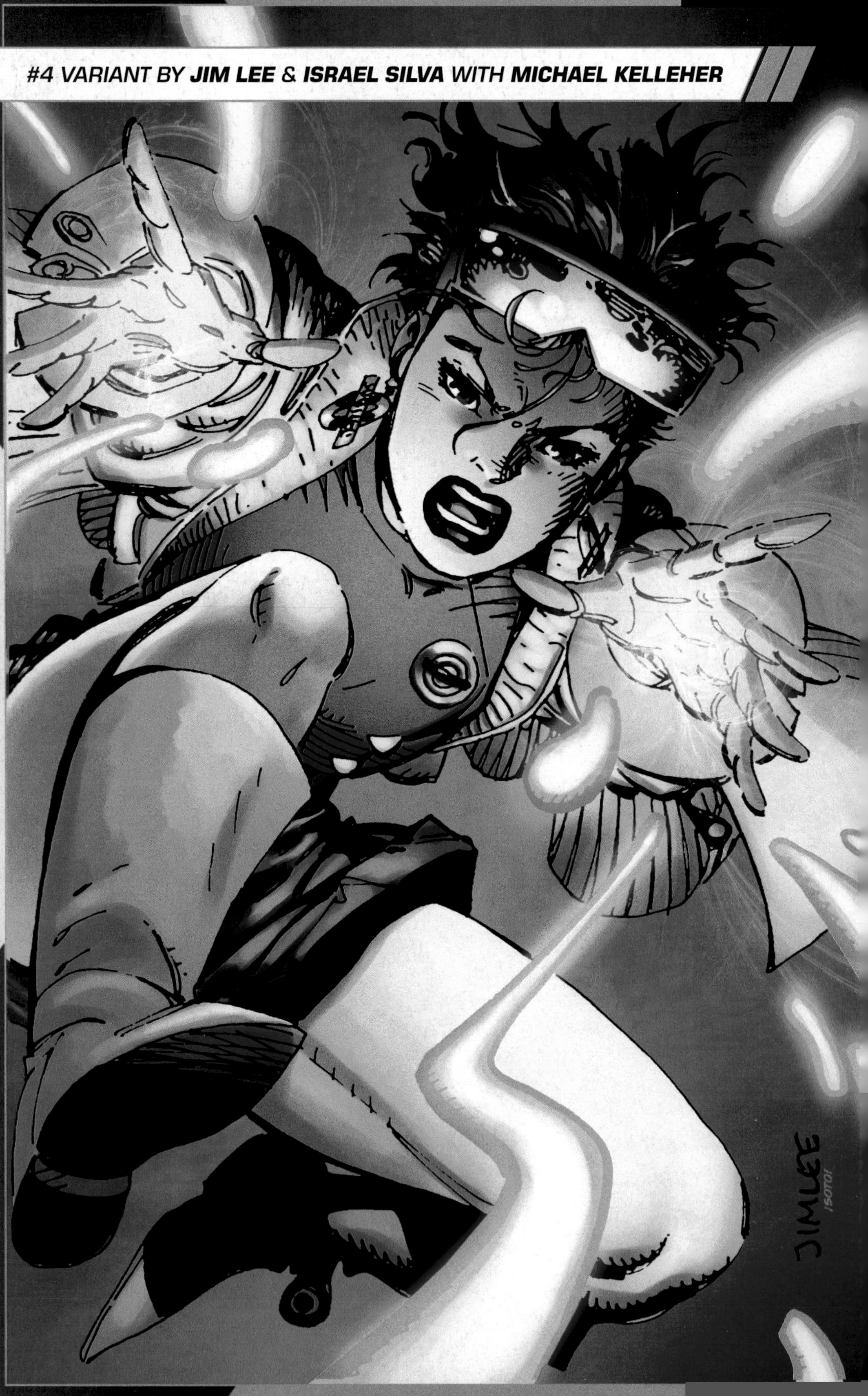